KENNETH JERNIGAN:

THE MASTER, THE MISSION, THE MOVEMENT

Compiled writings of
Dr. Kenneth Jernigan
with editorial introduction
and notes on the text

A publication of the
National Federation of the Blind

1800 Johnson Street
Baltimore, Maryland 21230

Kenneth Jernigan, November 13, 1926,
October 12, 1998

Table of Contents

Preface i

Introduction: The Man Within the Movement 1

Part I: Beyond the Barricades:
  Marching into the Millennium 15
  "The Federation at Fifty" 15
  "Shifting Balances in the Blindness Field" 34
  "Reflections and Comments on the
  World Blind Union" 54

Part II: The Building Blocks of Freedom:
  Mobility, Equality, and Independence 71
  "Blindness: Handicap or Characteristic" 72
  "A Definition of Blindness" 88
  "The Nature of Independence" 92

Part III: Plain Talk and Home Truths:
  Sowing the Seeds—Creating the Kernel Books 111
  Editor's Introduction to *What Color Is the Sun* 112
  "Growing Up Blind in Tennessee" 113
  "Competing on Terms of Equality" 125
  Editor's Introduction to *As the Twig Is Bent* 145
  "To Park or Not to Park" 147
  "Making Hay" 150
  Editor's Introduction to *The Journey* 156
  "The Value of Planning" 158
  Editor's Introduction to *Standing on One Foot* 163

"Standing on One Foot" 165

"The Hook on the Doctor's Door" 170

Editor's Introduction to *Toothpaste and
    Railroad Tracks* 175

"Of Toothpaste and Shaving Cream" 177

"Tapping the Charcoal" 183

"Beginnings and Blueprints" 189

"The Revolution of the Kernel Books" 194

"The Day After Civil Rights" 212

Editor's Introduction to *Like Cats and Dogs* 215

"The Sounds and Smells of Sixty Years" 218

Editor's Introduction to *Wall-to-Wall
    Thanksgiving* 224

"Don't Throw the Nickel" 226

"The Continuing Saga of the Kernel Books" 232

Editor's Introduction to *Gray Pancakes and
    Gold Horses* 233

"The Barrier of the Visible Difference" 235

Editor's Introduction to *To Touch the
    Untouchable Dream* 243

"Even I" 246

**Part IV: We Know Who We Are:
    From Confrontation to Emerging Harmony** **253**

The Pitfalls of Political Correctness:
    Euphemisms Excoriated 255

The Future of Specialized Services
    for the Blind 259

On the Nature of Mental Discipline
    and Sonnets 272

Preface

This volume tells of the convergence of a master teacher and the organized blind movement—of Dr. Kenneth Jernigan and the National Federation of the Blind. For almost half a century, the two were linked inseparably, virtually indistinguishable one from the other. Thus, when the blind of America heard the name Dr. Kenneth Jernigan, they thought of the National Federation of the Blind. When they heard of the National Federation of the Blind, they thought of Dr. Jernigan. This one name came to symbolize the organized blind movement, and the movement found its voice in this man.

When did it happen that these two became one? Was it in 1949, when young Jernigan joined the Federation? Was it in 1952, when he attended his first National Convention? Was it later during that convention at the time of his initial election to the Federation's Board of Directors? Did it happen in 1958 when Jernigan became director of statewide programs for the blind in Iowa? Or was it at the point when he became President of the Federation in 1968?

It is impossible to say, of course, exactly when and where the process of mutual convergence had its origin. It may be that the spirit of the man was foreshadowed in the harsh life of the boy on the Tennessee farm in rural America where he spent his early years of blindness and isolation. What we do know is that Dr. Kenneth Jernigan was born on November 13, 1926, and that he died seventy-one years later on October 12, 1998, within a few miles of the Baltimore headquarters of the movement he embodied and personified.

In the course of that lifetime, Dr. Kenneth Jernigan forged out of the raw materials and spare resources of his bleak, lean boyhood a powerfully resilient character and a pragmatic outlook on life. What emerged from his childhood isolation is a determined spirit of independence and self-reliance, coupled with the recognition that cooperative effort is essential for survival. Through his college and teaching years, he developed habits of scholarly learning and intellectual inquiry. Dr. Jernigan came to manifest a distinctive aura of personality—a presence, which projected with unmistakable certainty the fundamental reality that the blind are not prevented from becoming teachers, strategists, leaders, and statesmen. Call it greatness. It is this rare and elusive quality of character that these pages illustrate from many of the speeches and writings, stories and poems, letters and messages of Dr. Jernigan. Let the texts reveal their truths, and let the body of writings illuminate the transcendent soul within.

Introduction

The Man Within the Movement

Incisive intelligence, scintillating wit, and unalterable determination are not the characteristics ordinarily associated with the blind, and even when they are present in the life of a blind individual, these traits are sometimes unrecognized because of the traditional misunderstanding and misperception so often associated with the blind. However, the life of one towering human being personified these characteristics and changed forever the prospects of blind people in our own country and in lands beyond our borders. This one man, Dr. Kenneth Jernigan, gathered about him the blind of more than a generation and gave to them his understanding, instilling in them during the process a method of thought and a spirit of living which altered the future for them all. What did this man know that so many others had missed? The answer is simple and, at the same time, complex. It cannot be given in a word, a paragraph, or a page. It must be observed in a habit of belief and a way of life.

Dr. Jernigan was an inspirational speaker at the convention podium, a tireless crusader for the rights of the blind, a powerful writer and editor of an endless stream of publications, a charismatic presence, and an unforgettable personality.

At the Iowa Commission for the Blind, Dr. Jernigan served as director of statewide programs for twenty years from 1958 to 1978, and in the process transformed the agency from the nation's worst to the nation's finest by every measure of performance. He also became the revered instructor to successive generations of disoriented blind students who arrived at the center without hope and left it as graduates without the stultifying fear that had stifled their progress before they arrived. During the time that Dr. Jernigan served as director, the blind of Iowa became known as the best-trained group of blind people anywhere in the world, and their performance lived up to the reputation. For twenty years the graduates of this program demonstrated leadership in communities throughout the United States.

His genius for persuasion was nowhere more apparent than in the long uphill struggle of the National Federation of the Blind (NFB), alone and beleaguered at the outset, against the entrenched and aggressive forces of the Blindness System. When the young Jernigan became active in the organized blind movement at the national level in the early 1950's, relations between the NFB and some of the agencies were deteriorating, and after a time resembled those of warring states. Dr. Jernigan learned his politics from the founder and then President of the Federation, Dr. Jacobus tenBroek, who spoke of the Federation in 1957 as an "embattled organization."

Kenneth Jernigan, successively Second Vice President and First Vice President during the decade, led the fight in the trenches and fired up the rhetoric from the platform. His language was not the fawning persuasion of a sycophant or a supplicant. His voice rang out and spoke to the heart with a note of resolve and determination tempered by humanity that was as stirring as it was unexpected. By 1976 the resonant voice of our leader, trained and tempered by Dr. tenBroek, stirred the convention with these words:

> As we make our advance and set our daily skirmish lines we come to the fight with gladness—not with cringing or fear. We come with a song on our lips and joy in our hearts, for we have seen the vision of hope and felt the power of concerted action and self-belief. In the conflict ahead we will take casualties. We know it and we are prepared for it. Whatever the price, we will pay it. Whatever the cost, we will bear it. The stakes are too high and the promise too certain to let it be otherwise. We are organized and moving forward. We will be free—and the sighted will accept us as partners and equals. We know who we are, and we will never go back. The vulture sits in the branches of a dead tree, and we know where the wings join the body. Our gaze will not waver. Our shaft will go straight to the mark, and the vulture will fall. My brothers and my sisters, the future is ours. Come! Join me on the barricades, and we will make it come true!

Dr. Jernigan's oratory remained as stirring and forthright through the remainder of his life as it was in 1976. However, it would gain other added elements. There were at least three intended audiences for his convention speeches, then and always. Primary among them were the blind. Next came the professionals in the field of work with the blind—some who had taken up arms against the Federation and many others who had come to work cooperatively with the organized blind movement to enhance opportunity and encourage independence for the blind. And finally, there was the vast undifferentiated public—the Great American Audience—that volatile and amorphous but absolutely critical element in the urgent struggle to achieve understanding. Dr. Jernigan spoke to us all, delineating the reality that nobody can live our lives for us, that we must do it for ourselves, that we cannot do it in isolation but must find a way to welcome our sighted brothers and sisters as friends, that we must also find a way to persuade our sighted colleagues to welcome us, that equality carries with it a certain standard we must be prepared to meet, and that in the process of all of this effort we must speak and act for ourselves in an organized body which has the power and strength to gain for us the goals we seek.

In 1940, when the Federation came into being, there had only recently been an effort to create a national focus to promote the interests of the blind led by the American Foundation for the Blind. This effort was of tremendous value, but it represented the interests of the agencies established to serve the blind, not the interests of the blind themselves. Through the leadership of our founder and first President, Dr. Jacobus tenBroek, the blind of America came to recognize that to speak for the blind, a representative must be elected by the blind. Thus, the Federation was formed to serve the interests of the blind in 1940, and it was different from anything else dealing with blindness that had preceded it. It was not an organization speaking for the blind; it was the blind who had decided to speak for themselves.

At the outset, the agencies possessed all of the instruments of power over the unorganized blind: the workers in the sheltered workshops, the operators in the vending stands, and the employees in certain other occupations were almost completely dependent for basic needs on the goodwill and favor of the administrators who controlled the service agencies for the blind. It was the goal of the Federation to break this strangle hold and to alter the balance of power by "organizing" sheltered shop workers and others into the Federation, while at the same time promoting legislation to protect the right of the blind to organize and to be consulted—the right to be heard.

Why did the conflict exist? If the blind and those established to give them service are all working for the betterment of the blind, how can there possibly be conflict? Dr. Jernigan addressed this question repeatedly, stating emphatically that the agencies cannot speak for us—the blind. At most they can speak with us. Certain officials in the field of work with the blind had misinterpreted their role. They had formed the belief that they were caretakers for the helpless—caretakers for the mind, the body, and the spirit of the blind. When they were informed that the blind were not so helpless after all, they did not believe it, and they fought to maintain the status quo. They insisted that the blind were just as helpless as they had always imagined them to be, and they declared their intention to fight any blind person who maintained to the contrary—especially the National Federation of the Blind.

As late as the 1970's and the first years of the 1980's, the field of work with the blind was still characterized by strife and confrontation. But during the eighties, as the National Center for the Blind evolved and expanded, the conflicted pattern of relationships began to shift markedly in the direction of dialogue and cooperation. Officials of agencies and programs for the blind came to work more harmoniously with the organized blind movement, and there emerged a growing recognition of the community of interest shared between the blind as consumers and the agencies as providers of services designed to meet their needs.

In the last years of his life, Dr. Kenneth Jernigan devoted more and more of his energy and intellect to welding the various entities in the blindness field into a cohesive force for the advancement of the interests of blind people. Although deep-seated suspicion and misunderstanding of the blind still exist within society, there is a growing recognition by officials of rehabilitation programs for the blind that blind people are normal—that they possess the same hopes and dreams, the same quirks and foibles possessed by all other members of society. At one time a number of officials in the structure of programs to serve blind people were more of a hindrance to the blind than a help. Full integration of the blind is the dream that the Federation and Dr. Jernigan worked so diligently to achieve. He hoped that the blind of the next generation might attain this objective, and he gave us the tools to continue the work. An increasing number of people within the structure of programs for the blind have accepted his vision of the future. The striking degree of unity and harmony that characterizes the field today is a validation of that commitment and a vindication of the prophecy made by Dr. Jernigan himself as early as 1973. In a speech entitled "Blindness: Is History Against Us?" he assessed the state of the struggle and ventured a long-term prediction in these dramatic terms:

While no man can predict the future, I feel absolute confidence as to what the historians will say. They will tell of a system of governmental and private agencies established to serve the blind, which became so custodial and so repressive that reaction was inevitable. They will tell that the blind ("their time come round at last") began to acquire a new self-image, along with rising expectations, and that they determined to organize and speak for themselves. And they will tell of Jacobus tenBroek—of how he, a young college professor (blind and brilliant), stood forth to lead the movement.

They will tell how the agencies first tried to ignore us, then resented us, then feared us, and finally came to hate us—with the emotion and false logic and cruel desperation which dying systems always feel toward the new, about to replace them.

They will tell of the growth of our movement through the '40's and '50's, and of our civil war. They will tell how we emerged from that civil war into the '60's, stronger and more vital than we had ever been; and how more and more of the agencies began to make common cause with us for the betterment of the blind.

They will also record the events of the 1970's when the reactionaries among the agencies became even more so, and the blind of the second generation of the National Federation of the Blind stood forth to meet them. They will tell how the reactionary agencies gradually lost ground and gave way before us. They will tell of new and better agencies rising to work in partnership with the blind, and of harmony and progress as the century draws to an end. They will relate how the blind passed from second-class citizenship through a period of hostility to equality and first-class status in society. But future historians will only record those events if we make them come true. They can help us be remembered, but they cannot help us dream. That we must do for ourselves. They can give us acclaim, but not guts and courage. They can give us recognition and appreciation, but not determination or compassion or good judgment. We must either find these things for ourselves, or not have them at all.

Twenty-three years later, Dr. Jernigan returned to the theme of his earlier prophecy and announced to another convention audience (meeting in Anaheim, California, in 1996) that

in broad terms the prediction has come true. The century draws to a close, and there is unprecedented harmony between agencies and organizations of and for the blind.

As for the future, the Federation's long-time leader expressed his confidence with these words:

I am absolutely certain of the general direction our organization will take. Our mutual faith and trust in each other will be unchanged, and all else will follow . . . . I know to the depths of my being that our shared bond of love and trust will never change and that because of it we will be unswervable in our determination and unstoppable in our progress.

And then, Dr. Jernigan uttered these memorable concluding words:

As I said in 1973, we have come a long way together in this movement. Some of us are veterans, going back to the '40's; others are new recruits, fresh to the ranks. Some are young; some are old. Some are educated, others not. It makes no difference. In everything that matters we are one; we are the movement; we are the blind.

Perhaps the most profound part of Dr. Jernigan's work occurred during the 1990's. During that time he organized a remarkable revolution: one without violence or riot, devoid of strife or confrontation, conceived entirely in the spirit of love and understanding—it is the "revolution of the Kernel Books." At the 1996 Convention of the National Federation of the Blind, Dr. Jernigan explained the unusual character and effect of this peculiar revolution, in which the only weapons were small paperback books. He wrote: *"Revolution, the dictionary tells us, is 'sudden or momentous change.' It is 'activities directed toward bringing about basic changes in the socioeconomic structure, as of a minority or cultural segment of the population.' By these standards, what we have achieved during the past five years in writing, publishing, and distributing the Kernel Books is a revolution. We have brought about a 'sudden' and 'momentous change' in attitudes about the blind, our own attitudes, and those of society. We have initiated 'activities directed toward' causing 'basic changes in the socioeconomic structure of a minority, a cultural segment of the population.' And we have done it in half a decade."* He pointed out that eleven of the Kernel Books were (in 1996) already in print and that three million copies of them were in circulation around the country. "Revolution?" he asked; "from these little books? Yes, revolution. Never mind that the tone is gentle and the message nonconfrontative. The effect is felt, and basic changes are being made in the socioeconomic structure."

The basic changes that were being made extended beyond the socioeconomic structure, as Dr. Jernigan was the first to realize. This was a revolution of the heart and the mind, bringing about a transformation in the attitudes toward blindness of the general public and generating nothing less than a quantum leap in the level of understanding of what it means to be blind. During all of his adult life Dr. Jernigan devoted his energy to the mission of creating opportunity for the dispossessed—for the blind of the United States and beyond. His labors often took the form of political activism and organizational expansion, and he never flinched from danger or avoided confrontation when it was necessary. As Dr. Jernigan so frequently said: "We want no strife or confrontation, but we will do what we have to do." It is highly desirable, he told us, to avoid conflict; but it is absolutely essential to be prepared to fight for your rights if there is no other way to secure them.

Although Dr. Jernigan was always a warrior prepared to do battle, he was also a teacher, a confidant to the blind, a devoted friend. He worked for the blind of every generation, but he had a special concern for the children. He jumped rope with them, constructed paper airplanes for them, showed them how to travel with a cane, played games with them, told them stories, and inspired in them a zest for learning and adventure. Thinking out loud, he said to us at one point, "The pattern of my life is established. The pattern for the children who will come after us is yet to be determined. Though they are not our biological offspring, they are (in every meaningful sense of the word) our

children—part of our family. We must build for ourselves, of course; but of more importance we must think
to the future for our children. We must find a way to
make it possible for them to create opportunity never
known in the lives of the blind of our own generation."
As he edited the Kernel Book entitled *As the Twig is
Bent*, he was thinking of the urgent need to continue
the process of building for the blind of the next generation. As the twig is bent so grows the tree.

By the latter part of the 1990's, Dr. Jernigan could
speak of "The Day After Civil Rights." That was the
title of his stunning banquet address delivered at the
1997 Convention devoted, (not coincidentally), both to
the phenomenon of the Kernel Books and to the need
for a new comprehensive philosophy and policy of understanding. The visionary leader of the blind saw
that the two elements were complementary, organi-
cally connected at the heart. The astonishing appeal
of the little books was due to their honest and unpre-
tentious narratives of everyday life as it is lived by
blind persons, narratives which emphasized quite
naturally the commonalties rather than the differences
in the lives of blind and sighted Americans. In the
humorous and poignant telling of these short anec-
dotes and true confessions there was, for every reader,
a sense of the familiar and a hint of recognition, a
shared secret, a moment of reflection, a thought to
ponder, a flash of a dream remembered. The blind
were heartened, cheered, and inspired; but so were
the members of the public.

The little books with the large print did more than
tickle the funny bone of America; they touched its heart
and lifted its spirit, and they have swept away the
mystery from the condition of blindness. For the mil-

lions of those who have become readers of the Kernel Books, blind men and women, blind boys and girls, can never again be easily dismissed as strangers. Through these real-life narratives they have come to be recognized as neighbors, and not just neighbors but friends.

The readers of these pages will observe that almost all of the material contained in this volume is drawn from the writings of Dr. Jernigan, composed during the 1990's. A previous volume delineating the history of the organized blind movement in the United States entitled *Walking Alone and Marching Together* by Dr. Floyd Matson incorporates many of Dr. Jernigan's outstanding addresses and thoughtful compositions composed before 1990. It would not be practical to include all or even most of what Dr. Jernigan wrote. Thus, this volume draws from the latter part of the compendium of Dr. Jernigan's work.

Dr. Jernigan changed the lives of blind people through his example and inspiration. He changed the lives of the sighted through his wisdom and writings. That was his mission, his purpose, and his goal. Dr. Jernigan taught us to think of tomorrow. The pattern of today is set, but the pattern of tomorrow can be affected by the work of today. Plan for tomorrow, next week, next month, or the year to follow, he told us. He himself did precisely as he recommended to us. He always planned for the future! He urged us to take the long view, and we have. His work did not come to a close when he drew his last breath, for he gave us a spirit and the mechanism for building a better future. He gave us his writings and his example, and he gave us the organized blind movement. His life was filled with ceaseless activity—with writing, with speaking,

with challenging, with teaching, with loving. His final message will live through the decades and be reflected in the generations to come. Believe in yourself, dream of the future, build for tomorrow, and never,
ever give up! And above all else, care for one another
with an abiding love which will provide the strength
and the inner moral fiber to make us unstoppable and
unbeatable!

Marc Maurer
Baltimore, Maryland
1999

Part I:
Beyond the Barricades:
Marching into the Millennium

Dr. Kenneth Jernigan understood the meaning of history. He took delight in studying and teaching it, and he was amused by the notion that he himself was a significant factor in making it. In 1990, at the convention of the National Federation of the Blind, on the occasion of our 50th anniversary, he delivered an outstanding address illuminating the causes that founded the National Federation. This address is entitled "The Federation at Fifty."

If the engineers of 1800 had possessed complete drawings for a transistor radio (one that could be bought today for $10), they couldn't have built it, not even if they had had billions or trillions of dollars. They lacked the infrastructure, the tools, the tools to build the tools, and the tools to build those; the plastics, the machines to make the plastics, and the machines to make the machines; the skilled work force, the teachers to train the work force, and the teachers to train the teachers; the transportation network to assemble the materials, the vehicles to use the network, and the sources of supply. All of this is generally recognized, but it is far less well understood that what is true of material objects is also true of ideas and attitudes. In the absence of a supporting social infrastructure of knowledge and beliefs, a new idea simply cannot exist.

So far as I can tell, there are only three possible reasons for studying history; to get inspiration, to gain perspective, or to acquire a basis for predicting the future.

In 1965 Dr. Jacobus tenBroek, the founder and leader of our movement, spoke at our twenty-fifth banquet, reviewing the first quarter century and charting the road ahead. We were meeting in Washington, and more than a hundred members of Congress were present. I was master of ceremonies, and some of the rest of you were also there. Tonight (twenty-five years later) we celebrate our Golden Anniversary, and the time has once again come to take stock. Where are we, where have we been, and where are we going?

In a sense the history of our movement begins in the distant past in the medieval guilds and brotherhoods of the blind in Europe, in the tentative stirrings of organization in China, and even earlier, but the National Federation of the Blind is essentially an American product. Its genesis is native. Although (as we all know) Dr. Jacobus tenBroek presided at the founding of the National Federation of the Blind in 1940 at Wilkes-Barre, Pennsylvania, he had a teacher (Dr. Newel Perry), who laid the foundations and served as precursor. And Dr. Perry, in turn, had a teacher, Warring Wilkinson.

Most of what we know about Wilkinson is contained in the eulogy which Dr. tenBroek delivered at the time of Dr. Perry's death in 1961, but our knowledge is sufficient to tell us that Wilkinson was a worthy teacher of the teacher of our founder. He was the first principal of the California School for the Deaf and Blind. He served in that capacity for forty-four years, from 1865 to 1909. He not only loved his students but also did what he could to move them toward the main channels of social and economic participation. Particularly, he saw the potential in young Perry, sending him from the California School for the Blind to Berkeley High to complete his secondary education. To do this Wilkinson (who was ahead of his time both in his understanding of education and the needs of the blind) had to overcome numerous obstacles.

I was fortunate enough to know Dr. Perry, meeting him when I moved to California in 1953. He was then eighty, and he spent many hours with me reminiscing about what conditions for the blind were like when he was a boy. He came to the California School for the Blind when he was ten; penniless, blind, his father dead, his home dissolved. Two years earlier he had lost his sight and nearly his life as the result of a case of poison oak, which caused his eyeballs to swell until they burst and which held him in a coma for a month. It was at the School, of course, that he first met Warring Wilkinson.

While going to high school (from which he graduated in 1892) he lived at the California School for the Blind. He also lived there while attending the University of California from 1892 to 1896. His admission to the University (as had been the case with high school) had to be secured over strong resistance. Again, Wilkinson was the pathfinder, young Perry his willing and anxious instrument. Wilkinson's role in Perry's life as a youth can hardly be overestimated: father, teacher, guide, supporter, in Perry's own words, "Dear Governor."

After graduating from the University, Dr. Perry devoted himself to further education and to the search for an academic job. He took graduate work at the University of California, meanwhile serving successively as an unpaid teaching fellow, a paid assistant, and finally as an instructor in the department of mathematics. In 1900, following a general custom of that day, he went to Europe to continue his studies. He did this for a time at the University of Zurich in Switzerland and then at the University of Munich in Germany. From the latter he secured in 1901 the degree of Doctor of Philosophy in Mathematics, with highest honors. He returned to the United States in 1902, landing in New York, where he was to remain until 1912. He had about eighty dollars in capital, a first-class and highly specialized education, and all of the physical, mental, and personal prerequisites for a productive career, except one, eyesight.

During this period he supported himself precariously as a private coach of university mathematics students. He also applied himself to the search for a university position. He displayed the most relentless energy. He employed every imaginable technique. He wrote letters in profusion. In 1905, he wrote to 500 institutions of every size and character. He distributed his dissertation and his published article on mathematics. He haunted meetings of mathematicians. He visited his friends in the profession. He enlisted the aid of his teachers. He called on everybody and anybody having the remotest connection with his goal.

Everywhere the outcome was the same. Only the form varied. Some expressed astonishment at what he had accomplished. Some expressed interest. One of these seemed genuine. He had a blind brother-in-law, he said, who was a whiz at math. Some showed indifference, now and then masked behind polite phrases. Some said there were no vacancies. Some said his application would be filed for future reference. One said ironically: 'For what, as an encouragement to men who labor under disadvantages and who may learn from it how much may be accomplished through resolution and industry?' Some averred that he probably could succeed in teaching at somebody else's college. Many said outright that they believed a blind person could not teach mathematics.

Many of these rejections may, of course, have been perfectly proper. Many were not. Their authors candidly gave the reason as blindness. Dr. Perry failed not because of lack of energy or qualification but because the necessary infrastructure of attitudes and beliefs did not exist to allow it to be otherwise; so he did not find a job in a university. Perhaps it was better for the blind (for those of us gathered here tonight) that he did not, but for him what pain! What absolute desolation and misery! And he had to face it alone; no family, no supporting organization of the blind, only himself and the bleak wall of continuing rejection year after year. He might have quit in despair. He might have become embittered. But he did not. Instead, he returned to California and settled down to build for the future. If he could not have first-class treatment for himself, he was absolutely determined that at least the next generation of the blind would not be denied.

He taught at the California School for the Blind from 1912 to 1947, and day after day, month after month, season after season he exhorted and indoctrinated, preached and prepared. He was building the necessary infrastructure of ideas and beliefs. Those who were his students went on to become his colleagues, and as the number grew, the faith was kept. There would be a statewide organization of the blind in California. It did not happen until 1934, but when it came, it was built on a solid foundation. And there would also be a National Federation of the Blind, but not yet.

Dr. Perry was to that generation what Warring Wilkinson had been to him. In the words of Jacobus tenBroek, his most brilliant student and the man who would lead the blind in the founding of their national movement: We were his students, his family, his intimates, his comrades on a thousand battlefronts of a social movement. We slept in his house, ate at his table, learned geometry at his desk, walked the streets interminably by his side, moved forward on the strength of his optimism and confidence.

Dr. tenBroek graduated from Berkeley High School in 1930 with, as he said, "plenty of ambition, but no money." He was prepared to enter the University of California but was denied state aid to the blind, a program then newly instituted as a result of Dr. Perry's efforts in sponsoring a constitutional amendment, which had been adopted by the voters of California in 1928. In Dr. tenBroek's words, "The reason for the denial was not that my need was not great. It was that I intended to pursue a higher education while I was being supported by the state. That was too much for the administrative officials." Almost without discussion, Dr. Perry immediately filled the gap. Just as Warring Wilkinson had earlier done for him, said Dr. tenBroek, "he supplied me with tuition and living expenses out of his own pocket for a semester while we all fought to reverse the decision of the state aid officials."

"It was," Dr. tenBroek said, "ever thus with Dr. Perry. The key to his great influence with blind students was, first of all, the fact that he was blind and therefore understood their problems; and second, that he believed in them and made his faith manifest. He provided the only sure foundation of true rapport: knowledge on our part that he was genuinely interested in our welfare."

So the new generation came to maturity, and Jacobus tenBroek was to be its leader. Born in 1911 on the prairies of Alberta, Canada, he was blinded by an arrow in a childhood game and moved to California to enter the school for the blind. He went on to earn five academic degrees: from the University of California at Berkeley a bachelor's in 1934, a master's in 1935, a law degree in 1938, and a Doctorate in Jurisprudence in 1940; and from the Harvard Law School a Doctorate in Jurisprudence in 1947. There is no need for me to talk to this audience about Dr. tenBroek's brilliance—his learned articles and books, his chairmanship of the California Board of Social Welfare, his scholarly pre-eminence and national acclaim, his writings on constitutional law that are still the authoritative works in the field. Rather, I would speak of the man; the warm human being who fought for acceptance, led our movement, and served as my mentor and role model, the man who was my closest friend and spiritual father.

When Dr. tenBroek was first trying to get a teaching position in the 1930's, the climate of public opinion was better than it had been a generation earlier, but he faced many of the same problems which had confronted Dr. Perry, and sometimes with identical letters from the same institutions. "It was," he said, "almost as if a secretary had been set to copying Dr. Perry's file, only changing the signatures and the name of the addressee."

Here is what Dr. tenBroek wrote to Dr. Perry in March of 1940. At the time he was studying at Harvard:

"Last November a large midwestern university was looking for a man to teach public law. Having read my published articles but knowing nothing else about me, the head of the department in question wrote a letter to the University of California inquiring whether I would be available for the position. Cal. replied that I would and accompanied the answer with a considerable collection of supporting material. However, when the department head learned that I was blind, the deal was off although none of the competing applicants had as good a paper showing. This incident seems to me of particular interest because, although I have been refused other jobs, this was the first instance in which blindness could be traced as the sole explanation for rejection. Of course, in other cases blindness was also the determining factor, but the fact could not be demonstrated as well."

There were other letters and other rejections, but on June 8, 1940, Dr. tenBroek was able to write to Dr. Perry:

"We have justification for hanging out the flags and ringing the bells. I have been offered and have accepted a job at Chicago University Law School. The job pays $1,800, is denominated a half-time position, and lasts for only a year. But it is a job nevertheless. And the Harvard people, who exerted no end of pressure to get it for me, regard it as an excellent opportunity. The position is designated 'tutorial fellowship' and consists in supervising the research of the first- and second-year law students. It involves no actual classroom teaching, except possibly by way of an occasional fill-in job."

This was how Dr. tenBroek (the man who fifteen years later was to win the Woodrow Wilson Award for the outstanding book of the year in political science and who was always the most sought-after professor at the University of California) was to begin his teaching career. Yet, even today there are sighted people (and also some of the blind people who ought to know better) who tell me that the blind are not victims of discrimination. Yes, the tenBroek job search was fifty years ago, but you know and I know that we have not yet come to first-class status and equal treatment in society. The framework of ideas and beliefs to make it possible, though long in the building, is still not complete. Warring Wilkinson, Newel Perry and his students, Jacobus tenBroek and the founders of our movement, and the Federationists of succeeding decades have worked year after year to improve the climate of public acceptance and make opportunity available for the blind, but the job is not yet finished. Each generation has built on the work of the one before it. Each has fought and hoped, dreamed and drudged for the one to follow, and also for the blind then alive.

What we have done must be seen in perspective; for no act of the past (no gain or denial) is irrelevant, and no present behavior of ours can be divorced from tomorrow. We are close to freedom, and we must finish the journey. 1940 was notable for something else besides Dr. tenBroek's debut at the University of Chicago. It was also the year of the founding of this organization. With the passage of the Social Security Act in 1935 the federal government had supplanted the states in providing assistance to the blind. In 1939 Congress and the Social Security Board combined to pressure the states having the most forward looking programs (chief among them California but also Pennsylvania, Missouri, and Wisconsin) to repeal their progressive laws. This supplied the immediate impetus for the formation of the Federation, but of course the momentum had been building for a generation. The event occurred at Wilkes-Barre on November 15 and 16, 1940, coincident with the convention of the Pennsylvania Federation of the Blind.

In a letter to Dr. Perry dated November 19, 1940, Dr. tenBroek said in part:

"The confab at Wilkes-Barre gave birth to an organization, the National Federation of the Blind, of which you, vicariously through me, are president. The long-range aims of the organization are the promotion of the economic and social welfare of the blind, and its immediate and specific aims are the sponsorship of the principle of Senate Bill 1766 and an amendment of the Social Security Act. Seven states were represented at the organizational meeting: Minnesota, Wisconsin, Illinois, Missouri, Ohio, Pennsylvania, and California. We arrived in Wilkes-Barre in the middle of Friday afternoon....On Saturday morning, while the Pennsylvania state meeting was going on, I had several back-of-the-scenes conversations with Pennsylvania leaders.... In the afternoon... we drew up a skeleton constitution, which we presented to a meeting of all of the delegates to the national meeting, beginning about four o'clock and ending about the same time twelve hours later.... The meeting was interrupted at 5:30 in the afternoon long enough to give the other delegates a chance to eat dinner, and the Pennsylvania leader (Gayle Burlingame) and me a chance to appear on the local radio, where we lambasted hell out of the Social Security Board."

On January 4, 1941, Dr. tenBroek wrote to Dr. Perry concerning the details of getting the new organization started. 'With the National Federation of the Blind not yet two months old,' he said, 'its permanence is definitely assured. The factor guaranteeing that permanence is the closely knit nucleus composed of Minnesota, Pennsylvania, and California. We three have now had enough experience with each other to know that we can make a go of it.... We can add to this trilogy the state of Wisconsin. I had a letter from Minnesota yesterday to the effect that they are ready to pay their assessment but that they wish assurance that Pennsylvania and California are also ready before they mail their check. I also had a letter from Pennsylvania stating that it is ready but wishes assurance that Minnesota and California are ready. I have written to both of these states requesting them to make out their checks, payable to the Treasurer of the National Federation, and to send them to me, with the stipulation that I shall not forward them to the Treasurer until I have the dues from each of the states of California, Pennsylvania, and Minnesota. Consequently, if California is ready, I suggest that you follow the same procedure....'

But the new president did not limit himself to procedural matters. The Federation immediately assumed its present-day role of working to improve the quality of life for the nation's blind. In a letter to Dr. Perry dated March 15, 1941, President tenBroek described the efforts he had been making to get changes in the administration of public assistance to the blind. Here, in part, is what he said:

"After a week in Washington I have more unsocial exchange to report than specific accomplishment.... Gradually working our way upward, Gayle Burlingame and I first presented our case to Jane Hoey, director of the Bureau of Public Assistance, and her associate, a lawyer named Casius. Next we went to Oscar Powell, executive director of the Social Security Board; and finally to Paul V. McNutt, administrator of the Federal Security Agency. Hoey is simply another social worker of the familiar type but with a higher salary than most. Casius has lost none of his qualities since Shakespeare described him, except that his wit has been sharpened by a little legal training. Powell is a very high calibre

man with a fine sense of argumentative values, a considerable store of good nature, and unusual perception.
He simply is not a believer in our fundamental assumptions. McNutt, on the other hand, is a lesser Hitler by
disposition and makes our California social workers look
like angels by comparison.

Hoey and Powell had argued that the new ruling of
the Board did not necessarily result in a reduction of a
recipient's grant by the amount of his earnings or other
income. McNutt took the position that it did and, moreover, that it should. 'Are you saying to us,' I asked
McNutt, 'that blind people should have their grants reduced no matter how small their private income and no
matter how great their actual need?' His answer was
that he was saying precisely that. I formulated the question in several other ways, only to get the same reply. I
can't say that I wasn't glad to get this official declaration from McNutt since it provides us with an official
declaration by the highest administrator of them all that
ought to be of immense propagandistic value to us.
Moreover, McNutt's conduct during the conference has
provided us with the most perfect example of the arbitrary and tyrannical methods of the Board that we could
hope to have. In the remaining week that I shall stay
in Washington, we shall attempt to carry our appeal to
the last administrative step. Senator Downey of California and Senator Hughes of Delaware are attempting
to secure for us appointments with Mrs. and President
Roosevelt.

As things stand, the only course open to the blind
of California is to urge the legislature to retain the blind
aid act in its present form and tell the federal government to go to hell. Even if we can get a favorable amendment to the Social Security Act, it certainly will not be
until after the California legislature adjourns."

This is what Dr. tenBroek wrote in 1941, and although we have often said in this organization that the
first task which the Federation faced after its founding

was to help the blind of the nation get enough money for bare survival, I sometimes wonder if we have made the point with sufficient clarity to convey the desperation of it. The report which was prepared following the 1941 convention of the Federation in Milwaukee says in part:

"Mr. Stephen Stanislevic of New York City reported as follows: 'The blind population of New York State is roughly estimated at 13,000. Of these, more than half are in New York City. A very small number of our people, a few hundred in all, are at present employed in sheltered industries, on government projects, at newsstands, or in miscellaneous enterprises. The majority depend for sustenance either upon private bounty or upon Social Security grants. The average monthly grant per individual is $27 in New York City and $23 in the upstate counties. This is the paltry pittance which the wealthiest state in our Union sees fit to dole out to those of its citizens who are blind. Mr. Hugh McGuire explained that in Indiana there are approximately 2,600 blind and that between 2,200 and 2,300 are drawing assistance with the monthly average of $20.'"

That was forty-nine years ago, and much has happened in the interim. Not that it happened by chance, of course. Mostly we made it happen. How many times since 1940 has the National Federation of the Blind led the way in social reform in this country, not only for the blind but also for others? To mention only three examples, we pioneered exempt earnings for the recipients of public assistance; we pioneered fair hearing procedures in rehabilitation and other public programs; and we pioneered jobs for the disabled in government service.

As I have already said, our first task as an organization was to initiate programs to enable the blind get enough to eat. In 1940 and the decades immediately following, most of the blind of this country were desperately poor, and there were almost no government programs to help. When people are hungry, little else matters. Later (although many of us were still in poverty, and, for that matter, are now) we worked on rehabilitation and employment, and today we emphasize civil rights and equal participation in society. But essentially our role is what it has always been—seeing that blind people get equal treatment and a fair shake.

It is not only in basics but also in detail that our operation today is often much the same as it was in past decades. Let me give you a rather specialized example. I have made a lot of banquet speeches at these conventions, and certain key ideas are central to them all. I can sum up the essentials in a few sentences. The real problem of blindness is not the blindness itself but what the members of the general public think about it. Since the agencies doing work with the blind are part of that general public, they are likely to possess the same misconceptions that are held by the broader society. The blind, too, are part of that broader society, and if we are not careful, we will accept the public view of our limitations and thus do much to make those limitations a reality. The blind are not psychologically or mentally different from the sighted. We are neither especially blessed nor especially cursed. We need jobs, opportunity, social acceptance, and equal treatment—not pity and custody. Only those elected by the blind can speak for the blind. This is not only a prime requisite of democracy but also the only way we can ever achieve first-class status.

These are the essential points of every banquet speech I have ever made. The banquet speeches are meant to be widely circulated. They have the purpose of convincing those in work with the blind and the public at large that they should rethink their notions about blindness. They also have the purpose of stimulating our own members to increased activity and added vigor. Hopefully the speech will be sufficiently inspiring, entertaining, and literate to make people want to listen to it, and later (when it is distributed) to read it. The difficulty is that just about the same thing needs to be said every year, but it has to be restated so that the listeners (and ultimately the readers) will feel that it is different, and maybe even new. After a while, putting it all together becomes quite a problem.

I don't think I ever talked about this matter with Dr. tenBroek, and I certainly did not attend the 1949 convention at Denver. With this background let me share some correspondence with you. Kingsley Price was a Californian, who became a college professor and was living in New York in the 1940's. In a letter dated April 8, 1949, Dr. tenBroek wrote to urge him to attend the Denver convention. "The problem does not arise," Dr. tenBroek said, "out of an unmixed desire to enjoy your company. I would like to get you to give the principal banquet address. This is something that I have not been able to dodge very often in the seven conventions that we have had. [Conventions were not held in the war years of 1943 and 1945.] The banquet address," Dr. tenBroek continued, "is a kind of focal point in which the problems of the blind, their peculiar needs with respect to public assistance, employment, and equal opportunity are formulated and presented both with an eye to rededicating and stimulating the blind persons present and an eye to enlightening and possibly converting the many sighted persons who have been invited to attend. For me, this has always been a job of rehashing and repeating certain central ideas. My imagination and new methods of statement have long since petered out. The next alternative is to get a new 'stater.' This is what I would like you to be. We would, of course, introduce you as a New Yorker since there are far too many Californians in the limelight as it is. We also, if we thought hard, could find one or two other chores about the convention for you to do. Please think this matter over as long as you want, but let me have an immediate answer." Among other things, Dr. tenBroek obviously wanted to get Price to become more active in the movement, and he probably thought the banquet speech might be a way to do it. There has always been a tendency for the successful members of a minority to try to avoid involvement. The only trouble with this behavior is that it won't work. At an earlier period many blacks tried to straighten their hair and hide in white society, but then they realized that it was better to make it respectable to be black. The corollary, if I need to say it, (and every one of us had better know and understand it) is that it is respectable to be blind. That's what the National Federation of the Blind is all about.

No blind person in this country is untouched by our successes or, for that matter, our failures, and no blind person can avoid identification with the rest of us. This is true regardless of how the blind person feels about it and regardless of how we feel about it. Blindness is a visible characteristic, and all of us are judged by each other whether we like it or not. The feeling I have toward those blind persons who try to hide in sighted society is not anger but pity, and, yes, I am talking about those who are regarded (and who regard themselves) as highly successful.

When Professor Price replied to Dr. tenBroek, he said that he might be able to come but would probably do a bad job making the banquet speech. He should not have been deceived by the light tone of Dr. tenBroek's letter of invitation, for Federation presidents take banquet speeches seriously. In a letter dated April 21, 1949, Dr. tenBroek set him straight:

"Dear Kingsley:

I am not now, nor on June 20th shall I be, in the least inclined to accept a bad job in the banquet address. If I were willing to accept a bad job, I can think of at least a hundred persons of assured competence to satisfy the requirement. The banquet address is the focal point of the whole meeting. It has come to be regarded as the most important thing that is done at a convention. Many people of influence in the community are invited to hear it. The Governor of the State often is present, and the occasion is used to give him instructions as to what his policy should be towards the blind. The address is expected to be of such a character that it can be published and circulated the nation over with some advantage to the blind.

The address must be on the subject of the nature of the problems of blindness, and the discussion should be frank and forthright. Amplification of points by way of personal experience is always helpful and attractive. One conclusion that must always be reached is that the blind should speak for themselves because they are the only persons qualified to do so.

I enclose a copy of my Baltimore address, which may give you an idea of what needs to be said. The same truths have to be retold, but the hope is that they will be dressed up in a new and fresh style, even to the point of appearing to be different truths.

One further word: It may be that the address will be broadcast direct from the banquet hall. Consequently, both speech and delivery need to be well in hand. I hope these admonitions are solemn enough to convince you of the importance of doing a good job and yet not so solemn as to scare you away. We are desperately in need of a new voice and a new brain to do this job, and a man from New York has geographical advantages as well.

Cordially yours,"

In considering our past I am mindful of the fact that except for inspiration, perspective, and prediction, there is no purpose to the study of history. Certainly we can find inspiration in the lives of Warring Wilkinson, Newel Perry, and Jacobus tenBroek. Often in lonely isolation they worked for a distant future which they knew they would never see but which is our present. Using meager resources that they could ill-afford to spare, they fought to build a framework of opportunities and benefits which constitute the underpinning and foundation of what we have today. How can we be unmoved by their story? It speaks to us across the years; calling us to conscience, giving us strength for the battles ahead, reminding us of our heritage, and underscoring our duty to those who will follow.

Yes, there is inspiration in our history, and it also gives us perspective. Otherwise we might become discouraged. Even today, with all of our work, more often than not when we come to one of these conventions and talk to the press, they assign their medical reporters to deal with us. They want to write stories about our guide dogs, the causes of blindness, and how capable we are because we can do the ordinary tasks of daily living, like cutting our food or finding our way.

But the balances are shifting. Each year a few more reporters are beginning to understand that our story is not one of physical loss, or courage in the face of deprivation, but lack of opportunity and denial of civil rights. A perfect example is the recent story in the *Wall Street Journal* about the blind who are running their own businesses. It contains not a scrap of pity, nor a wasted word about those who (though blind) are valiantly struggling to earn a living. Of course, it contains drama, but it is the drama of a people fighting to rise to first-class status in a society which treats them like children and wonders why they object.

Recently I went to the White House and talked with the President of the United States about the problems we are having with the airlines and the Federal Aviation Administration. We are being excluded from exit row seats on airplanes, but year after year the Federal Aviation Administration has said that there is no issue of safety in our sitting there. Now (because of pressure by the airlines) they have changed their minds. As we have become painfully aware, the issue of seating is only one tiny part of an overall pattern of bullying and harassment which blind persons face today in air travel. The difficulty which always confronts us when we try to discuss this issue is the talk we get about compassion and how commendable it is that we are trying to be independent—all of which is a bunch of nonsense. If we pose a hazard in exit row seats, we shouldn't sit there, and we wouldn't want to. If we don't pose a hazard in exit row seats, then we have as much right to sit there as anybody else, and to try to make us move is an infringement of our civil rights. In either case compassion has nothing to do with it.

When I tried to convey these ideas to President Bush, his response made it clear that he had been thoroughly briefed, and by somebody who hadn't the faintest idea about the issues. In answer to my question the President said that if there was no evidence that we constituted a greater hazard than others in exit row seats, he would put an end to the rule if he had the power to do so, which, of course, he has. I wasn't very hopeful about the outcome because of two things. President Bush kept avoiding the word *blind*, gingerly referring to us as the non-sighted, and he said that Secretary of Transportation Skinner had personally tested an airplane door to see whether an individual without sight could open it, which is comparable to my going (with my lack of experience) to a hospital to see what can be done with surgical instruments.

The President assigned his lawyer, Boyden Gray, to look into the matter and get back to me. The results were what might have been expected. Mr. Gray did not talk to us, nor did he look at the video tape of our test evacuation of an airplane. Instead, he talked with Secretary of Transportation Skinner, who told him that we constituted a safety hazard, which data he ceremonially transmitted to me.

So was it just an exercise in futility? Not at all. This is where perspective helps. In 1940 Dr. tenBroek was not able even to get a hearing from President Roosevelt even though two United States senators tried to help him do it. Moreover, my talk with President Bush was only one brief skirmish in our long airline fight, and the history of our past efforts tells us that we will ultimately win. It is true that Dr. tenBroek did not get to talk with President Roosevelt, but it is also true that most of the Social Security reforms for which he fought have been adopted, and mostly they have been adopted through the efforts of the National Federation of the Blind.

Likewise, we lost the recent motion to cut off debate on our airline bill in the United States Senate, but we had fifty-six votes. And when has any other group in the blindness field ever been able to bring a bill of its own to the floor of the United States Senate and have it be the pending business of that body for several days? Never, and never with the number of votes we mustered. Again, this was only a single skirmish in an individual battle in a long war; a war which has been going on for more than a century, a war which we are winning, and a war which we intend to finish.

Yes, our history provides us with both inspiration and perspective, and it also gives us the basis for prediction. Of course, no individual can be sure of what will happen tomorrow, but I feel absolutely certain that this organization will continue to grow and lead the way in improving the quality of life for the blind. The outward appearance of the issues may shift, but the basics will not change—not until we have achieved equal treatment and first-class status in society. And we will achieve it.

In examining our past I have not attempted to assess my own role and contributions. How could I? I have been too close, loved too deeply, put too much of my life into the process. All I can say is this: When Dr. tenBroek was dying, I made certain pledges to him. I have tried to keep those pledges. I shall always try to keep them. And when in 1986 I thought the time had come that the movement would best be served by my leaving the presidency, I did it. The decision was not easy, but I think it was right. I believe that President Maurer was the best person we could have chosen for the position and that he will lead this organization into the twenty-first century—stronger, more vibrant, and more committed than it has ever been. And there is something more: I think the new generation that is on the horizon will provide leaders and members who will be present fifty years from now when we meet for our hundredth anniversary. We must never forget our history; we must never dishonor our heritage; we must never abandon our mission. With love for each other and faith in our hearts we must go the rest of the way to equal status and first-class membership in society. Let us march together to meet the future.

In 1992, Dr. Jernigan offered an analysis of progress and change within programs for the blind during the twentieth century, with particular emphasis on the expanding role of the blind in shaping the future and determining their own destiny. In the beginning of the century programs to serve the blind were dominant. However, blind people tasted freedom and became more active, more articulate, and more insistent on speaking and acting for themselves. The mechanism for this change was the National Federation of the Blind. In an address to the convention of the Federation held in Charlotte, North Carolina, Dr. Jernigan gave us what is, perhaps, the most robust brief analysis of the relationships among entities dealing with the blind that has been created. Entitled, "Shifting Balances in the Blindness Field," this is what Dr. Jernigan said:

The German scientist Max Planck said: "A new truth usually doesn't triumph by convincing its opponents and making them see the light but rather because its opponents eventually die and a new generation grows up that is familiar with it." In more prosaic language I say that those who base their actions on yesterday's perceived truths (whether real or imagined) are poorly equipped to deal with today's realities and are likely to have much time for reflection in tomorrow's leisure of unemployment.

Today we are talking about the future of services for the blind. The fact that we are, along with the popularity and recurrence of the theme, means that there is a felt need and that there are problems. But we are talking about something more. We are talking about the shifting balances in the blindness system of this country. We are talking about the governmental and private agencies, blind consumers, and the relationship between consumers and professionals. In a broader sense we are talking about the very survival of the blindness field as we have known it.

The most notable thing about the blindness field is how different it is today from what it was twenty or thirty years ago. From the 1920's to the 1960's the unquestioned leader among the governmental and private agencies doing work with the blind in this country was the American Foundation for the Blind, and there was a reasonable amount of coherence and unity. As to the organized blind movement, the National Federation of the Blind didn't even exist until 1940, and it didn't become a major factor in the field for quite a few years after that. Today everything has changed. If what I am about to say is to do any good at all, it is absolutely essential that we deal with facts, not just wishes or claims or fantasies.

Let me begin with the American Foundation for the Blind. It was established in 1921, and its mission was fairly clear. It was to coordinate the efforts of the professionals in the blindness field throughout the country, help create and guide new agencies, do research, serve as a mechanism for resources and referrals, and generally act as a focal point for agency activities. Realistically viewed, most of those functions no longer exist as prime objectives.

In the 1920's the Foundation was instrumental in establishing and providing initial guidance to quite a number of state agencies. In Iowa, for instance, where I was formerly director, the American Foundation for the Blind worked in 1926 and 1927 with the state legislature and the school for the blind to establish the Iowa Commission for the Blind. It sent staff members to help get programs started and to find and train personnel. The same was true in a number of other states. That mission no longer exists. Today the state agencies are well established, and they don't now generally look to the Foundation for guidance; nor do they feel any particular loyalty to it. Rather, they look to their state-federal relationships, their own national organizations and committees, mechanisms within their state borders, and alliances with consumer organizations. This is not to criticize but simply to state facts.

In the twenties and thirties the American Foundation for the Blind, if not alone in the work, was certainly the principal leader in developing specialized tools and appliances for the blind: Braille watches, measuring devices, household aids, and the like. The Foundation also took the lead in developing the talking book machine, and for a time it was virtually the only organization producing talking book records. All of that has now changed. The Foundation is a relatively minor participant in the production and sale of specialized tools, aids, and appliances. It does not even sell or ship these from its own premises but relies on a catalog fulfillment company to do the work. If the Foundation were to go completely out of the specialized tools and appliances business today, there would scarcely be a ripple. The Foundation is, by no means, the principal manufacturer or distributor. That part of its original mission is now largely (and in the main, successfully) finished.

As to the production of talking book records, the Foundation still does it, but there would be no great problem to anybody but the Foundation if it ceased the activity. Others have now taken the lead in the field. Again, this is no criticism. In fact, quite the contrary. It emphasizes the success of the Foundation's pioneering effort.

The Foundation played a key role in helping design and pass some of the principal legislation which determined the direction of the blindness field and which still underpins many of the opportunities that we as blind people enjoy, but that was decades ago. The golden age of the Foundation's influence in shaping federal legislative and administrative policy was probably the 1930's and the early '40's when the Books for the Blind program of the Library of Congress was established, Title X (the Public Assistance for the Blind section of the Social Security Act) was adopted, the Randolph-Sheppard Act was passed, the Rehabilitation Act (Barden-La Follette, 1943) was amended to include the blind, and a whole new spate of other legislative and administrative policies came into being. Indeed, the Foundation did not single-handedly make these achievements, having at times to compromise with others in the field and even now and again failing altogether to get its own way—but few would argue that the Foundation was not at the center of the action or the dominant force.

That, however, was more than fifty years ago, and the 1990's bear little resemblance to the 1930's and '40's. Certainly the Foundation is no longer a controlling factor in legislative or executive decisions concerning the blind. We who are blind now speak for ourselves through our own organization, the National Federation of the Blind, and we are the most powerful force in such matters in Washington and the state capitals today. Of course, the governmental and private agencies for the blind still have a major presence in legislative and executive decisions concerning blindness, but they speak with many voices—and certainly with no dominance or central influence on the part of the Foundation. Again, I cannot emphasize too strongly that what I am saying is not meant as criticism but only as a recognition of fact.

The Second World War and the period immediately following brought a shift in emphasis for the Foundation. Because of the thousands of children who developed retrolental fibroplasia (today we would call it retinopathy of prematurity), there was a crisis in education. In California, for instance, where I was living at the time, there were in the early 1950's more than 1,200 young RLF children who were blind—and the residential school could handle only about 200. What was to be done? RLF had largely been conquered, and when the wave of hundreds of blind children had passed through the population, there was every reason to believe the number would return to normal. It made neither economic nor political sense for the state of California to build five or six new residential schools for the blind. It was simply not in the cards. At the same time the parents were not going to permit their blind children to stay at home and not have an education. The answer was obvious. They would have to be placed in the public schools in their local areas—which, incidentally, made the endless arguments (arguments often stimulated by the Foundation) about which environment is better for the education of a blind child, the residential or the public school, not only pointless but downright harmful and diversionary. Regardless of the quality of the training or the competence of the teachers, most of these children were necessarily going to be trained in the public schools in their home communities.

To its credit, the American Foundation for the Blind stepped into the breach. It had a major new mission, the establishment of university programs to train teachers of blind children, the recruitment of the teachers, the finding of teachers to teach the teachers, and the development of educational materials to make the process possible. Important as that mission was (and it was extremely important), it has long since passed. The university programs to train special education teachers for the blind are now completely mature. They demonstrate no special loyalty to the Foundation nor any evidence of following its leadership or asking it to coordinate their efforts. In fact, as adult children are wont to do, they often find themselves competing with the Foundation for money and leadership. Whatever else may be said for the loose national confederacy to which most of the university programs belong—that is, the Association for Education and Rehabilitation of the Blind and Visually Impaired (AER)—the organization is not now controlled or dominated by the American Foundation for the Blind. This is true despite the fact that the Foundation was instrumental in establishing many of the university programs and that in the 1970's it gave sizable amounts of money to the AER, which at the time was using another name.

As a natural concomitant of its work with the university programs, the Foundation began to organize and give direction to parents of blind children. In fact, a few years ago the Foundation was instrumental in organizing NAPVI (the National Association for Parents of the Visually Impaired). It provided a staff member to the organization, gave direction and leadership to it, and helped it set policy. Recently, however, the Hilton Foundation gave the Perkins School for the Blind a $15,000,000 grant, running over a five-year period; and Perkins effectively took control of NAPVI, giving it many tens of thousands of dollars, much more than the Foundation could possibly muster. The Foundation competed for the Hilton grant, but it lost—another sign of the shifting balances in the blindness field.

With respect to those shifting balances, there is still another factor. The Parents of Blind Children Division of the National Federation of the Blind is now probably the major force in the field. Certainly its magazine, *Future Reflections*, is the largest circulation publication for parents and educators of the blind, as well as the most influential. In any case the Foundation (to the extent that it has any part left to play in organizing and directing the activities of parents of blind children) is now only a minor participant.

Once more I repeat that I am not being critical. The American Foundation for the Blind filled a need with respect to the education of blind children and the counseling of their parents which could not have been filled by anybody else at the time and which absolutely demanded attention. It is simply that this part of the Foundation's mission has now been largely accomplished. There are those who would argue (in fact, I am one of them) that some of the Foundation's advice to the parents and many of its policy guidelines to the universities were custodial in nature, overly defensive about what was called professionalism, and more involved with complexity and prestige than common sense and the good of the child—but these criticisms must be viewed in context. When considered from the distance of the years and the magnitude of the task undertaken, the criticisms soften and take perspective. There was no viable alternative, and the Foundation did what it could with the knowledge it had and the resources it possessed. It deserves our appreciation, not our spleen.

The Second World War brought other changes besides those affecting the education of blind children. It moved the United States to the center of the stage in world affairs. Among other things, this meant that our country would take the leading role in helping other nations develop programs for the blind. The American Foundation for the Blind was the natural leader and coordinator.

It played a principal part in establishing the World Council for the Welfare of the Blind, and in November of 1945 it took control of the American Braille Press for War and Civilian Blind and renamed it the AFOB (the American Foundation for Overseas Blind). The AFOB was technically a separate organization, but its board was almost identical to that of the Foundation. Throughout the world in the forties and fifties the Foundation was generally recognized as the leading force in the blindness field in the United States and as our chief spokesman in overseas matters.

All of that has now changed. In the late sixties and early seventies the AFOB went through an alteration. It changed its name to Helen Keller International, began to acquire a different board from that of the Foundation, and ultimately broke the ties almost completely. Then, in the changing climate of public opinion about overseas projects, Helen Keller International very nearly went bankrupt. It is now largely financed (and, therefore, in reality substantially controlled) by the U.S. government and spends the major part of its money (a sizable budget) in prevention of blindness projects in other countries. Meanwhile the American Foundation for the Blind no longer has preeminence in overseas activities.

In 1984 the International Federation of the Blind and the World Council for the Welfare of the Blind (the two major world organizations in the field) merged to become the World Blind Union. The North America/ Caribbean Region of the World Blind Union consists of organizations of and for the blind in Canada, the English-speaking nations of the Caribbean, and the United States, and is generally recognized by other countries as the principal mechanism for action affecting the blind in this part of the world—particularly, regarding overseas matters. The Foundation is a member of the regional structure, but it is certainly not dominant.

I have already alluded to the $15,000,000 grant which the Perkins School received from the Hilton Foundation. Some of this money is being spent inside the United States, but much of it is being used to develop projects and give aid overseas. With respect to dollars spent in overseas aid, Perkins is now a major factor— and with money goes influence. I think it is fair to say that (with the exception of providing a certain amount of professional literature) the American Foundation for the Blind does not today have any significant commitment, influence, or mission beyond the borders of this country. This is in no way to belittle or take away from the work which the Foundation did in this area in the past or the work which it may do in the future. It is simply to state facts as I believe them to be at present.

Let me turn next to NAC (the National Accreditation Council for Agencies Serving the Blind and Visually Handicapped). In the 1960's the American Foundation for the Blind created COMSTAC (the Commission on Standards and Accreditation). It financed COMSTAC and provided it with an executive director. The objective was to establish for agencies in the blindness field a system of accreditation, which the Foundation hoped would come to be universally accepted, bringing influence to the Foundation and harmony to the field. The exact opposite occurred. After a brief existence, COMSTAC established NAC, which confidently announced that it would be completely self-supporting in no more than five or six years and that it would encompass most of the agencies.

What followed is a study in failure. NAC was never accepted by even as many as twenty percent of those that it wanted to accredit. Through the sixties, the seventies, and the eighties it bled the Foundation financially and politically, a black hole of controversy and cost. NAC has been the Foundation's Vietnam—and (as with America's Vietnam) disentanglement, admission of mistakes, and loss of face have been bitter medicine to swallow. My conversations with Foundation officials indicate that the Foundation has spent more than $9,000,000 on NAC. It has now stopped the expenditures, and NAC is in its death throes. Even so, the Foundation understandably finds it difficult to make a clean break and a public statement that the chapter of its Vietnam must be closed and left in the past.

In a number of discussions during the past few months, Carl Augusto (the recently appointed president and chief executive of the Foundation) has talked with me quite frankly about the condition and future of his organization. I gather from him that the Foundation's assets have dropped from a worth of about forty million dollars four or five years ago to a present value of something over twenty-four million and that the hemorrhaging (though slowing) continues. I also understand that the Foundation eliminated some twenty percent of its staff positions during 1991, making massive layoffs. In my opinion this does not mean that the Foundation will go bankrupt or cease to be a major participant in the affairs of the blind, nor do I think it would serve the best interests of the blind if such were the case. Rather, I think it means that the Foundation must redefine its mission, free itself from its Vietnam, and accept the realities of the present day.

As to redefining its mission, the Foundation has recently been working on the matter. Under date of January 15, 1992, Mr. Augusto sent me a letter concerning extensive planning sessions the Foundation conducted during 1990 and 1991, and along with the letter he enclosed a statement entitled the "AFB Mission." Here it is:

The mission of AFB is to enable persons who are blind or visually impaired to achieve equality of access and opportunity that will ensure freedom of choice in their lives. AFB accomplishes this mission by taking a national leadership role in the development and implementation of public policy and legislation, informational and educational programs, diversified products and quality services.

To advance this mission, AFB works to: develop and disseminate knowledge, programs, and products that can be used by professionals providing service to persons who are blind or visually impaired, by educational institutions, by legislators, by employers, and by others in a position to widen and improve equal access; to initiate or join with coalitions of other organizations, when appropriate, to accomplish specific goals or objectives; to promote the positive image of persons who are blind or visually impaired in the media and the community, and to provide a diversified and stable funding base for the organization to ensure ongoing support for the strategies and activities required.

The mission statement [the document continues] *calls for AFB to move toward a more selective national leadership role in effecting the fundamental changes required to achieve equality of access and opportunity for persons who are blind or visually impaired. It defines AFB's national leadership role as an information broker, an agent of change, a leader, and innovator.*

That is what Mr. Augusto sent me as the Foundation's new mission statement, and I can only say that I find it somewhat disappointing. It seems to me that it is too much couched in generalities and does not contain enough that is different from yesterday's largely finished activities. It announces almost no new initiatives, no specifics, and no clear direction for the future. Perhaps the Foundation will go back to the drawing board and further define its role and how it intends to achieve it. I hope that it will, for the blind and the blindness field need the Foundation—not a Foundation looking back to the past but the kind of creative organization of the formative years—vital, resilient, determined, and innovative.

It is a positive sign that the Foundation and the Federation have been working together with increasing closeness during the past decade. Bill Gallagher and I have become warm personal friends, and Carl Augusto shows an interest in continuing to strengthen the ties. He was at last year's convention and indicated a positive desire to speak on this year's program. These things would not have been possible twenty years ago.

In this discussion of shifting balances in the blindness field, why have I spent so much time on the American Foundation for the Blind? The answer is simple. The Foundation has played such a major part in the development of the blindness system in this country during the past seventy years that any meaningful discussion of where we are and where we are going must take it into account and give it significant emphasis.

But there are other forces to be considered. One of them is the AER (the Association for Education and Rehabilitation of the Blind and Visually Impaired). The AER resulted from a merger between the AAIB (American Association of Instructors for the Blind, which later changed its name to the Association for Education of the Visually Handicapped) and the AAWB (the American Association of Workers for the Blind). The AAIB was established in the middle of the last century, and the AAWB came into being in 1905. The merged organization (AER) was meant to encompass most of the professionals in work with the blind in both Canada and the United States. It has a large membership on paper and is potentially the leading force among the agency professionals—but the potential has never been realized, and there seems little likelihood that it will. The problem is that AER has almost no central authority. It is so loosely knit that in many ways it is an organization in name only. Its constituents show no prime loyalty to it and no ability to act in concert on tough questions and meaningful issues. It has many members but little influence, and it is likely to stay that way.

Let me illustrate. In the summer of 1988 at an AER convention in Montreal a number of us decided to try to see if we could pull the blindness field in Canada and the United States together for concerted action. Accordingly, the Committee on Joint Organizational Effort (JOE) was established. Those invited to attend as initial members (it was thought we might later expand the membership) were the Canadian National Institute for the Blind, the Canadian Council of the Blind, the

AER, the American Foundation for the Blind, the National Library Service for the Blind and Physically Handicapped, the American Council of the Blind, the Blinded Veterans Association, and the National Federation of the Blind. The first JOE meeting was held in March of 1989 at the National Center for the Blind in Baltimore and was hosted by the National Federation of the Blind. All who were invited attended except the American Council of the Blind, which thereby emphasized and increased its growing isolation from the main stream of the blindness field.

Although the first JOE meeting spent much of its time smoothing tensions and establishing relationships, it dealt with substantive issues as well. One of these involved Braille literacy. After much discussion we unanimously agreed upon the language of a statement. Present as representatives of AER were its immediate past president, its then current president, and its president elect—presumably the top leaders of the organization. Most of us left that meeting feeling that we had achieved a binding agreement. Yet, the AER board agonized, wanted to water down the statement, and ultimately rejected it.

At the second meeting of the Committee on Joint Organizational Effort, which was held at the Canadian National Institute for the Blind in Toronto in November of 1990, the need to find a way to increase Braille literacy was further discussed. At the third JOE meeting, held at the American Foundation for the Blind in New York in January of this year, Braille literacy was again considered. Once more, AER was represented by its immediate past president, its current president, and its president elect. After much discussion and refinement of language we unanimously agreed upon the following statement:

Recognizing that ongoing assessment and due process are requirements of the law, the members of the Committee on Joint Organizational Effort endorse the principle that in planning the educational program for a blind or visually impaired child, these guidelines be followed:

- If reading and writing are to be taught and if the parent or parents and the decision makers for the school want the child to be taught Braille, this should be done.

- If reading and writing are to be taught and if the parent or parents and the decision makers for the school want print to be taught, this should be done.

- If the parent or parents and the decision makers for the school cannot agree, then both Braille and print should be taught.

This was the statement we agreed upon, and if it had been any milder, it would have been worthless. Also, remember that it had been discussed over a three-year period at three succeeding meetings and that top AER officials had participated throughout the process. Yet, under date of April 12, 1992, Dr. William Wiener, president of AER, sent a memorandum to the members of the Committee on Joint Organizational Effort entitled "Recent JOE Agreements." Here is what he said:

As you may know, because AER is a membership organization, its Board of Directors requires that major policy decisions of the Association be reviewed by its duly elected representatives. Based on this policy, the officers of the Association that attended the last JOE meeting presented our agreements for confirmation by the Board of Directors. It is the purpose of this memorandum to report the decisions that were made.

In general the Board is supportive of the efforts of the JOE to discuss issues that affect blind people. Because our differences are sometimes great, it should not be viewed as negative when consensus is not reached. It is felt by the Board that honest discussions will re-

sult in an increased ability to understand each other and that agreement is not a required outcome.

The Board was appreciative of our efforts to reach consensus on the issue of Braille Literacy. After a lengthy discussion, however, the Board voted not to support our concluding agreement. The Board felt that the wording of the agreement left the statement open to different interpretations. A statement that can be viewed differently by different groups serves no useful purpose. The Board did, however, endorse that AER supports the goal that no child should ever find the implementation of legislation an obstacle to his or her best educational process. The JOE discussions on this issue have been useful as they have inspired the Board of AER to move ahead to define its own position on Braille Bills. As President, I have appointed an Ad Hoc Board Committee chaired by Toni Heinze to develop a statement that clearly defines our beliefs. It will not be "model legislation" but rather important points to be considered in formulating a position on any particular version of the Braille Bills. I believe this will be a useful tool as we move forward to insure that blind children and adults receive the best possible education and rehabilitation.

It is our goal to complete this task by our biennial meeting in Los Angeles. I will be sure to share this information with the Committee on JOE as soon as it has been approved by the AER Board.

There you have the AER memorandum—and there you also have, in AER's own language, the reason why it is not, and cannot be, the leader of the governmental and private agencies in this country or, for that matter, even a strong force in their conduct. The AER totally rejected the actions of its top leaders on what should have been almost a non-controversial issue, and even if the Board had approved, there is no reason to believe that the individual agencies and members of AER would have paid any attention or altered their policies in the slightest. Again I remind you that I am not criticizing. I am only stating facts as I see them and suggesting that those in the blindness field (all of us) must either avoid the world of fantasy and face reality or risk destruction.

Let me next turn to the ACB (the American Council of the Blind). It was formed in 1961 at the end of the NFB's civil war, partly from people who were expelled from our organization and partly from those who quit. It, too, has an identity crisis and a problem of mission. At first its goal seemed simple—hate the National Federation of the Blind and get revenge. But that was over thirty years ago, and a new generation has risen. Hate and negativism are poor materials for long-term building, and thoughts of revenge are mostly the dream of the weak and the solace of the dispossessed. At our conventions you will observe that the American Council of the Blind is rarely thought of or mentioned, but at their meetings the circumstances are different. We are frequently the topic of discussion and the subject of snide allusion.

As to mission, the Council has a growing problem. In the sixties and seventies, when the American Foundation for the Blind and some of the other agencies were in bitter conflict with us, the ACB was used as a buffer. When there was a hotly contested issue, the agencies could trot the Council out and say: "The Federation does not represent the blind. Here is another consumer organization, which agrees with us." In short, the Council served as a company union. But that was before the 1980's when the Federation and an increasing number of the agencies started drawing closer and working in partnership. As the process continues and accelerates today, the Council not only ceases to be an asset to the agencies as a company union but actually becomes an embarrassment and a liability. It does, that is, unless it is willing to change its stance and join with the rest of us in trying to build a new basis for positive partnership in the field. At a minimum this would mean stopping the pretense that it is the largest organization of the blind in the country (a claim which nobody, including its own members, takes seriously anyway) and ceasing the hate campaigns—in short, leaving fantasy and facing reality. The American Council of the Blind can be a real force for constructive action if it will, and we will gladly work with it if it takes that road.

There are, of course, numerous other organizations and agencies in the blindness field, but many of these have not taken a significant role in the politics of it. The Blinded Veterans Association, for instance, falls into this category. Comparatively small and generally respected, it has traditionally limited its activities to matters concerning veterans. The National Council of State Agencies for the Blind, the organization of residential schools, the organization of state vision consultants, the National Council of Private Agencies for the Blind, and a number of other such groups have been loosely associated and have generally not attempted to exert much influence outside their particular specialties—and even in those areas of specialty, they have largely been forums for discussion and exchange of information rather than rallying points for broad-based, united action. Obviously all of this can change, and there is a good deal of evidence that in some instances it will. The balances are shifting.

In addition to the groups I have mentioned, there are individual agencies which have a national constituency and scope of operation that potentially give them influence far beyond what they have ever developed or chosen to use. I think of the Hadley School for the Blind, Recording for the Blind, and the American Printing House for the Blind as prime examples. All three of these agencies are reaching out to play broader roles than they have ever attempted before, and their presence is being felt.

The Rehabilitation Services Administration and the National Library Service for the Blind and Physically

Handicapped of the Library of Congress are also factors in the equation. They have broad constituencies and will necessarily play key roles in determining the nature and effectiveness of the blindness system in the years ahead. They will influence and be influenced by the coalitions which are built and the philosophies which are developed. With the leadership that they currently have, it seems clear that they will make positive contributions.

Then, there are the vendors of technology. They, too, are becoming an important part of the mix. Thirty years ago they did not exist, and such technology as we had came almost exclusively from the American Foundation for the Blind and the American Printing House for the Blind. Today the situation is totally different. There are an increasing number of commercial and non-profit producers and distributors of both high and low tech items, and their influence is growing. Their products affect our lives, and their sales representatives and service personnel mingle with us on a continuing basis. Whether they want to or not (and, for that matter, whether either they or we like it or not), they will necessarily be a significant factor in the discussions and alliances that are shaping the future of the blindness system.

Of course, technology has brought major changes in the lives of the sighted just as it has in the lives of the blind, but there is a significant difference. When the sighted moved from medievalism to the industrial revolution, then to the automobile, the airplane, and later to the electronic age, they had 200 years to do it, and there was time for adjustment and acclimatization—but not so with us. Our move from medievalism to electronics has happened in less than thirty years, with all of the upheaval such compression brings. Yes, technology is changing our lives—and there are political as well as technological implications.

So the vendors and distributors of technology will play an important part in determining the course of the blindness system, and there are also others who will. Some of the agencies in New York and other parts of the country, for instance, now have financial resources (more than one of them with upwards of fifty million dollars) which far exceed those of the American Foundation for the Blind or the others I have mentioned. Will they choose to become factors in the national mix? They could—and some of them may. Perkins, for instance, (although possibly a little less wealthy than a few of the rest) is well financed and energetically led. Whether it will choose to raise its profile and whether that will be good or bad will turn entirely on its motives and actions.

Whatever all of this may prove, surely there can be no doubt about at least one thing. The blindness field in this country is in ferment, and the old alignments and power bases are gone, gone forever. New forces are emerging. New balances are being struck. Will this be good or bad, positive or negative? It depends on what choices we make, what wisdom we show, and how responsibly we act.

So far, I have talked about others. Let me now say a few words about us, about the National Federation of the Blind. What does the new reality mean for the Federation? Well, for one thing, it means that we must be careful not to get too big for our pants. We may be (and I think we unquestionably are) the strongest force in the affairs of the blind in this country today—but we are not the only force. There are others, and their views must be taken into account. If we make the mistakes of some of those who were leaders in the blindness field in the past, if we fail to reach out in cooperative good will, our momentum will slow. Our progress will stop. We do not want to boss or lord it over others. We know what that feels like. We have been treated that way too often ourselves to want to do it to anybody else.

But let nobody misunderstand what I am saying. We are just as determined as we always were, never again to be treated like second-class citizens or kept from having a say in our own destiny. We have had a bellyful of that—and we are strong enough to see that it doesn't happen again. We still have teeth, and we know how to use them.

The blindness system in our country today is seriously threatened. Unless it can pull itself together in true partnership (with all, or at least the major participants, working in mutual respect), it may very well perish. Budgets are tightening; the environment is deteriorating; population is rising; and resources are dwindling. In addition, other disability groups (once disorganized and invisible) are finding their voice and reaching for power. They are now a growing force to be reckoned with, and there is no turning back.

As we look ahead, the future is bright with promise. We as an organization are stronger than we have ever been, and we are prepared to work in partnership with any and all who are interested in helping the blind move toward opportunity, equality, and freedom. These are the things we want, and these are the things we intend to have—opportunity, equality, and freedom. A measure of our progress can be seen in the increasing number of governmental and private agencies and members of the public who are joining with us in common cause, but the real indicator of our progress is what is happening within us as blind people. By the thousands and tens of thousands we have gained confidence, determination, and self-respect—and no force on earth can turn us back. This is the meaning of all I have said. This is the message of the shifting balances in the blindness field. Let us join together, and we will make it come true!

Shortly after the World Blind Union was formed in Riyadh, Saudi Arabia, in 1984, Dr. Jernigan became active within this world organization of the blind. By 1987, he had become president of the North America/Caribbean Region of the World Blind Union, a position he held until the fall of 1997. For ten years Dr. Jernigan traveled the world, speaking to individuals and organizations of the blind, planning international activities, and bringing hope and inspiration to blind people throughout the globe. He recognized that the task of bringing independence to blind people in every culture is monumental. Nevertheless, he reflected that the old joke about eating an elephant has within it a truth. "You eat an elephant one bite at a time, and the task, no matter how big, must be approached one act and one blind person at a time." Dr. Jernigan outlined his efforts within the World Blind Union in a report contained in the Braille Monitor for January 1995. This report entitled "Reflections and Comments on the World Blind Union" offers a brief overview of his dynamic work. This is what he said:

REFLECTIONS AND COMMENTS ON
THE WORLD BLIND UNION

by Kenneth Jernigan

At the end of the second World War America, England, and the countries comprising the British commonwealth were riding high. There seemed to be a feeling that a new day of progress and prosperity was dawning and that the English-speaking countries of the world were destined to lead the way in achieving it (and also, by and large, in paying for it). In this universal spirit of hope and brotherhood (no, not sisterhood—we hadn't got to that point yet) all were to receive assistance. There were Marshall Plans, foreign aid, and the United Nations.

Nobody was to be forgotten—and, of course, that included the blind. So in 1949 the World Council on the Welfare of the Blind was established. It met in Rome; elected Colonel Baker (the head of the Canadian National Institute for the Blind) as its president; and planned to meet again in five years, leaving interim matters to its officers and executive committee. The organization (generally called the WCWB) claimed to represent not only the governmental and private agencies but also the blind. And, indeed, there were organizations of the blind in its membership, including the National Federation of the Blind.

The problem was that many of the European organizations were hybrids. They called themselves organizations of the blind, and their claim had legitimacy. They had blind members; they had elections; and mostly they had blind officers. But they were also agencies, in that they provided rehabilitation and other services to the blind—very often the only such services in their countries. Moreover, their principal financing usually came from government, and their leaders were paid as service providers. This is not the place to discuss whether that was a better or worse model than we were using but simply to note that it was different. There were obvious advantages to the hybrid model—a steady source of income, paid leadership with time to develop programs, and a rather persuasive method of recruitment. In fact, when I was in Denmark four or five years ago, I asked how many members that country's organization of the blind had. I was given an answer. I then asked what the total blind population of the country was, and again I was given an answer. The two numbers were virtually the same.

On the other hand, there were disadvantages. If a blind person is dissatisfied with the behavior or services he or she receives, how can an effective appeal be made? The entire atmosphere of the operation will discourage appeals, as well as the very notion of adverse interests or freedom of choice.

Whether the advantages outweigh the disadvantages is a question that can be argued, but one thing is indisputable. When a group of representatives from different countries gather to talk about methods and procedures, communication is made difficult by the different kinds of organizations that call themselves organizations *of* the blind. Sometimes the subject can be touchy. I remember, for instance, a meeting in London a few years ago at which I said that in the United States an organization *of* the blind would not be defined in the same way as it would in some European countries, and I received an angry response from one of my esteemed European colleagues—which, of course, changed nothing since the facts are still the facts.

But back to the World Council on the Welfare of the Blind (the WCWB). In its early years it was largely run by the American Foundation for the Blind, the CNIB, and the British. It was characterized by quinquennial conventions, agency control, and professional articles and papers. It wielded relatively little influence in the blindness field in the United States—taking a backseat, for instance, to the American Foundation for Overseas Blind, which later split away to become Helen Keller International.

During the 1950's and 60's the participation of the National Federation of the Blind in WCWB activities was constant but mostly perfunctory. By the mid-1960's we felt that a worldwide organization *of* the blind should be established—not just an organization composed of and led by the blind but also an organization undiluted in its purpose of representing the blind. We were not seeking to build a force that would be hostile to the agencies but the establishment of a world organization that would avoid combining the functions of both service provider and service receiver—an organization that would serve as a balance to the agency-controlled WCWB. As I have often said, the organized blind of the United States do not wish actually to administer the agencies. If we did, another organization would have to be formed to serve as a watchdog on us and to represent the interest of consumers in dealing with us.

Much of the spadework in creating the new international organization was done by Dr. Isabel Grant, who traveled throughout the world to promote the establishment of independent organizations of the blind. At the 1964 convention of the National Federation of the Blind in Phoenix, Arizona, the preliminaries were commenced, and later that summer in New York the International Federation of the Blind (the IFB) was brought into being. Dr. tenBroek became its first president, and I drafted its constitution.

From the beginning it was touch and go with the IFB, for many of its members were also members of the WCWB. More important, their primary identification was with the agencies and service providers. Of course, the NFB was also a member of the WCWB, but its distinction from the agencies was more pronounced than that of organizations of the blind in many other countries—particularly some of those in Europe.

Let me not be misunderstood. A number of the organizations of the blind in Europe (particularly, those in England) did not perform agency functions. They were, by the most rigorous definition, organizations *of* the blind, representing the blind. But the English organizations were weakened by being specialized—one serving as a labor union and another as the rallying point for blind people in the professions.

Despite its problems, the International Federation of the Blind (IFB) had a promising beginning. New organizations of the blind began to emerge throughout the world, and a convention was planned for 1969 in Sri Lanka (at that time Ceylon). But in 1968 Dr. tenBroek, who had been not only the president of the IFB but its driving force, died. Almost immediately the IFB went into a sharp decline.

With Dr. tenBroek's death I became president of the National Federation of the Blind, and my time for the next few years was spent in building and expanding the NFB. Technically I served as the NFB's delegate to both the WCWB and the IFB, but any real participation on my part was virtually nonexistent. So was any meaningful influence by either the IFB or WCWB on matters dealing with the blind in this country. There were no regular meetings of U.S. delegates, no exciting proposals or initiatives, and no tangible programs or results.

Meanwhile, the IFB increasingly moved into the WCWB's orbit. First there were suggestions and then a growing pressure to merge the two organizations. What was contemplated was not a true combining of equals but a takeover of the weakened IFB by the WCWB. This move was resisted by some of the independent organizations *of* the blind, especially some in Asia and Africa. It was also resisted by us, but our resistance was at the token level, lacking priority or a sense of urgency. Through the decade of the 1970's we were chided by a number of blind leaders throughout the world for not taking leadership and rallying the forces of the International Federation of the Blind to bring to fruition the work we had started a decade earlier. Whether we should have adjusted our priorities and given emphasis to international affairs is probably not worth debating in the present circumstances. The fact is that we didn't.

By the early 1980's it was clear that the IFB would be absorbed by the WCWB and that our choices were to accept the situation or form a new international organization of the blind with safeguards to prevent subversion. In 1984 a joint meeting of IFB and WCWB was held in Riyadh, Saudi Arabia for the purpose of merging the two organizations. As a symbolic statement for the record, the National Federation of the Blind withdrew from the International Federation of the Blind prior to the Riyadh meeting, but we retained our participation in the merged organization by continuing to be members of the WCWB. It seemed to be an honest recognition of the actuality of the situation.

We did something else, which in retrospect was probably a mistake. We declined to go to the Riyadh meeting, which combined the IFB and the WCWB to create the World Blind Union (the WBU). The American Foundation for the Blind also boycotted the meeting. In the vacuum, the representative of the American Council of the Blind, Grant Mack, was elected president of the newly established North American region (later the North America/Caribbean Region) of the World Blind Union. The Mack presidency was an interim matter that lasted for a few weeks until permanent elections could be held.

That was the situation in the fall of 1984 when the six delegates from the United States and the four from Canada met in a hotel in Washington to conduct the first regional meeting of the WBU on this continent. The newly written WBU constitution emphasized geographic regions, and North America was one of seven— the other six being Africa, Asia, East Asia Pacific, Europe, Latin America, and the Middle East.

At the Washington meeting Bill Gallagher, who at that time was head of the American Foundation for the Blind, was elected regional president. Incidentally and for the record, I nominated him. I did it despite the fact that the American Foundation for the Blind and the National Federation of the Blind had traditionally disagreed, sometimes rather stridently. Relations between the two organizations had begun to thaw in the early '80's, a process which was in its early stages in 1984 but which would continue through the rest of the decade and beyond. Bill Gallagher played a major part in the improving cooperation, and it seemed fair to me to recognize the fact. That was one, but only one, of my reasons for nominating him.

It was at that Washington meeting in 1984 that I first met Dr. Euclid Herie and that our cooperative relations with the Canadians began. It was also at that meeting that the basic outlines of our regional WBU structure and procedures were established.

In 1986 the World Blind Union executive committee met in New York, and a number of Federationists (including Marc Maurer, who had just been elected president of the NFB) attended. It was the first time that I really got to know Sheikh Abdullah Al-Ghanim of Saudi Arabia, who served as WBU president from 1984 to 1988. The Sheikh wears well, and my respect for his competence and integrity has steadily increased as the years have passed.

In 1987 Bill Gallagher resigned as regional president, and I was elected to finish his term. I was reelected in 1988 and again in 1992. Sometime during the '80's the English-speaking countries of the Caribbean joined our region. Thus, we had (and still have) twelve WBU delegates—six from the United States, four from Canada, and two from the Caribbean.

The regional structure of the World Blind Union has served as a principal vehicle for the growing harmony in the blindness field in our country—a process which began in the '80's and is today a dominant theme. As to the situation with respect to the World Blind Union at large, the circumstances are totally different. The allocation of WBU delegates and the overall functioning of the organization are not in accord with reality. Therefore, it is not surprising that some of the results have been what they have been and that strains exist. Europe, for instance, has more than ten times as many delegates as our entire region. Yet, it would be hard to make a rational argument that Europe (with all due respect to its admitted greatness and traditions of excellence) is ten times stronger, wiser, or more virtuous than we are. Certainly it does not have ten times our population, and while we are on the subject of population, Europe has more delegates than Asia.

The allocation of delegates is not the only problem. The functioning of the organization is such that it is virtually impossible to bring about change by amending the constitution. Officers' meetings often seem hampered by personalities, procedures, and questionable issues (see the following article in this issue of the *Braille Monitor*).

Even more serious, perhaps, is the seeming tendency of some of the leaders to flirt with what has been called the cross-disability or pan-disability movement— the notion that all disability groups should come together in a common effort to approach problems. Through a resolution initiated by our region, the 1988 World Blind Union assembly in Madrid voted unanimously that we should not merge with other disability groups but should clearly keep our separate identity and concentrate on problems faced by the blind. Despite this fact and the fact that all of the WBU leaders insist that they support this policy, the trend of the organization seems otherwise.

A good example is the WBU's dealings with the United Nations. The WBU does not insist on separate negotiations with the UN but combines with other disability groups. It does this on the grounds that the UN won't have it any other way. Yet, this pressure to merge (this insistence that we pretend that all disability groups have common interests and common problems) is no different from the pressure the NFB constantly faces from Congress, state legislatures, and the general public. But we don't surrender to it, and our resistance is successful. It is more than that. It is one of the principal sources of our strength. I think the WBU could do likewise if it were determined and if it were convinced of the justice of its cause.

Another prime example is the case of the International Disability Foundation (IDF), which I discussed at length in the April, 1994, *Braille Monitor*. Through the leadership of Arne Husveg, President of the European Blind Union, the WBU officers and executive committee have decided to take office space in the proposed International Disability Center that the International Disability Foundation intends to establish in the Netherlands at The Hague. If the WBU takes office space with other disability groups in the so-called International Disability Center and shares staff with them, I don't see how the organization can be perceived as maintaining a meaningful separate identity. Moreover, I don't see how the WBU can reasonably object to fund raising in the name of the blind by the IDF. Explanations or anger won't change the reality of what is occurring. In fact, I question the legality of the decision to participate in the IDF in view of the Madrid resolution on maintaining separate identity.

With regard to IDF fund raising in Canada and the United States, the organizations of and for the blind in our region are solidly united. In that connection, the following letter to David Blyth, president of the World Blind Union, is self-explanatory:

Baltimore, Maryland
November 22, 1994

Dear David:

As you will see from the enclosed minutes, the North America/Caribbean region met on November 4, 1994. Among other things, we discussed the International Disability Foundation and its fund-raising activities. As regional president, I was instructed to write this letter to you and to state in the strongest possible terms our determination not to have the IDF or any other group raise funds either directly or indirectly in the name of the blind in the United States and/or Canada without our prior consent. We feel that the IDF's own literature makes it clear that IDF is raising funds in this region on a continuing basis and that action must be taken to put a stop to it.

Perhaps the determination and concern of the region can best be shown by calling your attention to the following portion of the minutes of our recent regional meeting. Item IV says in part:

A discussion was held concerning the International Disability Foundation (IDF) and the fund raising it is doing. Mr. Sanders said that perhaps we should write a letter to the World Blind Union president, reviewing the Melbourne discussion concerning IDF and the fact that it is WBU policy that funds may not be raised in a country without the consent of that country's delegation. Dr. Jernigan asked whether the delegates wanted him to send a letter to President Blyth concerning the matter. It was moved by Mr. Sanders and seconded by Mr. Cylke that such a letter be sent. The motion carried.

Dr. Herie said that the WBU president, like all of the rest of us, is bound by the policy adopted in Madrid in 1988 and that if IDF should come to Canada with cross-disability fund raising, CNIB would publicly and vigorously oppose it. Dr. Herie said that mega fund-raising campaigns serve no useful purpose. The United States delegates strongly agreed and were unanimous in feeling that if IDF is raising funds in the United States, there must be determined and concerted public opposition. Dr. Spungin said that she did not want our letter to be too weak. Mr. Sanders said that we should remind the WBU president of the policy concerning fund raising and request that an official letter be sent to the International Disability Foundation saying that the North America/Caribbean region has not approved IDF fund raising in our countries and that such fund raising must cease immediately if it is now in progress and must not be undertaken without our written consent.

There was unanimous approval of this course of action, and Dr. Jernigan said that he would write such a letter, first reviewing its exact wording with other regional delegates so that there could be no mistake that it represented the determined and concerted opinion of all of us.

Dr. Jernigan outlined the letter as he proposed to write it: We feel that fund raising is occurring, and we ask the WBU president to write a clarifying letter that it should not go forward.

Dr. Herie: Add that if it goes forward, our region will take steps to let the public and government know that we do not sanction it.

Mr. Sanders: And we will circulate our letters.

Mr. Magarrell: Make it clear that it is a total regional position.

Mrs. Braak: Also reiterate this issue involves the cross disability policy adopted by the 1988 General Assembly.

Mrs. McCarthy moved and Dr. Spungin seconded that our letter be to this effect. The motion carried unanimously. Dr. Jernigan appointed Mrs. McCarthy, Dr. Spungin, and Dr. Herie to work with him on the wording of the letter to the World Blind Union president.

This is what our minutes say, and I think the unanimity and intent are clear. As to our evidence of IDF's fund-raising activity, I was surprised at the recent Amman meeting that there was even any question about it. The IDF's own summer, 1994, publication lays it out in plain language. Here is what it says:

SHARING KING OLAV'S CAR

[*Photo*: The restored Cadillac limousine of King Olav V will be on permanent display in the Norwegian-American museum at Vesterheim in Iowa.]

Companies on both sides of the Atlantic are contributing to the joint IDF project to place King Olav's 1951 state car in the Norwegian-American museum in the USA.

The car was donated by King Harald, and all proceeds will go to the Foundation's work. "It will be a permanent tribute to a great monarch and humanitarian," said Hans Hoegh.

Norwegian companies have already made contributions, ... plus a number of donations from private individuals.

Interest now moves to the USA where full page adverts have been gifted by *The Norway Times* and *The Western Viking*.

This is what the IDF's publication says, and if "interest now moves to the U.S.A.," if there have been a "number of donations from private individuals," and if "all proceeds will go to the Foundation's work," it is hard to see how this can be called anything else except fund raising. Of course, there is all manner of other evidence: talk of art sales, individual contacts, and much more. Yet, when I raised the question in Amman, it was simply brushed aside as if the person responding didn't know what I was talking about.

David, we want to work cooperatively with you and do what we can to help promote the objectives of the World Blind Union. We are not seeking confrontation. We want to do our part in helping fund the activities of the organization. At the same time, we think it is reasonable to insist that the policies adopted by the WBU General Assembly be strictly and scrupulously followed. We are asking you to send to the IDF and anybody else who is concerned a straightforward, unequivocal letter setting forth the policy about fund raising and saying that the policy will be enforced. We would like a copy of that letter so that the organizations in our region may be reassured.

If this can not be done, quickly and clearly, then the organizations in our region will feel that they have no choice except to take immediate, widespread, and determined public action.

Sincerely,

Kenneth Jernigan, President
North America/Caribbean Region
World Blind Union

Under date of December 1, 1994, I received a letter from Pedro Zurita, Secretary General of the World Blind Union, enclosing information calculated to show that the IDF is not raising funds in the United States. Canada was not mentioned. The letters were from Mr. Hans Hoegh, Secretary General of the International Disability Foundation, and from someone named Rio D. Praaning, whose title is not given but who is described as speaking for the Building Foundation for the International Disability Centre in The Hague. It will be seen from the dates that the letters sent me by Mr. Zurita could not be in response to my November 22 letter to David Blyth. Rather, they are attempts to answer questions I raised about the IDF at the WBU officers meeting in Amman, Jordan, September 26-28, 1994. According to my reading, the letters do not satisfy the concern but confirm it. Here they are to speak for themselves:

Geneva, Switzerland
24 November 1994

To: Mr. Pedro Zurita
    Secretary General World Blind Union

Re: Your Letter dated 14 November 1994

Subject: IDF Fund-raising in the USA

IDF:
His Majesty, King Harald donated his father's Cadillac from 1951 to the IDF. We sold shares in this car to Norwegian Americans.

American Friends of IDF:
no fund-raising

Building Foundation of The Hague:
On our request Rio Praaning has sent you a report on the fund-raising activities of the Building Foundation in the United States.

Yours sincerely

Hans Hoegh
Secretary General
The International Disability Foundation

Brussels, Belgium
22 November, 1994

Dear Mr. Zurita,

Through Mr. Hans Hoegh I received your request for information concerning the fundraising for the construction of the International Disability Centre through the Building Foundation.

Please be informed that we have focused our activities on the Middle East and Asia. However, some interested multinational companies in the U.S. may provide a variety of forms of assistance to the centre, particularly due to their interest in Europe.

After the first donation of His Majesty the Sultan of the Sultanate of Oman - the sum of USD 300,000 will be transferred to our account this week - we have been informed that the Gulf Cooperation Council is considering a major donation to the Centre. Contacts in Hong Kong and Japan have indicated similar positive positions. We expect final and formal decisions in December 1994/January 1995.

I trust this will satisfy your request, but I should be happy to provide you with further information at your request.

Yours sincerely,

Rio D. Praaning

These are the letters, and I don't see how they can be interpreted to mean anything else but fund raising. If Norwegian Americans are, as it is put, sold shares in a car for charitable purposes, does their descent from Norwegian stock make them less American, or the solicitation less a solicitation? Does the fact that, as it is said, certain "interested multinational companies in the United States may provide a variety of forms of assistance to the Centre, particularly due to their interest in Europe," make that assistance not be a fund raising activity? I wonder whether the Norwegian Americans will claim their purchases of shares in the car as deductions on their federal income tax. I wonder whether the multinational companies will do the same with respect to their "assistance" to the IDF. And I also wonder whether the authorities that regulate charitable activities in the various states will want registration of these transactions as charitable solicitations.

With all of these problems, the WBU is still the only organization today which has worldwide membership and claims to speak for the blindness field. Our choices are simple. We can form a new international organization of the blind with appropriate safeguards to prevent subversion, and either stay in the WBU or get out of it; we can withdraw from the WBU and concentrate on regional affairs; we can maintain nominal membership in the WBU but limit our participation and largely write it off; or we can continue to participate and try to reform and improve the organization. Whatever we do, our actions should be upbeat and positive, but this does not mean that we should allow ourselves to be intimidated or dissuaded from expressing our opinions or seeking change because somebody may accuse us of being negative or disruptive. Our conduct should be orderly and courteous—but it should also be honest, vigorous, and purposeful. We should remember that by not following one course of action we necessarily follow another. Above all, we should not just drift into whatever we do. We should do it deliberately and with planned precision.

Part II:
The Building Blocks of Freedom: Mobility, Equality, and Independence

When the National Federation of the Blind was founded in 1940, the prevailing attitude about blindness was that the blind were helpless, that blindness signified inferiority, and that (with rare exceptions) those who are blind are incapable of productive activity. The philosophy of the Federation indicated that this tragic view of blindness was incorrect. By personal example, by public presentation, and by the written word, Dr. Jernigan sought to change this perception. In a continuing stream of speeches and articles he explained and demonstrated the principle that blind people (taken as a cross section of society) are the same as sighted people except that they cannot see. Blind people are not weird, but normal; not peculiar, but similar to you and your neighbor. Blindness need not be a handicap unless it is misunderstood. This concept was articulated in detail in an address first delivered to a convention of the National Federation of the Blind held in the 1960's. This speech, reprinted a number of times, is, "Blindness: Handicap or Characteristic." This is what Dr. Jernigan said:

From the Editor Emeritus: The first formal presentation of "Blindness—Handicap or Characteristic" was when I gave it as the banquet speech at the 1963 convention of the National Federation of the Blind in Philadelphia. However, I had been developing the ideas embodied in it for more than a decade, using them in classes at the Tennessee School for the Blind and later at the California and Iowa orientation centers.

After the Philadelphia convention I made a few revisions and gave the speech again in Albuquerque—in either 1963 or 1964. I don't remember which. In any case it was at a district meeting of Governors' Committees on Employment of the Handicapped for a number of southwestern states. The version presented at that time is the one we have used ever since, and I think it is fair to say that it has been (and still is) regarded as a cornerstone of our philosophy. It has probably been the subject of more attacks than most documents we have ever issued, and it has also been, according to many Federationists, a great help to them in forming their ideas about what blindness is and what it isn't.

I think I haven't revised "Blindness: Handicap or Characteristic" for at least three decades, nor do I think it needs much revising now. It still represents the basic core of what I believe about blindness. It occurs to me, however, that a number of newer Federationists may not be familiar with this germinal document, so I thought it might be well to print it again in the Monitor.

When I wrote it, I was director of the Iowa Commission for the Blind, and I have left it that way. Even so, a certain amount of superficial changing has been done. Here and there I have given a nod to political correctness, and I have done some jumping backward and forward in time. This leaves a few rough edges, but the body of the document is left intact. So here, with the exceptions I have mentioned, is "Blindness: Handicap or Characteristic" as I wrote it over thirty years ago:

It has been wisely observed that philosophy bakes no bread. It has, with equal wisdom, been observed that without a philosophy no bread is baked. Let me talk to you then about philosophy—my philosophy about blindness—and, in a broader sense, my philosophy concerning handicaps in general.

One prominent authority recently said, "Loss of sight is a dying. When, in the full current of his sighted life, blindness comes on a man, it is the end, the death, of that sighted life...It is superficial, if not naive, to think of blindness as a blow to the eyes only, to sight only. It is a destructive blow to the self-image of a man...a blow almost to his being itself!"

This is one view, a view held by a substantial number of people in the world today. But it is not the only view. In my opinion it is not the correct view. What is blindness? Is it a "dying"?

No one is likely to disagree with me if I say that blindness, first of all, is a characteristic. But a great many people will disagree when I go on to say that blindness is *only* a characteristic. It is nothing more or less than that. It is nothing more special, more peculiar, or more terrible than that suggests. When we understand the nature of blindness as a characteristic—a normal characteristic like hundreds of others with which each of us must live—we shall better understand the real needs to be met by agencies serving the blind, as well as the false needs which should not be met.

By definition a characteristic—any characteristic—is a limitation. A white house, for example, is a limited house; it cannot be green or blue or red; it is limited to being white. Likewise every characteristic—those we regard as strengths as well as those we regard as weaknesses—is a limitation. Each one freezes us to some extent into a mold; each restricts to some degree the range of possibility, of flexibility, and very often of opportunity as well. Blindness is such a limitation. Are blind people more limited than others?

Let us make a simple comparison. Take a sighted person with an average mind (something not too hard to locate); take a blind person with a superior mind (something not impossible to locate)—and then make all the other characteristics of these two exactly equal (something which certainly is impossible). Now, which of the two is more limited? It depends, of course, on what you want them to do. If you are choosing up sides for baseball, then the blind person is more limited— that is, he or she is "handicapped." If you are hunting somebody to teach history or science or to figure out your income tax, the sighted person is more limited or "handicapped."

Many human characteristics are obvious limitations; others are not so obvious. Poverty (the lack of material means) is one of the most obvious. Ignorance (the lack of knowledge or education) is another. Old age (the lack of youth and vigor) is yet another. Blindness (the lack of eyesight) is still another. In all these cases the limitations are apparent, or seem to be. But let us look at some other common characteristics which do not seem limiting. Take the very opposite of old age—youth. Is age a limitation in the case of a youth of twenty? Indeed it is, for a person who is twenty will not be considered for most responsible positions, especially supervisory or leadership positions. He or she may be entirely mature, fully capable, in every way the best qualified applicant for the job. Even so, age will bar the person from employment. He or she will be classified as too green and immature to handle the responsibility. And even if the person were to land the position, others on the job would almost certainly resent being supervised by one so young. The characteristic of being twenty is definitely a limitation.

The same holds true for any other age. Take age fifty, which many regard as the prime of life. The person of fifty does not have the physical vigor he or she had at twenty; and, indeed, most companies (despite recent legislation to the contrary) will not start a new employee at that age. When I first wrote those words in the 1960's, the Bell Telephone System (yes, it was the Bell System at that time) had a general prohibition against hiring anybody over the age of thirty-five. But it is interesting to note that the United States Constitution has a prohibition against having anybody under thirty-five run for President. The moral is plain: any age carries its built-in limitations.

Let us take another unlikely handicap—not that of ignorance, but its exact opposite. Can it be said that education is ever a handicap? The answer is definitely yes. In the agency which I headed (I was director of the Iowa Commission for the Blind from 1958 to 1978) I would not have hired Albert Einstein under any circumstances if he had been alive and available. His fame (other people would have continually flocked to the agency and prevented us from doing our work) and his intelligence (he would have been bored to madness by the routine of most of our jobs) would both have been too severe as limitations.

Here is an actual case in point. When I was director of the Iowa Commission for the Blind, a vacancy occurred on the library staff. Someone was needed to perform certain clerical duties and take charge of shelving and checking books. After all applicants had been screened, the final choice came down to two. Applicant A had a college degree, was seemingly alert, and clearly had more than average intelligence. Applicant B had a high school diploma (no college), was of average intelligence, and possessed only moderate initiative. I hired applicant B. Why? Because I suspected that applicant A would regard the work as beneath him, would soon become bored with its undemanding assignments, and would leave as soon as something better came along. I would then have to find and train another employee. On the other hand, I felt that applicant B would consider the work interesting and even challenging, that he was thoroughly capable of handling the job, and that he would be not only an excellent but also a permanent employee. In fact, he worked out extremely well.

In other words, in that situation the characteristic of education—the possession of a college degree—was a limitation and a handicap. Even above-average intelligence was a limitation, and so was a high level of initiative. There is a familiar bureaucratic label for this unusual disadvantage: it is the term "overqualified."

This should be enough to make the point—which is that if blindness is a limitation (and, indeed, it is), it is so in quite the same way as innumerable other characteristics to which human flesh is heir. I believe that blindness has no more importance than any of a hundred other characteristics and that the average blind person is able to perform the average job in the average place of business, and do it as effectively as the average sighted person similarly situated. The above average can compete with the above average, the average with the average, and the below average with the below average—provided (and it is a large proviso) that he or she is given training and opportunity.

Often when I have advanced this proposition, I have been met with the response, "But you can't look at it that way. Just consider what you might have done if you had been sighted and still had all the other capacities you now possess."

"Not so," I reply. "We do not compete against what we might have been, but only against other people as they now are, with their combination of strengths and weaknesses, handicaps and limitations." If we are going down that track, why not ask me what I might have done if I had been born with Rockefeller's money, the brains of Einstein, the physique of the young Joe Louis, and the persuasive abilities of Franklin Roosevelt? (And do I need to remind anyone, in passing, that FDR was severely handicapped physically?) I wonder if anyone ever said to him:

"Mr. President, just consider what you might have done if you had not had polio!"

Others have said to me, "But I formerly had sight, so I know what I am missing."

To which I might reply, "And I was formerly twenty, so I know what I am missing." Does this mean that I should spend my time grieving for the past? Or alternatively should I deal with my current situation, sizing up its possibilities and problems and turning them to my advantage? Our characteristics are constantly changing, and we are forever acquiring new experiences, limitations, and assets. We do not compete against what we formerly were but against other people as they now are.

In a recent issue of a well-known professional journal in the field of work with the blind, a blinded veteran, who is now a college professor, puts forward a notion of blindness radically different from this. He sets the limitations of blindness apart from all others and makes them unique. Having done this, he can say that all other human characteristics, strengths, and weaknesses belong in one category—and that with regard to them the blind and the sighted are just about equal. But the blind person also has the additional and unique limitation of blindness. Therefore, there is really nothing the blind person can do quite as well as the sighted person, and he or she can continue to hold his or her job only because there are charity and goodness in the world.

What this blind professor does not observe is that the same distinction he makes regarding blindness could be made with equal plausibility with respect to any of a dozen—perhaps a hundred—other characteristics. For example, suppose we distinguish intelligence from all other traits as uniquely different. Then the person with above 125 IQ is just about the same as the person with below 125 IQ—except for intelligence. Therefore, the college professor with less than 125 IQ cannot really do anything as well as the person with more than 125 IQ—and can continue to hold his or her job only because there are charity and goodness in the world.

"Are we going to assume," says this blind professor, "that all blind people are so wonderful in all other areas that they easily make up for any limitations imposed by loss of sight? I think not." But why, I ask, should we single out the particular characteristic of blindness? We might just as well specify some other. For instance, are we going to assume that all people with less than 125 IQ are so wonderful in all other areas that they easily make up for any limitations imposed by lack of intelligence? I think not.

This consideration brings us to the problem of terminology and semantics—and therewith to the heart of the matter of blindness as a handicap. The assumption that the limitation of blindness is so much more severe than others that it warrants being singled out for special definition is built into the very warp and woof of our language and psychology. Blindness conjures up a condition of unrelieved disaster—something much more terrible and dramatic than other limitations. Moreover, blindness is a conspicuously visible limitation, and there are not so many blind people around that there is any danger that the rest of the population will become accustomed to it or take it for granted. If all of those in our midst who possess an IQ under 125 exhibited, say, green stripes on their faces, I suspect that they would begin to be regarded as inferior to the non-striped—and that there would be immediate and tremendous discrimination.

When someone says to a blind person, "You do things so well that I forget you are blind—I simply think of you as being like anybody else," is that really a compliment? Suppose one of us went to France, and someone said: "You do things so well that I forget you are an American and simply think of you as being like anyone else." Would it be a compliment? Of course, the blind person should not wear a chip on the shoulder or allow himself or herself to become angry or emotionally upset. The blind person should be courteous and should accept the statement as the compliment it is meant to be. But the blind person should also understand that it is really not complimentary. In reality it says: "It is normal for blind people to be inferior and limited, different and much less able than the rest of us. Of course, you are still a blind person and still much more limited than I, but you have compensated for it so well that I almost forget that you are my inferior."

The social attitudes about blindness are all-pervasive. Not only do they affect the sighted but the blind as well. This is one of the most troublesome problems which we have to face. Public attitudes about the blind too often become the attitudes of the blind. The blind tend to see themselves as others see them. They too often accept the public view of their limitations and thus do much to make those limitations a reality.

Several years ago Dr. Jacob Freid (at that time a young teacher of sociology and later head of the Jewish Braille Institute of America) performed an interesting experiment. He gave a test in photograph identification to black and white students at the university where he was teaching. There was one photograph of a black woman in a living room of a home of culture—well furnished with paintings, sculpture, books, and flowers. Asked to identify the person in the photograph, the students said she was a "cleaning woman," "housekeeper," "cook," "laundress," "servant," "domestic," or "nanny." The revealing insight is that the black students made the same identification as the white students. The woman was Mary McLeod Bethune, one of the most famous black women of her time, founder and president of Bethune-Cookman College, who held a top post during Franklin Roosevelt's administration, and a person of brilliance and prestige in the world of higher educa-tion. What this incident tells us is that education, like nature, abhors a vacuum, and that when members of a minority group do not have correct and complete infor-mation about themselves, they accept the stereotypes of the majority group even when they are false and un-just. Even today, after so many years of the civil rights movement, one wonders how many blacks would make the traditional and stereotyped identification of the photograph—if not verbally, at least in their hearts.

Similarly with the blind—the public image is ev-erywhere dominant. This is the explanation for the at-titude of those blind persons who are ashamed to carry a white cane or who try to bluff sight which they do not possess. Although great progress is now being made, there are still many people (sighted as well as blind) who believe that blindness is not altogether respectable.

The blind person must devise alternative techniques to do many things which would be done with sight if he or she had normal vision. It will be observed that I say alternative, not substitute techniques, for the word "sub-stitute" connotes inferiority, and the alternative tech-niques employed by the blind person need not be infe-rior to visual techniques. In fact, some are superior. Of course, some are inferior, and some are equal.

In this connection it is interesting to consider the matter of flying. In comparison with the birds, humans begin at a disadvantage. They cannot fly. They have no wings. They are "handicapped." But humans see birds flying, and they long to do likewise. Humans cannot use the "normal," bird-like method, so they begin to devise alternative techniques. In jet airplanes humans now fly higher, farther, and faster than any bird that has ever existed. If humans had possessed wings, the airplane would probably never have been devised, and the infe-rior wing-flapping method would still be in general use.

This matter of our irrational images and stereotypes with regard to blindness was brought sharply home to me in the early 1960's during the course of a rehabilitation conference in Little Rock, Arkansas. I found myself engaged in a discussion with Father Carroll, a well-known leader in the field of work with the blind at that time. Father Carroll held quite different views from those I have been advancing. The error in my argument about blindness as a characteristic, he advised me, was that blindness is not in the range of "normal" characteristics. Therefore, its limitations are radically different from those of other characteristics falling within the normal range. If a normal characteristic is simply one possessed by the majority in a group, then it is not normal to have a black skin in America or a white skin in the world at large. It is not normal to have red hair or to be over six feet tall. If, on the other hand, a normal characteristic is simply what this or some other authority defines as being normal, then we have a circular argument—one that gets us nowhere.

In this same discussion I put forward the theory that a person who was sighted and of average means and who had all other characteristics in common with a blind person of considerable wealth would be less mobile than the blind person. I had been arguing that there were alternative techniques (not substitute) for doing those things which one would do with sight if one had normal vision. Father Carroll, as well as several others, had been contending that there was no real, adequate substitute for sight in traveling about. I told the story of a wealthy blind man I know who goes to Hawaii or some other place every year and who hires sighted attendants and is much more mobile than any sighted person I know who has ordinary means since most of the people I know can't go to Hawaii at all. After all of the discussion and the fact that I thought I had conveyed some understanding of what I was saying, a participant in the conference said—as if he thought he was really making a telling point, "Wouldn't you admit that the wealthy man in question would be even more mobile if he had his sight?"

This brings us to the subject of services to the blind, and more exactly to their proper scope and direction. There are, as I see it, four basic types of services now being provided to blind persons by public and private agencies and volunteer groups in this country. They are:

1. services based on the theory that blindness is uniquely different from other characteristics and that it carries with it permanent inferiority and severe limitations upon activity;

2. services aimed at teaching the blind person a new and constructive set of attitudes about blindness— based on the premise that the prevailing social attitudes, assimilated involuntarily by the blind person, are mistaken in content and destructive in effect;

3. services aimed at teaching alternative techniques and skills related to blindness; and

4. services not specifically related to blindness but to other characteristics (such as old age and lack of education), which are nevertheless labeled as "services to the blind" and included under the generous umbrella of the service program.

For purposes of this discussion, categories three and four are not relevant since they are not central to the philosophical point at issue. We are concerned here with categories one and two. An illustration of the assumptions underlying the first of these four types of services (category one) is the statement quoted earlier which begins, "Loss of sight is a dying." At the Little Rock conference already mentioned, Father Carroll (who was the one who made the statement) elaborated on the tragic metaphor by pointing out that "the eye is a sexual symbol" and that, accordingly, the man who has not eyes is not a "whole man." He cited the play *Oedipus Rex* as proof of his contention that the eye is a sexual symbol. I believe that this misses the whole point of the classic tragedy. Like many moderns, the Greeks considered the severest possible punishment to be the loss of sight. Oedipus committed a mortal sin. Unknowingly he had killed his father and married his mother. Therefore, his punishment must be correspondingly great. But that is just what his self-imposed blindness was—a punishment, not a sexual symbol.

But Father Carroll's view not only misses the point of *Oedipus Rex*—it misses the point of blindness. And in so doing it misses the point of services intended to aid the blind. For according to this view what the blind person needs most desperately is the help of a psychiatrist—of the kind so prominently in evidence at several of the centers and agencies for the blind throughout the country. According to this view what the blind person needs most is not travel training but therapy. Blind persons will be taught to accept their limitations as insurmountable and their difference from others as unbridgeable. They will be encouraged to adjust to their painful station as second-class citizens and discouraged from any thought of breaking and entering the first-class compartment. Moreover, all of this will be done in the name of teaching them "independence" and a "realistic" approach to their blindness.

The two competing types of services for the blind—categories one and two on my list of four—with their underlying conflict of philosophy may perhaps be clarified by a rather fanciful analogy. All of us recall the case of the Jews in Nazi Germany. Suddenly, in the 1930's, the German Jews were told by their society that they were "handicapped" persons—that they were inferior to other Germans simply by virtue of being Jews. Given this social fact, what sort of adjustment services might we have offered to the victim of Jewishness? I suggest that there are two alternatives—matching categories one and two on my list of four.

First, since the Jews have been "normal" individuals until quite recently, it will, of course, be quite a shock (or "trauma" as modern lingo has it) for them to learn that they are permanently and constitutionally inferior to others and can engage only in a limited range of activities. They will, therefore, require a psychiatrist to give them counseling and therapy and to reconcile them to their lot. They must "adjust" to their handicap and "learn to live" with the fact that they are not "whole men and women." If they are, as the propaganda would have it, "realistic" they may even manage to be happy. They can be taken to an adjustment center, where they may engage in a variety of routine activities suitable to Jews. Again, it should be noted that all of this will be done in the name of teaching them how to accept reality as Jews. That is one form of adjustment training.

In the case of Nazi Germany, of course, the so-called "adjustment training" for the Jews passed the bounds of sanity and ended in the death camps of the Holocaust. The custody and control with which we as blind persons deal do not generally in present-day society express themselves in such barbarous forms, but it should be remembered that blind babies were uniformly exposed on the hillsides to die in earlier times. Today's custodial attitudes about the blind are more often than not kindly meant—especially if the blind are submissive and grateful and if they are willing to stay in their places. In fact, with respect to the blind, the day of custodialism is hopefully passing.

We know what happened to the Jews and others in Nazi Germany who rejected the premise that Jewishness equalled inferiority. The problem was not in Jewishness but in the perceptions of others. Any real so-called "adjustment" would have needed to involve equal treatment and human rights. The problem was centered not in the individual but in society and society's perception of the individual. In such circumstances (even if anybody had been inclined to use one) the psychiatrist would not have been helpful. The so-called professionalism of the Nazi psychiatrist would have made no difference since such professionals likely had the same misconceptions about Jews as the rest of Nazi society. The emphasis could not be on resignation; it had to be on rebellion. That is how it might have worked if even the rudiments of civilization had continued, but Hitler's madness put an end to dialogue, and to a great deal more.

Even though we live in a different country and a different time, there is much we can learn by contemplating the interaction between Nazi society and the Jews. False perceptions about minorities that begin as nothing more than distaste or a feeling of superiority can magnify to a point of separation from reality. What seemed unthinkable yesterday can become acceptable today, commonplace tomorrow, and fanatical dogmatism the day after that. Both minorities and majorities can be dehumanized in the process.

Be that as it may, we must deal with the problems of our own time and society (and in our case, particularly with the problems of the blind). We must do it with all of the understanding and freedom from preconception we can muster. There are still vast differences in the services offered by various agencies and volunteer groups doing work with the blind throughout the country. At the Little Rock conference to which I have already referred, this was even more apparent than it is today, and the differences of philosophy repeatedly surfaced. For instance, when blind persons come to a training center, what kind of tests do you give them, and why? In Iowa (at least this is how it was in the '60's) and in some other centers, the contention is that the blind person is a responsible individual and that the emphasis should be on his or her knowing what he or she can do. Some of the centers represented at that Little Rock conference in 1962 contended that blind trainees needed psychiatric help and counseling (regardless of the circumstances and merely by virtue of their blindness) and that the emphasis should be on the center personnel's knowing what the student could do. I asked them whether they thought services in a training center for the blind should be more like those given by a hospital or those given by a law school. In a hospital the person is a "patient." This is, by the way, a term coming to be used more and more in rehabilitation today. (That is what I said in 1962, but I am glad to say that more than thirty years later we have made a considerable amount of progress in this area.)

With respect to patients the doctors decide whether they need an operation and what medication they should have. In reality "patients" make few of their own decisions. Will the doctor "let" him or her do this or that?

In a law school, on the other hand, the "students" assume responsibility for getting to their own classes and organizing their own work. They plan their own careers, seeking advice to the extent that they feel the need for it. If students plan unwisely, they pay the price for it, but it is their lives. This does not mean that the student does not need the services of the law school. He or she probably will become friends with the professors and will discuss legal matters with them and socialize with them. From some the student will seek counsel and advice concerning personal matters. More and more the student will come to be treated as a colleague. Not so the "patient." What does he or she know about drugs and medications? Some of the centers represented at the Little Rock conference were shocked that we at the Iowa Commission for the Blind "socialized" with our students and invited them to our homes. They believed that this threatened what they took to be the "professional relationship."

Our society has so steeped itself in false notions concerning blindness that it is most difficult for people to understand the concept of blindness as a characteristic, as well as the type of services needed by the blind. As a matter of fact, in one way or another, the whole point of all I have been saying is just this: Blindness is neither a dying nor a psychological crippling. It need not cause a disintegration of personality, and the stereotype which underlies this view is no less destructive when it presents itself in the garb of modern science than it was when it appeared in the ancient raiment of superstition and witchcraft.

Throughout the world, but especially in this country, we are today in the midst of a vast transition with respect to our attitudes about blindness and the whole concept of what handicaps are. We are reassessing and reshaping our ideas. In this process the professionals in the field cannot play a lone hand. In fact, the organized blind movement must lead the way and form the cutting edge. Additionally it is a cardinal principle of our free society that the citizen public will hold the balance of decision. In my opinion, it is fortunate that this is so, for professionals can become limited in their thinking and committed to outworn programs and ideas. The general public must be the balance staff, the ultimate weigher of values and setter of standards. In order that the public may perform this function with reason and wisdom, it is the duty of the organized blind movement to provide information and leadership and to see that the new ideas receive the broadest possible dissemination. But even more important, we must as blind individuals—each of us—examine ourselves to see that our own minds are free from prejudice and preconception.

These thoughts caused much speculation about the nature of blindness. In response to a request for a definition of the term, Dr. Jernigan identified the essential characteristics. Here is the definition of blindness:

Before we can talk intelligently about the problems of blindness or the potentialities of blind people, we must have a workable definition of blindness. Most of us are likely familiar with the generally accepted legal definition: visual acuity of not greater that 20/200 in the better eye with correction or a field not subtending an angle greater than 20 degrees. But this is not really a satisfactory definition. It is, rather, a way of recognizing in medical and measurable terms something which must be defined not medically or physically but functionally.

Putting to one side for a moment the medical terminology, what is blindness? Once I asked a group of high school students this question, and one of them replied—apparently believing that he was making a rather obvious statement—that a person is blind if he "can't see." When the laughter subsided, I asked the student if he really meant what he said. He replied that he did. I then asked him whether he would consider a person blind who could see light but who could not see objects—a person who would bump into things unless he used a cane, a dog, or some other travel aid and who would, if he depended solely on the use of his eyesight, walk directly into a telephone pole or fire plug. After some little hesitation the student said that he would consider such a person to be blind. I agreed with him and then went on to point out the obvious—that he literally did not mean that the definition of blindness was to be unable to see.

I next told this student of a man I had known who had "normal" (20/20) visual acuity in both eyes but who had such an extreme case of sensitivity to light that he literally could not keep his eyes open at all. The slightest amount of light caused such excruciating pain that the only way he could open his eyes was by prying them open with his fingers. Nevertheless, this person, despite the excruciating pain he felt while doing it, could read the eye chart without difficulty. The readings showed that he had "normal sight." This individual applied to the local Welfare Department for Public Assistance to the Blind and was duly examined by their ophthalmologist. The question I put to the student was this: "If you had been the ophthalmologist, would you have granted the aid or not?"

His answer was, "Yes."

"Remember," I told him, "under the law you are forbidden to give aid to any person who is not actually blind. Would you still have granted the assistance?" The student said that he would. Again, I agreed with him, but I pointed out that, far from his first facetious statement, what he was saying was this: It is possible for one to have "perfect sight" and still in the physical, literal sense of the word be blind.

I then put a final question to the student. I asked him whether if a sighted person were put into a vault which was absolutely dark so that he could see nothing whatever, it would be accurate to refer to that sighted person as a blind man. After some hesitation and equivocation the student said, "No." For a third time I agreed with him. Then I asked him to examine what we had established.

1. To be blind does not mean that one cannot see. (Here again I must interrupt to say that I am not speaking in spiritual or figurative terms but in the most literal sense of the word.)

2. It is possible for an individual to have "perfect sight" and yet be physically and literally blind.

3. It is possible for an individual not to be able to see at all and still be a sighted person.

What, then, in light of these seeming contradictions is the definition of blindness? In my way of thinking it is this: One is blind to the extent that he must devise alternative techniques to do efficiently those things which he would do if he had normal vision. An individual may properly be said to be "blind" or a "blind person" when he has to devise so many alternative techniques—that is, if he is to function efficiently—that his pattern of daily living is substantially altered. It will be observed that I say *alternative* not *substitute* techniques, for the word *substitute* connotes inferiority, and the alternative techniques employed by the blind person need not be inferior to visual techniques. In fact, some of them are superior. The usually accepted legal definition of blindness already given (that is, visual acuity of less than 20/200 with correction or a field of less that 20 degrees) is simply one medical way of measuring and recognizing that anyone with better vision than the amount mentioned in the definition will (although he may have to devise some alternative techniques) likely not have to devise so many such techniques as to alter substantially his patterns of daily living. On the other hand, anyone with less vision than that mentioned in the legal definition will usually (I emphasize the word *usually*, for such is not always the case) need to devise so many such alternative techniques as to alter quite substantially his patterns of daily living.

It may be of some interest to apply this standard to the three cases already discussed:

First, what of the person who has light perception but sees little or nothing else? In at least one situation he can function as a sighted person. If, before going to bed, he wished to know whether the lights are out in his home, he can simply walk through the house and "see". If he did not have light perception, he would have to use some alternative technique—touch the bulb, tell by the position of the switch, have some sighted person give him the information, or devise some other method. However, this person is still quite properly referred to as a blind person. This one visual technique which he uses is such as small part of his overall pattern of daily living as to be negligible in the total picture. The patterns of his daily living are substantially altered. In the main he employs alternative techniques to do those things which he would do with sight if he had normal vision—that is, he does if he functions efficiently.

Next, let us consider the person who has normal visual acuity but cannot hold his eyes open because of his sensitivity to light. He must devise alternative techniques to do anything which he would do with sight if he had normal vision. He is quite properly considered to be a "blind person."

Finally, what of the sighted person who is put into a vault which has no light? Even though he can see nothing at all, he is still quite properly considered to be a "sighted person." He uses the same techniques that any other sighted person would use in a similar situation. There are no visual techniques which can be used in such circumstances. In fact, if a blind person found himself in such a situation, he might very well have a variety of techniques to use.

I repeat that, in my opinion, blindness can best be defined not physically or medically but functionally or sociologically. The alternative techniques which must be learned are the same for those born blind as for those who become blind as adults. They are quite similar (or should be) for those who are totally blind or nearly so and those who are "partially sighted" and yet are blind in the terms of the usually accepted legal definition. In other words, I believe that the complex distinctions which are often made between those who have partial sight and those who are totally blind, between those who have been blind from childhood and those who have become blind as adults are largely meaningless. In fact, they are often harmful since they place the wrong emphasis on blindness and its problems. Perhaps the greatest danger in the field of work for the blind today is the tendency to be hypnotized by jargon.

How does a blind person achieve independence? Does it happen automatically, or is there a process that must be followed? Should a blind person assert this independence on every possible occasion?

After reviewing writings of Dr. Jernigan, a number of young blind people posed these questions to him, and he responded. In an address delivered to the 1993 Convention of the National Federation of the Blind, in Dallas, Texas, Dr. Jernigan explained in detail what blindness as a characteristic means and how it should be approached. This is what he said:

> Shortly after last year's convention, I received a number of letters from students at the Louisiana Center for the Blind. It was clear that the letters were written as the result of discussions held at the Center and that, although the apparent topic was independent mobility, the real issue was independence in general, and how blind persons should live and behave. I want to share those letters with you, then tell you how I answered them, and finally say a few things about what I think independence really is. The letters are all dated July 23, 1992. Here is a composite of them:

> Dear Dr. Jernigan:

> I am a sophomore in high school. Right now, I am in a teenage program that the Louisiana Center for the Blind is sponsoring. It is the STEP program. That means Summer Training and Employment Project. We are allowed to get jobs and make money as well as have classes.

A few weeks ago I attended the national convention. I really enjoyed all your speeches and everything. People noticed that you and Mr. Maurer walked sighted guide sometimes, *[I interrupt to call your attention to the almost code-word use of the term "sighted guide." Not "walking with a sighted guide" or "walking with a sighted person" or "holding the arm of a sighted person," but "walking sighted guide." This makes it clear that the concept of "sighted guide" has been the topic of considerable conversation. But back to the letter.]* and we thought you all would never walk sighted guide, because you all are so highly involved in the NFB. I never thought sighted guide was OK until then. So why did you all use sighted guide? I know there are many reasons why this might be. We discussed this in one of our talk times and came up with one reason this might be. We know that you all have to be at meetings all the time, and it would be faster if you would use sighted guide. *[I interrupt again to call your attention to the use in the following sentences of the depersonalized "it." Now, back to the letter.]* I am sure you don't use it so much that you lose your cane travel skills. I am not trying to say this is wrong. I was just wondering why you do this. Someone brought up that if we, as the people being trained at the moment, were caught using sighted guide, they would fuss at us. And I realize that you are not the one in training, so it is not wrong. We couldn't use sighted guide, because we might want to use it more than the cane if we use too much of it.

Yours truly,

———————————————

Dear Dr. Jernigan:

During this past convention in North Carolina some of us noticed that you did not walk with a cane. I do not understand this at all. I can understand that you have to be in many places in a short amount of time at the conventions, and that might be the reason you went sighted guide. But I also know that when you came for a tour of the Center, you also went sighted guide. We do not understand this.

We all have our own theories as to why you went sighted guide, but we want to get the correct answer straight from the horse's mouth.

Your fellow Federationist,

_____

That's a very clear-cut letter, and I am pleased to be called that end of the horse. Here is the last one:

Dear Dr. Jernigan:

This year I came to Charlotte to attend my third national convention of the NFB. I am currently a student at the Louisiana Center for the Blind in the STEP program for blind teenagers. This program stresses cane use, Braille literacy, employment readiness, and self-confidence based on achievement. While at the convention I heard from a friend that you were never actually seen using your cane. I discussed this with a group of friends, and it was decided that you most likely had many places to go and had to get to them quickly. This made sense, and the question seemed settled. Then one of the group remembered you using sighted guide during a tour you took of the Center while passing through Ruston on the way to the Dallas convention in 1990. This was such a hectic situation, and the question was no longer settled because the only alternative travel technique anyone noticed you using was sighted guide.

I do not mean this letter to imply any disrespect towards you, the Federation, or its many achievements. If the Federation had not pushed so hard for independence for the blind, I would have no grounds on which to write this letter. It is because of my own personal convictions about independence that I ask why the figurehead of the NFB is not himself using the alternative techniques that his student, Joanne Wilson, has been teaching for nearly ten years in Ruston.

I would prefer to end the letter on a positive note. I realize that you are responsible for the training I am currently receiving, and I am grateful for it. I am not implying that you have no cane skills, because I do not honestly know.

Sincerely,

These are straightforward letters, seriously written. They raise fundamental questions, questions that deserve a reasoned answer. Here is the expanded substance of what I wrote:

Baltimore, Maryland
July 29, 1992

Under date of July 23, 1992, the three of you wrote to ask me why I didn't travel alone with a cane during the national convention in Charlotte and why on a visit to the Louisiana Center in 1990 I took a sighted person's arm instead of walking alone with a cane. I appreciate your letters and will tell you why I do what I do.

In the first place let us assume that I didn't have any cane travel skills at all. This might be comparable to the situation of a parent who had no education but dreamed of an education for his or her child. That parent might preach the value of education and might work to send the child to high school and then to college. The parent might, though personally uneducated, feel tremendous satisfaction at the learning and accomplishment which his or her effort had made possible. In such circumstances what attitude should the child have toward the parent? The child might be critical of the parent for his or her poor grammar and lack of education and might even be ashamed to associate with the parent—or the child might feel gratitude for the sacrifice and the work that had made the education possible.

This is not an apt analogy since I have perfectly good cane skills, but it has elements of truth about it. When I was a child, there were no orientation centers or mobility training. The only canes available were the short heavy wooden type, and we youngsters associated carrying a cane with begging, shuffling along, and being helpless.

It was not until I finished college and had taught for four years in Tennessee that I first carried a cane. It was made of wood and had a crook handle. I might also say that it was longer than most of those in vogue at the time, forty inches. I started using it in 1953, just before going to California to work at the newly established state orientation center for the blind. The Center had been in operation for only a few months and had enrolled only four or five students by the time of my arrival.

In those days the California Center was using 42-inch aluminum canes. They were a tremendous improvement over the 40-inch wooden cane I had been carrying, and I immediately adopted the new model. Even so, it seemed that something better was needed. I worked with the person who had been employed as the travel teacher, and we experimented with different techniques and canes.

In the mid-1950's the solid fiberglass cane was developed. It was first made by a blind man in Kansas, but we at the California center popularized it and brought it into general use. We also worked to improve the tip. Our students received intensive training, those with any sight using blindfolds (or, as we called them, sleep shades), and our students and graduates were identifiable in any group of blind persons because of their competence and ease in travel. Since they had enjoyed the benefit of our study and experimentation, as well as intensive instruction and the time to practice, many of them probably became better travelers than I—and I felt pride and satisfaction in the fact. We were advancing on the road to freedom and independence.

In 1958 I went to Iowa as director of the state commission for the blind, and I carried with me the experience and knowledge I had acquired in California plus a 48-inch fiberglass cane and a head full of new ideas and hopes for the future. I hired a young sighted man who had no experience at all with blindness and spent several days giving him preliminary instruction in mobility, using blind techniques. First I had him follow me all over Des Moines, watching me use the cane while crossing streets and going to various places. Then, he put on sleep shades, and I worked with him to learn basic skills. Next I sent him to California for three or four weeks to gain further experience and to compare what I had taught him with what the California Center was doing. Finally he came back to Des Moines, and I spent several more weeks working with him until (though sighted) he could (under blindfold) go anywhere he wanted safely and comfortably using a cane.

During all of that time I worked with him on attitudes, for unless one believes that he or she is capable of independence as a blind person, independence in travel (as in other areas) is not truly achievable. This travel instructor's name is Jim Witte, and he developed into one of the best I have ever known.

Iowa students rapidly became the envy of the nation. You could single them out in any group because of their bearing, their confidence, and their skill in travel. As had been the case in California, some of them undoubtedly traveled better than I, and I felt a deep sense of fulfillment in the fact. Joanne Wilson (the director of your own Louisiana Center) was one of those students, and I am sure she has told you how it was at the Iowa Center—how students were treated, what was expected of them, the relationship between staff and students, our dreams for the future, and how we set about accomplishing those dreams. Arlene Hill (one of your teachers) was also an Iowa student. Both Joanne and Arlene are living examples of what we taught and how it worked. So are President Maurer, Mrs. Maurer, Peggy Pinder, Ramona Walhof, Jim Gashel, Jim Omvig, and at least fifty others in this audience.

It was in Iowa that we developed the hollow fiberglass cane. It was an improvement over the solid cane, lighter and more flexible. We also gradually began to use longer and longer canes. They enabled us to walk faster without diminishing either safety or grace. As I have already told you, I started with a 40-inch wooden cane. Then I went to 42-inch aluminum—and after that to solid fiberglass, then to hollow fiberglass, and (three or four years ago) to hollow carbon fiber. As to length, I went from 40 inches 42, then to 45, 48, 49, 51, 53, 55, and 57. At present I use a 59-inch cane. It seems about right to me for my height and speed of travel. Will I ever use a still longer cane? I don't know—but at this stage I don't think so. Obviously there comes a time when a longer cane is a disadvantage instead of a help.

I've told you all of this so that you may understand something of my background and approach to independence in travel, and independence in general. The doctors who established the medical schools a hundred years ago were (with notable exceptions) not generally as competent and skilled as the doctors they trained, for they did not have the benefit of the kind of concentrated teaching they themselves were providing. Obviously they could not stand on their own shoulders. Through their students they extended their dreams into the future, building possibilities that they themselves had not known and could never hope to realize.

So it is with me in relation to you. You are the third generation of our mobility trainees, having the benefit of what I have learned and also of what Joanne and the other Iowa graduates have learned. Unless you make advances over what we have done, you will, in a very real sense, fail to keep faith with those who have gone before you and those who will follow. In this context I would expect and hope that some of you will become better travelers (and, perhaps, better philosophers and teachers) than I, and if you do, I will take joy in it.

Having said all of this, let me come back to my own travel skills. During the 1950's I traveled completely alone on a constant basis throughout this entire country, going to almost every state and dealing with almost every kind of environment—urban area, city bus, taxi, complicated street crossing, rural setting, hired private car, country road, and almost anything else you can imagine. During late December and early January of 1956 and 1957, for example, I traveled alone to fourteen states in eleven days, writing testimony for the NFB's Right to Organize bill. It was no big deal, and not something I thought about very much. It was simply a job that had to be done, and the travel was incidental and taken for granted. I have taught travel instructors and have developed new techniques and canes. I travel whenever and wherever I want to go in the most convenient way to get there—and sometimes that means alone, using a cane.

Once when I was in Iowa, students observed that I walked to a barber shop one day with another staff member, and they raised with me some of the same questions you have raised. That afternoon in our business class (you may call it by some other name—philosophy or something else) I dealt with the matter. I told the students some of the things I have told you, and then I went on to say something like this:

"Although what I have told you should mean that even if I couldn't travel with much skill at all I might still not merit your criticism, we don't need to leave it at that. Follow me. We are going to take a walk through downtown traffic—and see that you keep up."

I took the lead, and we walked for eight or ten blocks at a fast clip. When we got back to the classroom, I didn't need to tell them what kind of travel skills I had. They knew.

Then, we talked about why I had walked to the barber shop with another staff member. In that particular instance I had matters to discuss, and I felt I couldn't afford the luxury of doing nothing while going for a hair cut. As a matter of fact, in those days I often made a practice of taking my secretary with me to the barber shop and dictating letters while getting my hair cut. Of course, I could have made a point of walking alone each time just to make a visible demonstration of my independence, but somehow I think that such insecurity might have made the opposite point and would certainly have been counterproductive.

In the Iowa days I was not only director of the state Commission for the Blind but also first vice president and then president of the National Federation of the Blind. Both were full-time jobs, requiring me to use to best advantage every waking minute.

I was up before 6:00 to go to the gym with the men students; I wrote over a hundred letters a week; I entertained legislators and other civic leaders an average of two or three nights a week to gain support for our program; I traveled throughout the state to make speeches; and I spent long hours working individually with students. Besides that, I handled the administrative details of the Commission and the NFB on a daily basis. At the same time I was doing organizing in other states and dealing with problems brought to me by Federationists throughout the country.

In that context it would have been a bad use of my time (and both Federationists and Iowa students and staff would have thought so) for me to spend much of my day walking down the street to make a visible show of my independent travel skills. I traveled alone when I needed to, and I gave demonstrations to students, legislators, and others when I needed to do that—but I never did either to convince myself or to establish in my own mind the fact of my capacity or independence. It didn't seem necessary.

So what about the NFB convention in Charlotte? I was in charge of convention organization and arrangements, and there were a thousand details to handle. There were four hotels and a convention center, each with its own staff and each requiring separate handling and a myriad of decisions. Sometimes I had not only one but two or three people with me as I went from place to place, talking about what had to be done and sending this person here and that person yonder.

Even so, I might (you may say) have refused to take the arm of one of the persons with me and used my cane to walk alone. But for what reason? When a blind person is walking through a crowd or down a street with somebody else and trying to carry on a meaningful conversation, it is easier to take the other person's arm. This is true even if you are the best traveler in the world and even if both of you are blind.

In fact, I contend that there are times when refusing to take an arm that is offered may constitute the very opposite of independence. If, for instance, you are a blind person accompanying a sighted person through a busy restaurant closely packed with tables and chairs, do you create a better image of independence by trying to get through the maze alone, with the sighted person going in front and constantly calling back, "This way! This way!" or by simply taking the sighted person's arm and going to the table? What is better about following a voice than following an arm? From what I have said, I presume it is clear which method I favor. Of course, if no arm is conveniently available, you should be prepared to use another method, regardless of how crowded the restaurant or how labyrinthine the path. In either case you should do it without losing your cool. But I'll tell you what alternative is not acceptable in such circumstance—pretending that you don't want anything to eat and not going at all. That's not acceptable.

But back to the convention. When you are trying to get through crowds quickly to go from meeting to meeting, and possibly also trying to find different people in those crowds in a hurry, the efficiency of sighted assistance multiplies. Incidentally, even if I were sighted and doing the things I do at national conventions, I would want two or three persons with me—to look for people in crowds, to send for this and that, and to talk and advise with.

As an example, consider what happened at last year's convention with respect to Secretary of Education Lamar Alexander. He has normal eyesight and is in every other way, so far as I know, able-bodied and energetic. I am sure that he can drive a car and walk vigorously. Yet, he sent an assistant to Charlotte a day in advance of his arrival. The assistant scouted out the convention and then went to the airport to meet the Secretary. The assistant drove the car from the airport to the convention, accompanied the Secretary into the meeting hall, went with him to the platform, met him at the edge of the platform when he finished speaking, and drove him back to the airport. If the Secretary had been blind, I wonder if somebody would have said, "Just look! He's not independent. He has to have a sighted person with him at all times, accompanying him everywhere he goes and driving his car."

Since I am not a student trying to learn to travel independently or to establish within my own mind that I can compete on terms of equality with others, and since I can and do travel by myself when that is most convenient, I feel no particular obligation to make a demonstration when it is more efficient to do otherwise. If I were a student, I should and would behave differently. As an example, I think a student should always use a rigid (not a collapsible) cane. But I generally use one that is collapsible. Why? Students often are uncomfortable with canes, and if they are allowed to use those that fold or telescope, they may tend to hide or conceal them because they think (even if subconsciously) that it will make them look less conspicuous. I have carried a cane for so long that I would feel naked without it, and I always carry one whether I am with somebody or not. Because they were so rickety, I refused to carry a collapsible cane until we developed the telescoping carbon fiber model. I pull it to such a tight fit that it doesn't collapse as I use it, and I almost never collapse it unless I'm in close quarters. Again, it is a convenience, and my sense of independence is not so brittle that I think I have to carry the rigid cane to prove to myself or others that I am not ashamed to be seen with it or uncomfortable about blindness.

When I was teaching orientation classes in California and Iowa, I often said to those in attendance that students at a center tend to go through three stages: fear and insecurity, rebellious independence, and normal independence—FI, RI, and NI. During fear and insecurity one tends to be ultra cautious and afraid of everything, even if at times putting on a good front. During rebellious independence one tends to be overly touchy, resenting anybody who attempts to offer him or her any kind of assistance at all, even when the assistance is appropriate and needed. In the rebellious independence stage one is likely to be a pain in the neck, both to himself or herself and others—but this is a necessary step on the road from fear and insecurity to normal independence. Unfortunately some people never get beyond it.

Hopefully one will eventually arrive at the stage of normal independence, with relatively little need constantly to prove either to oneself or others that one is capable of independence and first-class citizenship. This means maturity in dealing with condescending treatment, and it also means flexibility in accepting or rejecting offers of assistance, kindness, or generosity. Sometimes such things should be graciously or silently taken, sometimes endured, and sometimes rejected out of hand—but the reason should never be because you doubt your own worth, have inner feelings of insecurity, or wonder whether you are inferior because of blindness.

Normal independence also means not rationalizing your fear or inability by saying that you are just doing what is convenient and efficient and that you don't feel the need to prove something when in reality you are just covering up the fact that you are as helpless as a baby—and it means not going so far the other way and being so touchy about your so-called independence that nobody can stand to be around you. It means getting to the place where you are comfortable enough with yourself and secure enough with your own inner feelings that you don't have to spend much time bothering about the matter one way or another. It means reducing blindness to the level of a mere inconvenience and making it just one more of your everyday characteristics—a characteristic with which you must deal just as you do with how strong you are, how old you are, how smart you are, how personable you are, and how much money you have. These are the goals, and probably none of us ever achieves all of them all of the time. Nevertheless, we are making tremendous progress—and we are farther along the road now than we have ever been.

I am pleased that you wrote me, and I am especially pleased that you are able to receive training at the Louisiana Center. It is grounded in Federation philosophy, and it is one of the best. You are getting the chance while you are young to learn what blindness is really like, and what it isn't like. You have the opportunity to profit from the collective experience of all of us— the things we tried that didn't work, and those that did. On the foundation of love and organizational structure which we have established, you can make for yourselves better opportunities than we have ever known—and I pray that you will. The future is in the hands of your generation, and I hope you will dream and work and build wisely and well.

Sincerely,

Kenneth Jernigan

That is what I wrote, and there have been a number of subsequent developments. One person, hearing these letters, said, "I can see your point, but don't you think you should try to be a role model?"

To which I replied, "I thought that was what I was doing."

Then, there was the letter I got about a month ago from a person who attended a seminar at the National Center for the Blind last Christmas. She said in part:

The discussion about the letter from the students at the Louisiana Center for the Blind has stuck with me and helped me in two ways. I no longer feel the deep embarrassment I had been experiencing about being unable to read Braille and having less-than-perfect travel skills. I remain painfully aware that I could be much more efficient than I am, particularly if I could read and write Braille, but I no longer feel that I am less worthy because of the lack. And, by the way, I hope to take care of my deficiencies in that area soon.

The discussion also helped me better to appreciate and respect my dad, who was blinded by an on-the-job accident when he was 26. After he became blind, he went to law school, and I have always admired his relatively quick adjustment to blindness. On the other hand, I have always felt somewhat embarrassed that when traveling he uses a sighted guide the majority of the time. (For instance, I was horrified and disbelieving when I heard my dad flew to Alaska by himself to go fishing without his guide dog or a white cane!) He has a guide dog but only used him when he was going to work. I have never seen him use a white cane although I have just learned that he used one while in his office at work. However, the seminar discussion helped me to understand that everyone's situation differs and that the opportunities available are not uniform. My dad has accomplished a lot: He was an administrative law judge until he retired last month; he is an avid fisherman; and he is as pro-Braille as anybody I have ever met.

That is what the seminarian wrote me, and her letter makes a point. It is simply this: We absolutely must not become so rigid and dogmatic about the means and precise details of achieving independence that we make ourselves and everybody else around us miserable. Down that road lies bigotry, as well as the loss of any real independence or true normality.

Usually when I go to bed at night, I read myself to sleep with a recorded book. A few months ago somebody took me to task for this. The person said something to this effect: "You should not read recorded books. You should use Braille. After all, the Federation advocates Braille literacy, and if you use tapes and talking books, you decrease the circulation of Braille from the libraries, and you also set a bad example. What kind of statement are you making? What kind of image are you creating? You have an obligation to serve as a role model."

I didn't argue with the person. It wouldn't have done any good. Yes, I use Braille; and as you know, I find it helpful. More than that. My life would be poorer without it. But Braille is a means. It is a vehicle, not an article of faith. I am conscious of the fact that I have an obligation to be a role model, and I do the best I can to meet the requirement. But the kind of role model I want to be (for anybody who cares to see me that way) is that of a competent, well-balanced human being, not a caricature. The fact that I don't want to die of thirst doesn't mean that I want to drown.

What is independence? I would define it this way. With respect to reading, it means getting the information you want with a minimum amount of inconvenience and expense. For me that means Braille, but it also means using live readers, recordings, and (despite my limited competence in that area) a certain amount of work with computers. For somebody else the combination may be different, but any active blind person who lacks skill in Braille will be limited—not necessarily unable to compete but definitely limited.

As to travel, independence is the ability to go where you want when you want without inconvenience to yourself or others. Probably none of us (blind or sighted) ever fully achieves that goal all of the time—and almost all of us achieve at least some of it some of the time. Usually we are on a continuum.

If I could not travel by myself without discomfort or great expense, there are times when it would be a real problem. What about the trip I made to Kansas City in May of this year to meet with local Federationists and speak at a JOB seminar? My wife had other things to do, and it would have been inconvenient to take somebody else. I went alone. Did I have any assistance during the trip? Yes. At times—when it was convenient for me and not inconvenient to others.

What about the time last month when I was called for jury duty? It would have been very difficult for a guide to have accompanied me to the jury box or the jury room—so, of course, I went by myself. Does that mean that nobody showed me where the jury box was or gave other assistance? No. It means that I went where I needed to go without inconvenience to me or those around me. That is what I call independence.

Just as with the sighted, there are times when you as a blind person want privacy—want to go somewhere (to see a boyfriend or girlfriend, for instance) without being accompanied by your daily associates, want to buy a present for a friend or a loved one, or just feel like following a whim. In such cases a dog or a cane is helpful. On the other hand, there are times when the assistance of a sighted person is extremely beneficial. Taken by itself, the use or lack of use of a sighted guide has very little, if anything at all, to do with real independence. In fact, the whole notion of independence (not just in mobility but also in everything else) involves the concept of doing what you want when you want, and doing it without paying such a heavy price (either monetarily or otherwise) that the thing is hardly worth having once you get it or do it.

In conclusion, I say to each member of this organization: Hold your head high in the joy of accomplishment and the pride of independence—but not because of dog or cane or human arm, and not because of your ability to read Braille or use a computer. These are the trappings of independence, not the substance of it. They should be learned, and used when needed—but they should be regarded only as means, not ends. Our independence comes from within. A slave can have keen eyesight, excellent mobility, and superb reading skills—and still be a slave. We are achieving freedom and independence in the only way that really counts—in rising self-respect, growing self-confidence, and the will and the ability to make choices. Above all, independence means choices, and the power to make those choices stick. We are getting that power, and we intend to have more of it. That is why we have organized. That is why we have the National Federation of the Blind. We know where we are going, and we know how to get there. Let anybody who doubts it put us to the test. My brothers and my sisters, the future is ours! Let us meet it with joy; let us meet it with hope; and (most important of all) let us meet it together!

Part III:
Plain Talk and Home Truths:
Sowing the Seeds—Creating
the Kernel Books

Nothing has had a more profound influence on the perception of blindness and blind people than the Kernel Books, edited by Dr. Kenneth Jernigan. These little paperback volumes contain first-person accounts by blind people of their own experiences. Each book includes a brief introduction by the editor along with a narrative about a portion of his life and thought. There are many contributors to the Kernel Books, but the segments written by Dr. Jernigan have a special sparkle.

In 1996, 1997, and 1998, Dr. Jernigan incorporated the material from the Kernel Books that he had written into major addresses delivered at conventions of the National Federation of the Blind. He observed in one of these addresses that the Kernel Books have altered the perception of blindness and changed the socioeconomic structure of our society. The changes that have been caused by these little books constitute nothing less than a revolution. Included here are some of the introductions to these books and all of the autobiographical material describing the experiences of the author. In those instances in which the material from the Kernel Book is incorporated within a larger address, the addresses have been reprinted here. The 1997 speech is of particular interest since it combines a new method of philosophical understanding with the experiences depicted in the Kernel Books. This address is entitled "The Day After Civil Rights." Dr. Jernigan worked for most of his long life to promote civil rights for the blind. He was no less interested in this endeavor at the end of his life than he had been in earlier times.

Yet, he recognized that, though this work is essential, it is not sufficient for full integration or the most meaningful of lives. It is only one element among many. The writings from the Kernel Books speak for themselves from the heart of the man who wrote them. In 1991, the Kernel Books were initiated with *What Color is the Sun*, which included this "Editor's Introduction" and Dr. Jernigan's article, "Growing Up Blind in Tennessee During the Depression."

EDITOR'S INTRODUCTION

by Kenneth Jernigan

For at least twenty years I have been appearing on radio and television and in the newspapers as the spokesman of the National Federation of the Blind, and lately something has been happening with increased frequency which I probably should have anticipated but didn't. Total strangers keep stopping me on the street or in the supermarket or airport to ask me about blindness. Well, not exactly about blindness as such, but about what it is like to be blind—about the everyday experiences and the ordinary happenings in the lives of blind people. I do the best I can to tell them, but usually neither they nor I have the time for me really to do it right. This book is an attempt to remedy that situation. Even so, I still don't know that I have done it right, but at least it is better than a hurried attempt in a super-market.

The persons who appear in the pages of the book are people that I know—friends, former students, colleagues in the National Federation of the Blind. Mostly they tell their own stories—stories of ordinary men and women who think about last night's dinner, today's taxes, and tomorrow's hopes and dreams. These are people I think you would like to know, so I am introducing them to you. And I am also telling you a little about myself. When you have finished reading these personal accounts and reminiscences I hope you will have a better picture of what it is like to be blind and how blind people feel. Mostly we feel just about the same way you do.

Kenneth Jernigan
Baltimore, Maryland
1991

GROWING UP BLIND IN TENNESSEE DURING THE DEPRESSION

by Kenneth Jernigan

I grew up on a farm in middle Tennessee during the depression—first the farm depression and then the one that everybody talks about. Life was not the way it is today. My father (though intelligent) had less than two weeks of formal schooling, and my mother (at least equally intelligent) did not finish the eighth grade. There were no books in our home except the family Bible, and we didn't get a newspaper or magazine.

We had no radio; no telephone; and until I was six, no automobile. It was the early thirties, and money was scarce. Hogs (when we had any) brought two cents a pound; and anything else we had to sell brought an equally low price.

I had an isolated existence. Except for the extremely elderly, I was the only blind person for miles around. My experiences in no way were like those of the sighted children I knew. Mostly until I was six, I had nothing to do and nobody to play with. Sometimes on Sundays my family and I would go to the home of one or the other of my grandparents for dinner and the day. I remember those times vividly.

The men (remember that this was rural Tennessee in the early thirties) would sit under a shade tree in the front yard and talk about the crops, the weather, and the price of hogs. The women would be in the kitchen preparing Sunday dinner and talking about children, what the neighbors were doing, and their gardens.

The boys and girls (usually a bevy of cousins were there on such occasions) would be in the barnyard playing hide and seek, tag, or some other game. I belonged to none of these groups. I circulated back and forth on the edges and hoped the day would end.

One thing more: Nobody had indoor toilets, so if I knew we were going somewhere for Sunday dinner, I would begin the day before to reduce my intake of liquids. It is embarrassing for a child of five to have to interrupt the men under the shade tree to ask if someone will take him down behind the barn to answer the call of nature.

I am sure that each person who attended those gatherings came away with different memories, memories that lingered through the years—playing with other children, talking with the men under the trees, or exchanging confidences in the kitchen.

Certainly I came away with memories. They revolve around a full bladder and a day of boredom. This is not to say that I felt abused or mistreated. Instead, I recognized (even at that early age) that the world was as it was; that nobody was trying to do me in; and that if I wanted to have a full life, I had better learn to plan and think ahead.

My parents loved me, but they didn't know how to deal with a blind child. They knew that they wanted the best for me, and I knew that I wanted out of that limited environment.

Every time I could, I got somebody to read to me. Read what? Anything—anything I could get. I would nag and pester anybody I could find to read me anything that was available—the Bible, an agriculture yearbook, a part of a newspaper, or the Sears Roebuck catalog. It didn't matter. Reading was magic. It opened up new worlds.

I remember the joy—a joy which amounted to reverence and awe—which I felt during those times I was allowed to visit an aunt who had books in her home. It was from her daughter (my cousin) that I first heard the fairy stories from *The Book of Knowledge*—a treasure which many of today's children have unfortunately missed.

My cousin loved to read and was long-suffering and kind, but I know that I tried her patience with my insatiable appetite. It was not possible for me to get enough, and I always dreaded going home, finding every excuse I could to stay as long as my parents would let me.

I loved my aunt; I was fascinated by the radio she had; and I delighted in her superb cooking—but the key attraction was the reading. My aunt is long since dead, and of course I never told her. For that matter, maybe I never really sorted it out in my own mind, but there it was—no doubt about it.

As you might imagine, I wanted to go to school as soon as I could, and I made no secret about it. But you had to be six, and when they said six, they meant *six*. School started in September, but I was not six until November 13, 1932. So I was not allowed to begin until the next quarter—January 9, 1933.

My parents loaded me into a car (a new second-hand Chevy bought especially for the occasion with hard earned savings) and took me to the residential school for the blind in Nashville fifty miles away. I entered the school grounds in early January of 1933 and didn't come out again until Easter when my parents took me home for the weekend.

That first year at the school for the blind in Nashville was quite an experience for me. I had never been away from my parents for any length of time in my whole life, and suddenly I was plopped down in the midst of twenty-five other small boys, who (though possessing certain cultural traits in common) came from widely diverse backgrounds and environments.

We called the woman who was in charge of us our supervisor. (We would have been outraged and humiliated by the term "housemother.") She was a genteel person, the elderly widow of a doctor; and she did the best she could to teach us manners and morals, keep us in order, and raise us right.

But even if she had had the sleuthing skills of a Sherlock Holmes and the energy of a strong young athlete, she couldn't have kept track of us all of the time. Although we obeyed her rules and paid the penalty when we didn't—that is, when she caught us (I might say here that a heavy paddle was much in evidence), primarily we made our own rules and governed ourselves—at least in matters relating to social interaction.

One of the more noteworthy customs of the school was a Saturday morning ritual involving the Scriptures. Shortly after breakfast the small boys (I don't know what happened to the girls) were plopped down on a bench and given the task of memorizing a chapter from the Bible. It didn't do any good to protest, object, or try to resist. You sat there until you memorized it, after which you were free to go play.

One's religion had nothing to do with it, nor did one's interest or aptitude. When you got the task done, you could go where you pleased and do what you liked. Meanwhile, you couldn't. And any time you spent trying to beat the system was just that much of the morning gone.

I suppose I need not tell you that I quickly concluded to learn my chapter with minimum delay, which I religiously (no play on words intended) did. As a result, I have been a devout Bible quoter ever since—and much, I might add, to my benefit and long-range satisfaction. Ah, well, children are not always in the best position to know what will stand them in good stead.

At home on the farm my family got up early, often around four o'clock. My dad would go to the barn to feed the livestock and milk the cows, and my mother would build a fire in the wood stove and cook breakfast. We would then eat, and by the time it was light, my dad would be in the field to start his day's work. I got up when the others did, for the table was one place where I was equal with the rest. It was not just food that I got there but an important part of the day's routine and ritual—a time when all of us were together in a common activity.

But at school it was all different. I went to bed that first night at the school for the blind in a strange city and in the biggest building I had ever seen—a building with running water, indoor toilets, electricity, steam heat, and a group of strangers.

And as might have been predicted, I woke up about four o'clock the next morning. It was not only that I was wide awake and in a strange setting. I had to go to the bathroom (simply had to), and I didn't know where it was or how to get there. I didn't think I should wake anybody else up, but I knew I had to do something—so I got up, went out into the hall, and began to hunt.

Somehow (I don't know how I did it, but somehow) I found the bathroom, but then I didn't know how to get back to my room. At this point I simply lay down in the middle of the hall and waited for something to happen. It was an experience which I still vividly remember.

But that was not all that happened that day. When the other boys got up, I went with them to the bathroom to wash my hands and face and get ready for the day. One of them (he was nine and big for his age) said, "Here, give me your hand. I'll show you where to wash."

I wasn't very sophisticated, but it was clear he was trying to put my hand into the toilet. I was outraged. My mother and father didn't believe a blind person could do very much, and they had restricted my movements and actions—but they loved me, and even spoiled me. Certainly they never mistreated me.

My anger took tangible form. I jerked away and resisted, accompanying my actions with sharp words. The nine-year-old (who, as I was to learn, made a practice of bullying the smaller children) was not pleased to have his fun spoiled and to be resisted in the presence of the other boy. He beat me up. In fact, it was but the first of several beatings that he gave me during the next few days.

It was clear that I was either going to have to find a way to solve the problem or lead a life of intolerable misery. There were a number of other six- and seven-year-olds in the same boat. So I got together with them, and we went to see him as a group—and this time we didn't lose the fight. Just to make certain, we kept at it for a while until there was absolutely no doubt that we hadn't lost the fight. He never bothered us again.

It was my first lesson in the worthwhileness of collective action. It was a valuable learning experience, one that I have never forgotten. It has stood me in good stead through the years and been a comfort to me in times of trouble—and I am sure that it always will.

If I should ever be foolish enough to doubt the necessity of the National Federation of the Blind, all I would need to do would be to remember that week of misery in January of 1933 when I was six. That nine-year-old that I confronted may long since have passed to his reward, but he did me a service and taught me a lesson.

The most exciting thing about starting to school was finally learning to read. But I soon found that Braille was hard to come by at the Tennessee School for the Blind. As a matter of fact, it was *rationed*.

In the first grade we were allowed to read a book only during certain hours of the day, and we were not permitted to take books to our rooms at night or on weekends. Looking back, I suppose the school didn't have many books, and they probably thought (perhaps correctly) that those they did have would be used more as missiles than instruments of learning if they let us take them out.

When we advanced to the second grade, we were allowed (yes, allowed) to come down for thirty minutes each night to study hall. This was what the "big boys" did. In the first grade we had been ignominiously sent to bed at seven o'clock while our elders (the second and third graders and those beyond) were permitted to go to that mysterious place called study hall. The first graders (the "little boys") had no such status or privilege.

When we got to the third grade, we were still not permitted to take books to our rooms, but we were allowed to increase our study hall time. We could actually spend a whole hour at it each night Monday through Friday. It was the pinnacle of status for the primary grades.

When we got to the "intermediate" department (the fourth, fifth, and sixth grades) we were really "growing up," and our status and prestige increased accordingly. We were allowed (I use the word advisedly—"allowed," not "forced") to go for an hour each night Monday through Friday to study hall, and during that time we could read books and magazines to our hearts' content.

True, the choice was not great—but such as there was, we could read it. Of course, we could not take books to our rooms during the week, but on Friday night each boy (I presume the girls had the same privilege) could take one Braille volume to his room for the weekend.

Before I go further, perhaps I had better explain that comment about the girls. The girls sat on one side of the room, and the boys sat on the other; and woe to the member of one sex who tried to speak or write notes to a member of the other. Girls, like Braille books, were difficult to get at—and all the more desirable for the imagining. But back to the main thread.

As I say, each boy in the "intermediate" department could check out one Braille volume on Friday night. Now, as every good Braille reader knows, Braille is bulkier than print; and at least four or five Braille volumes (sometimes more) are required to make a book. It is also a matter of common knowledge that people in general and boys in particular (yes, and maybe girls, too) are constantly on the lookout for a way to "beat the system." What system? Any system.

So on Friday nights we boys formed what would today be called a consortium. One of us would check out volume one of a book; the next, volume two; the next, volume three; et cetera. With our treasures hugged to our bosoms we would head to our rooms and begin reading.

If you got volume three (the middle of the book), that's where you started. You would get to the beginning by and by. Now, girls and Braille books were not the only items that were strictly regulated in the environment I am describing. The hours of the day and night fell into the same category. Study hall ended at 8:00, and you were expected to be in your room and in bed by 9:40, the time when the "silence bell" rang. You were also expected to be trying to go to sleep, not reading.

But as I have said, people like to beat the system; and to us boys, starved for reading during the week, the hours between Friday night and Monday morning were not to be wasted. (Incidentally, I should say here that there were usually no radios around and that we were strictly forbidden—on pain of expulsion, and God knows what else—to leave the campus except for a brief period on Saturday afternoon—after we got big enough, that is, and assuming we had no violations on our record which required erasure by penalty.)

In other words the campus of the Tennessee School for the Blind was what one might call a closed ecology. We found our entertainment where we could.

Well, back to Friday night and the problem of books. Rules are rules, but Braille can be read under the covers as well as anywhere else; and when the lights are out and the sounds of approaching footsteps are easy to detect, it is virtually impossible to prohibit reading and make the prohibition stick.

The night watchman was regular in his rounds and methodical in his movements. He came through the halls every sixty minutes on the hour, and we could tell the time by his measured tread. (I suppose I need not add that we had no clocks or watches.)

After the watchman had left our vicinity, we would meet in the bathroom (there was one for all twenty-six of us) and discuss what we had been reading. We also used the occasion to keep ourselves awake and exchange Braille volumes as we finished them.

It made for an interesting way to read a book, but we got there—and instead of feeling deprived or abused, we felt elated. We were beating the system; we had books to read, something the little boys didn't have; and we were engaged in joint clandestine activity.

Sometimes as the night advanced, one of us would go to sleep and fail to keep the hourly rendezvous, but these were minor aberrations—and the weekend was only beginning.

After breakfast on Saturday morning some of us (not all) would continue reading—usually aloud in a group. We kept at it as long as we could, nodding off when we couldn't take it any more. Then, we went at it again.

Let me be clear. I am talking about a general pattern, not a rigid routine. It did not happen every weekend, and even when it did, the pace was not uniform or the schedule precise. We took time for such pleasantries as running, playing, and occasional rock fights.

You can understand that after I had been in school for a few weeks, I contemplated with mixed feelings the summer vacation which would be coming. I loved my family, but I had been away from home and found stimulation and new experiences. I did not look forward to three months of renewed confinement in the four-room farm house with nothing to do.

Then, I learned that I was going to be sent a Braille magazine during the summer months. Each month's issue was sixty Braille pages. I would get one in June, one in July, and one in August. What joy! I was six, but I had learned what boredom meant—and I had also learned to plan. So I rationed the Braille and read two pages each day. This gave me something new for tomorrow. Of course, I went back and read and re-read it again, but the two new pages were always there for tomorrow.

As the school years came and went, I got other magazines, learned about the Library of Congress Braille and talking book collection, and got a talking book machine. By the time I was in the seventh grade I was receiving a number of Braille magazines and ordering books from three separate libraries during the summer. Often I would read twenty hours a day—not every day, of course, but often. I read *Gone With the Wind*, *War and Peace*, Zane Grey, and hundreds of others.

I read whatever the libraries sent me, every word of it; and I often took notes. By then it was clear to me that books would be my release from the prison of the farm and inactivity. It was also clear to me that college was part of that program and that somehow I was going to get there. But it was not just escape from confinement or hope for a broader horizon or something to be gained. It was also a deep, ingrained love of reading.

The background I have described conditioned me. I did not feel about reading the way I see a lot of people viewing it today. Many of today's children seem to have the attitude that they are "forced," not "permitted," to go to school—that they are "required," not "given the privilege and honor," to study.

They are inundated with reading matter. It is not scarce but a veritable clutter, not something to strive for but to take for granted. I don't want children or the general public to be deprived of reading matter, but I sometimes think that a scald is as bad as a freeze. Is it worse to be deprived of books until you feel starved for them or to be so overwhelmed with them that you become blase about it? I don't know, and I don't know that it will do me any good to speculate.

All I know is that I not only delight in reading but believe it to be a much neglected joy and a principal passport to success, perspective, civilization, and possibly the survival of the species. I am extremely glad I have had the opportunity and incentive to read as broadly as I have, and I believe my life is so much better for the experience that it borders on the difference between living and existence.

The world today is much different for everyone from what it was when I was a child. And for blind people it is a better world with more opportunities and a better future ahead because we have worked with each other and with generous and caring sighted people to make it so. I believe there are few problems in life that can't be solved when people do what they can for themselves and join together to help others. I am grateful for the help I have received in my lifetime and try to do my share to make the world a better place for all of us.

In 1992, Dr. Jernigan spoke of his own changing attitude about blindness in an article entitled, "Competing on Terms of Equality" from the Kernel Book *The Freedom Bell.* This is what he said:

COMPETING ON TERMS OF EQUALITY

by Kenneth Jernigan

As Federationists know, Job Opportunities for the Blind (JOB) is a project jointly sponsored by the U. S. Department of Labor and the National Federation of the Blind. At a JOB seminar held in Baltimore late in 1980, I made the following remarks. They were substantially reprinted in the Summer and Fall, 1981, issues of *Dialogue* magazine.

I believe that whether or not blind persons have ready access to the job market is important not only to blind people who are employed but to those who may be seeking employment. It is important to every segment of the blind population. People who are past the employment years are affected by whether blind persons can get jobs.

To make this clear, all I have to say is this: During the years when a black person in this country could not find employment except in shoeshining or in the very lowest paid of janitorial jobs, it affected the way society treated every black person—those who were not hunting employment as well as those who were. And so in that sense every blind person has a stake in what happens in our JOB project and in upgrading jobs for blind persons.

Whether or not we believe that as blind persons we really are as good as others—that is, whether we believe we are employable—has something to do with how we look at ourselves—what kind of confidence we will have, how we will expect people to treat us, and what we will expect we can do. I know (and probably you do, too) situations where blind people, men or women, have got themselves engaged to sighted people and the families of the sighted persons have been moved almost to violence, thinking their child had gone mad by wanting to marry a blind person. It's all tied up with jobs. In the past we haven't known blind people who have had jobs that were prestigious in the community. We haven't known blind people who were persons that other people hoped they could be like, and had to come to for favors, and all the other things that make for desirability.

The trouble is that blind people, being part of the culture, have accepted that notion of themselves too often and have, therefore, done much to make it come true. It's a vicious circle.

I know many people who say, "Of course, I believe that as a blind person I am as good as anybody else." Very often they simply don't know what they are saying. Very often they are lying in their teeth, but usually don't know it.

Let me give you an example from my own experience. I went to college. I had, I believe, a rather pleasing personality. We all think we have a pleasant personality, I suppose. But I had some objective evidence. I could use mine to some good effect when I wanted to.

Early in my freshman year I went to one of my professors and said to him, "I want to do everything that's needed. I don't want any special favors or privileges. I want to compete on terms of equality with the other students here. I really want to be able to perform, and I believe I can. As I have said, I don't want you to give me special favors or privileges. Once in a while there may be a few things that I will need to do a little differently, but I hope there won't be many such things and that they won't be sufficient to make a difference in my overall performance.

"Specifically," I said, "since fitting footnotes onto a sheet of typing constitutes some problem, I would hope that I would be able to omit footnotes from term papers and themes. I shall certainly do all the research involved, and will type the papers myself."

That is what I told my professor. It sounds pretty good. Don't you think? It's a fairly plausible argument. I put all of the right words: "no special favors, no special treatment, no unreasonable privileges." Then, I asked the professor: "Is it all right if I proceed in that manner?"

His answer was blunt and to the point.

"Hell no," he barked. "It's not all right. Look, you have come here telling me that you can compete on terms of equality, and you have made all of this speech about how you want to do it on equal terms with everybody else. You also say you are capable of doing competitive work in college. Now, you either can or you can't.

"I could let you get by without the footnotes and probably nobody would criticize me for it. But when you are through with my classes and are graduating, you are going to want a recommendation. At that time you'll get your feelings hurt if I say, 'He's not capable of competing on terms of real equality with others, but he can do a good job considering that he's blind.' You won't like it if I say that. Therefore, you are either going to pass my courses in such a way that I can honestly give you good recommendations, or I'll flunk you. Take it either way you want it."

That was one of the finest things that ever happened to me, because I had gone there with a good line prepared to snow the man, and I am not sure that I even knew that I was trying to do it. I typed his papers, by the way, and put the footnotes on them. There was no problem at all in doing it. I am afraid that if he had permitted it, I might have taken the easy way out and paid a terrible price for it.

Not all blind persons are as lucky as I was. Too many are faced with people who say to them, "You don't need to do this." Unfortunately too many blind people accept the proffered assistance and (more often than not) never realize the high price they pay for the success they achieve in avoiding whatever it is they get out of or are talked into not doing.

When you are blind, how do you manage to do the different things you need to do? Very often we begin by assuming that we need a lot more so-called "accommodation" than we do. Remember: There is no such thing as a free lunch. You pay for everything.

I want to jump forward to a talk that I had with an executive from IBM not long ago. I don't think the blind person involved would mind if I told you, because she and I laughed about it later—but it wasn't funny to her at the time.

We had a blind woman come here to the National Center for three months to work with us on the talking typewriter that IBM has developed. She had tried to get jobs in the past and had had one that hadn't worked out very well. We put her on the talking typewriter, and we all made good speeches. You know the pattern: "This will be a good chance to test out the machine, but also you'll be treated like any other employee."

She had a tendency to go and sit down in other people's offices and talk. She was blind, and everybody had always told her that she was a genius if she could do anything at all—and, of course, we all like to be told we're geniuses, every one of us. We all like to be told that we are wonderful. Often the reason we are told such things is not complimentary, but we don't recognize it. Often the reasoning is something like this: "Considering that you're blind, it's wonderful that you can do what (if you were sighted) would be taken as just an ordinary thing." That's not complimentary.

Anyway, this woman came in one day to Mrs. Walhof (who was her supervisor) and said she had done 50 form letters in a given period of time. She was obviously pleased about it and wanted to be petted for it. But Mrs. Walhof said, "That's not enough. If you think that way, you won't be able to compete on terms of equality. It's not enough."

The woman was crushed. She cried and felt ill-used. And so the lady from IBM who was in charge of training came in pretty soon and said to me: "I think you are being a little hard on her. You know, that's really quite good for a secretary. I want to talk to you about her because I think she feels that she's a little hard pressed. Maybe you are expecting too much."

I said, "Look. You stick to handling typewriters, and let me handle training blind people. Part of the problem we as blind people have is directly traceable to people like you. Without ever meaning to do it, you have kept blind people from getting jobs because of your lousy attitudes." After that kind of hard beginning I softened it down a bit. I had started out with shock tactics on her, but we got to be very good friends. I said to her, "Tell me (and really be honest): If this woman were sighted and a good secretary, would you regard her performance on those letters as satisfactory?"

After some hesitation she said: "Well, no, I guess I wouldn't. But after all, you've got to take into account that she does have extra problems."

"No, I don't have to take that into account," I said. "That's exactly why blind people don't have jobs. A blind typist does not need to perform at less capacity than a sighted typist. You don't believe that a blind person can perform up to capacity; and so, of course, you're having trouble with blind persons getting jobs. It's your own fault."

A couple of weeks later the IBM trainer came back to me, having visited around the country, and said, "I've thought about it a lot, and I want to tell you something. I've been to some other places (these other training sites we have) and the typists there expect me, because I'm sighted, to do everything from carry their coffee to go out and shop for them." She said, "They're not really being expected to perform up to par, and I guess I'd always taken it for granted that they shouldn't be. But I had to do something about it, and this person you have here may really become employable as a result of what you're doing. I was wrong."

"Okay, I'm glad you can see that," I said. "We are going to help the person we are training become able to be a really good secretary."

Then I got the IBM executive into my office (the one who was in overall charge of the talking typewriter project), and we had a long talk. I had come to know him. We had spent as much as eight or ten hours together, and we could talk frankly.

"You have asked me about your IBM Talking Typewriter," I said to him. And he said, "Yes, because we're having trouble selling it. We're not sure the market is out there."

"I think I could help you learn how to sell more of those typewriters," I said. "I think it's your own fault that you're not selling them.

He asked why.

"Because you haven't learned the lesson that the Gillette Razor people learned so well," I told him. "They wanted to sell blades, but they realized that they had to sell razors, too. Suppose they were selling blades and thought they were good, but they thought their razors were so bad that they were second-rate and inferior. Then the Schick people would have it all over them. They'd beat them in sales every time.

"You people wrote a special manual for blind operators of the Mag Card II typewriter, and it was one of the poorest pieces of business I've ever seen. You had a token blind woman employed at IBM who didn't believe in herself, but you people thought she was a genius because she was able to perform at all, and you had to give her something to occupy her time. What resulted was a manual written up specially for blind people. I don't know whether she wrote it, or whether you had somebody else do it. Maybe you had some more blind people employed. I don't know. Some of my colleagues and I tried the manual, and it didn't work. It assumed that the blind were morons. So we scrapped it and taped your regular manual for the Mag Card Typewriter and used it to train blind people. We got jobs for a lot of them.

"Now, you are going out and trying to sell your talking typewriter, but you don't really believe that blind people can perform on a par with others. How are you going to sell employers on buying talking typewriters to employ people that you don't really believe are employable? That's your problem."

"Well," he said, "I hadn't looked at it like that. I don't know. Maybe that's it, but I just hadn't looked at it that way."

"Let me put the question to you another way," I said. "Do you believe that you are necessarily more fortunate than I simply because you're sighted and I'm blind?"

He said, "Well, yeah, I guess I do."

Then, I said, "Okay. Let's see what it is that you think you have that makes you that way—whether it's the natural wish of every person to feel superior to somebody and the insecurity which all of us have (at least, a little of it) or if it's really that you've got that much on the ball. Let's see what it is you've got.

"Let me tell you the test I use. The world is competitive. It always will be. There isn't any way to make it otherwise. Whether we're under Communism, Fascism, the church, or a so-called democracy—it doesn't matter whether the capitalists run it, or the labor unions. It's competitive. Anybody who tells you otherwise is deceiving you—and probably is doing quite well in the world, as he moves on while you stay behind to meditate on the merits of his philosophy.

"Let's take it on that basis. By *competitive* I mean this: There are fewer things out there to fill wants than there are wants for those things. Therefore, necessarily whatever it is-whether jobs, honors, loaves of bread, dollars, cars, women, men, liquor, houses, Bibles, whatever—there are always fewer of whatever it is than there are people who want it. Somebody is going to get left out. I'm telling you that I don't think blind people have to get left out any more often than sighted people. I believe there are too many other things involved.

"Let me speak to you. You and I are at least fairly close to the same age. Are you really sure that if you want something in the world and I want it, and you and I both set out to get it with all we can—are you sure you're going to beat me out and get it?"

"Well, no," he said.

I said, "I'm not either. Think about it. I don't know whether you're more fortunate than I or not. You may be. But I doubt it."

He said he hadn't looked at it like that.

"That's one reason I might get whatever it is we are competing for and you might not," I said.

Now, let me leave the IBM typewriter and my conversation with the IBM executive. Let me go back and talk to you about the specifics of jobs. When I was in California at the Orientation Center for the Blind, I talked with people all along about blindness, trying to help blind persons come to realize that they could compete on terms of equality with others. I remember an individual who was an electrician before he became blind. He was 32 years old. He had been an electrician since before he was 20. One Sunday afternoon when he was working in his back yard a grinder blew up and blinded him. We got him at the Orientation Center very shortly afterward.

He came in with a kidding rather shallow kind of bravado, a sort of gaiety. He said he knew that he could learn to perform as a blind person as well as he'd ever performed as a sighted person.

It was obviously phony. It was clear he didn't believe anything of the sort. After he had been there about two or three weeks, he said to me, "I have really been thinking about it, and in a sense I guess blindness may have been a good thing for me, because it caused me to re-evaluate my life and make the changes that I would like to have made all along. I never really was happy as an electrician. I think I'd like to get into another line of work."

"What would you like to do?" I asked.

"Something that would let me get out and travel around," he said.

"Like what?" I asked.

"Maybe I could do piano tuning," he said.

I'm sure I don't have to tell you what that meant. He thought that was what blind people could do, and he was still trying to tell himself that he was a brave fellow, and maybe he really halfway convinced himself that's what he wanted to do.

All I said was, "We'll think about it." I changed the subject and began talking to him about the weather, and passed on.

After he had been at the center four or five months, he said to me one day, "You know, I was really phony about that piano tuning. I guess I thought that was all I could do as a blind person. But I've sort of changed my mind. Now, I can see some things that I didn't then. I don't want to be a piano tuner. What I really would like to do is go to college."

"Tell me about it," I said. "Tell me why."

"I think I would like to get into some sort of work helping my fellow blind," he said.

I said, "You know, you are an awful liar."

In these days of civil rights I suppose he could have hailed me up before the courts for having abused him. I might have had truth as a defense. I don't know.

Anyway, his response was: "But how could a blind person be an electrician?"

"I don't know," I said. "I'm not an electrician. I don't know anything about electricians. Let's work on it. You know something about being an electrician, and I know something about blindness. I don't know whether you can be an electrician, but let's try it. Let's see what you can do."

Well, we did. He went back and got a job as a full-time electrician, and he worked at it quite well and satisfactorily. But I might have taken him seriously, or he might have taken himself seriously in those earlier false starts. If he hadn't had some help in becoming deconditioned to what society had taught him to believe, he would have had a different kind of existence.

He taught me a lesson, too, by the way. He said, "You tell me that you believe a blind person ought to have an equal opportunity to be an electrician. Your house has some wiring problems. How about if I come over and work on your house? Are you willing for me to do that?"

I said, "Yes, I guess so if you'll give me some idea about how you propose to do it."

To which he said, "I'm a licensed electrician. Would you ask a sighted man to give you that kind of proof?"

I said, "No, I really wouldn't."

"Well, why, then, do you discriminate against me?" he asked.

I had taught him fairly well, I suppose. "Mark up a point for you," I told him. "I don't care how you do it. If you believe you can do it, come and have a whack at it."

When you get a job, much of what happens to you is, of course, determined by whether the job is suitable for you and whether your employer and your colleagues give you an equal chance. But it also has to do with the way you approach it—what you believe you can do. Here are some examples from my own experience:

Once upon a time I sold life insurance—a most interesting occupation. I had a big rate book in print. I don't know how each of you would have tried to deal with it, but I could not always afford to hire somebody to go with me and read it for me. I was trying to make a living, not be an executive. I couldn't put it into Braille. I didn't have enough reader time for that and even if I had, it would have meant carrying around volumes. So that wouldn't have been practical.

I had another problem: The company kept changing the rate book as new policies and procedures came along. So what was I to do?

I could have asked my prospective customers to look up the information I needed, but that wouldn't have worked because the book contained information I didn't want them to have. I wasn't trying to hoodwink them. But if you're a wholesaler, you don't ask the people you're selling to to look in the manufacturer's catalog and see what kind of markup you make. It isn't good psychology. Besides, most of my clients would not efficiently have been able to find what I wanted. But what would have been even worse was that it would have destroyed their confidence in me. They wouldn't have believed that I was competent to handle their insurance business if I had done it that way.

So what did I do? I could have cried about it or said, "Well, that shows a blind person can't be an insurance salesman. Right there it is. I tried, but tell me how I'm going to do it?" People often come to me and say, "Here is this job. Tell me how I'm going to do it."

I can't. I'm not motivated to sit down and spend a day or two of my time trying to figure out something which, if it can be figured out, they ought to be figuring out themselves. If it can't be figured out, why should I spend my time trying to do what can't be done?

I either had to figure this out or stop selling insurance. By the way, when I'd tried to get the insurance job, the first company had said they wouldn't hire me but would let me sell in the name of another established agent and split commissions with him if I wanted to. I said no, I didn't think I'd do that. Then, I went off and found a company that would put me on.

So I tried to discover if there was any way to figure out shortcuts to work with the rate book, a formula. I learned that if I knew the annual premium on a policy, the semiannual premium (if a client preferred to pay it that way) would be 51 percent. The quarterly was 26 percent, and the monthly premium was 10 percent. So right there I saved myself lots of columns. It isn't very hard to figure out 51 percent of something, or 26 percent, or 10 percent. Ten percent is easy—all you have to do is move a decimal.

Then, I started on the other end of it, the hard part. I learned that if I knew what an individual of a given age would be charged for a particular policy, there was a formula by which I could determine what that particular policy would cost an individual of any age. I arbitrarily took age 26, and (knowing the premium on an ordinary life insurance policy for a person of that age) I could figure the semiannual, quarterly, or monthly premium for a person of 50, 60, or any other age. Since we mostly sold fifteen or twenty kinds of policies (there were a few exotic things, but they were not ordinarily sold), I could put all the information I needed (name of policy and annual premium for age 26) on a Braille card or two and put them in my pocket so nobody would even know I was looking at them.

It occurred to me that my competitors might also have such data available. Rate books are rate books. So I thought, "If ours are like that, I wonder what theirs are like." So I lured some of my competitors out to my house to sell me insurance and deduced a number of things about their policies—unraveled the formula and found that they worked.

One lonesome, rainy night I went to see a fellow who was quite well-to-do, a man who could buy (and intended to buy) a relatively large life insurance policy. It was going to make somebody a whopping good commission. There are always fewer things than there are people wanting them, and in this case a lot of us wanted his insurance business—but only one of us was going to get it. And it didn't matter whether you explained it, or called yourself blind, or said, "I can tell you why I didn't do it." Only one thing counted: did you or didn't you? That was the test.

So I went over to see him, and he said he'd been thinking about buying this insurance. I said, "Well, if you do, it will cost you this amount.

"Suppose," he said, "I decided I want to pay it on a semi-annual, twice-a-year, basis?"

"You could do that," I said, "and if you did, it would cost you this amount.

"I've considered buying from this other company," he said.

"Well," I answered, "they're a good company, and if you buy the policy from them, it will cost you this." And I went on to tell him as honestly as I could the advantages and disadvantages of the other company's policy and of mine.

Then, he said, "I'm going to give you my insurance business, because I think you know what you're doing. I had a fellow out here the other night who didn't know a thing. Every time I asked him any question he had to look it up in that little book he had."

Now, I'm as lazy as anybody else. We all have a tendency to that, and there's nothing wrong with being lazy if you properly understand that it means extracting as much as you can for the labor you exert. That's perfectly proper. It's just that a lot of people don't know how to be lazy. If you'll work hard up front, it will allow you more time to do whatever it is you want to do, and you can do it more effectively, and have more time left over to do something else. If I had had sight, the chances are I never would have been motivated to have hunted up all that stuff and reasoned it out. But once I did, it proved to be a tremendous advantage and an asset. Yet, a lot of people would have told me that I was handicapped in selling insurance because I was blind and couldn't read my rate book. And they would have been right—unless I did something about it.

I want to tell you something else. I did a stint teaching school, and I want to tell you some of the methods I used. They are not the only methods a teacher might use, but they worked for me. I taught for a while in a school for the blind, in a day when blind teachers were not highly regarded. The question was: Could I carry my own weight, and (specifically) could I keep discipline?

At the beginning of the first class I made a speech to the students. I said to them, "We are entering on a new relationship." (That sounds nice and bureaucratic, doesn't it?) "We're entering on a new relationship, and we can live at peace, or we can engage in war. If we engage in a peaceful relationship, all of us can live happily. On the other hand, if you choose to go to war with me, I have certain advantages that you do not possess. You may have some that I don't possess—and some that I haven't thought of. But let me tell you what mine are.

"I can give you assignments, or not. I can assign things to you in a minute or two that will give you a great deal of trouble, either to do or find ways of avoiding doing. One day (whether you now know it or not) it will help you if you have nice recommendations written on your reports from me—not a lot, but it will help some.

"But beyond that, if you try to engage in conflict with me, there are times when you will succeed in putting things over on me, because all of the brains didn't come here when I got here. So you'll win sometimes. But on the other side of that is this: All of the brains didn't come here when you came, so you'll lose sometimes, and I will catch you. It remains to be seen, then, whether or not I can make it desirable for you to try to live in peace with me. I choose peace if I can have it, but I will engage in war if I must." I made them that speech and passed on.

I had a student named Johnny Lindenfellow, who was at that time in the seventh or eighth grade. He took every occasion to be as mangy as he knew how, and he was an expert at it. I tried to reason with him; I tried to be good to him; I pleaded with him about the good of the school and humanity; I talked with him about living and letting live. But nothing worked. There was no getting along with him. Nothing made any difference. In fact, whenever I would lay some punishment on him, he seemed to glory in it as being proof that he was a tough customer.

So I changed tactics. One day when he had done something I didn't like, I said, "Johnny, you will please stay after class."

I could feel him expand with pleasure. He knew I wasn't allowed to kill him, that there was some limit as to what I could do.

After class, when we were alone, I said, "Johnny, it's been a long conflict between you and me, and I want to tell you now what I'm going to do. As you know, I teach other English classes in this school. In about two hours I'm going to be teaching an English class, and I'm going to provoke an incident in that class so that somebody misbehaves. It's not difficult to think up some way to get it done. Then, I will say to the student who misbehaves, 'Why can't you be a *good little boy* like Johnny Lindenfellow?' I will do that over and over and over until I make you the most hated boy in this school. You will fight fifty times every day. I will call you a *good little boy* to every class I have until the day comes that they will beat you to death. You will fight all of the time."

"You wouldn't do that to me," he protested.

"Oh, but I would!" I said. "It's clear that I can think it up... I did; I've already told you about it. And I *will* do it."

He said, "Look, I'd like to get along."

"So would I," I said. "I'm perfectly willing to have it either way, peace or war. You have declared psychological war on me, and I'm no longer prepared to be passive about it. I'm going to pull out all the stops and go to war with you now."

"Look, I want to get along," he reiterated.

"Fine," I said, and he and I became the best of friends and had no more trouble.

That is one way you can maintain discipline. It didn't hurt him. It probably helped him. It certainly helped me.

I discovered another very effective technique, which is translatable beyond school. One day I found a student engaging in an infraction of the rules. I said nothing about it until the next day. Then, in the middle of the class period, I interrupted what I was saying and remarked: "Yesterday, Frances, you violated this rule (and I specified). Your punishment is this." Without another word I returned to the discussion. Nobody said much, but I could hear people thinking about it. In a day or two I caught somebody else doing something, and didn't mention that for two days. The next time I let it go three days—then, a week—then, two weeks—and then, three. Thus, the culprit never knew whether he or she had been detected in crime, and the agony of the suspense cut down on the pleasure considerably. The students never knew whether they had been caught— or when the ax would fall. A lot of times teachers forget that they were once students themselves, and they don't put any ingenuity into the psychological warfare which some students take joy in waging and always win.

We had a rule in my class. If anybody brought anything in and left it there and I found it, that individual had to sit down and punch out a whole sheet of full Braille cells, using a dull stylus and an old slate that wasn't in good alignment. The work had to be done in my presence so that I knew the individual had done it. That was also the rule if a person didn't bring whatever was supposed to be brought to class—book, paper, or whatever.

Once when I was keeping library, the president of the senior class brought me a written book report. I got called away from the library desk. When I left at the end of the period, I forgot to take the report with me. The next day when he came to my English class, the student walked up to my desk and handed the report to me. He said not a word. He just stood there. He had obviously primed all of his fellow students. Everybody simply sat and waited.

"You've got me dead to rights," I said. "Furthermore, you have done something else. You have stripped away all of the things that might have muddied the water. You didn't come and demand that I do anything. You didn't make me a speech. You just brought the evidence and laid it out. Therefore, today in library I will bring the slate and stylus and come and sit at your table. In your presence I will punch each and every dot and present you with the completed page."

I would like to be able to tell you that I deliberately planned that piece of drama—that I knowingly planted the book report and calculatedly forgot it in the hope that he would do what he did. But I didn't. I wasn't sharp enough. However, I hope I learned enough from the experience that I would do it next time—assuming, of course, there ever is a next time. It worked wonders. It made the students feel that I was willing to be flexible, that I wasn't stuffy, that I took seriously the rules which I made, and that I was not above the law. It did a lot of positive things, and if I had had the wisdom to think, I would certainly have staged it, just the way it happened. But I didn't. I simply saw the possibilities in the situation and took advantage of them. Somebody has wisely said that luck is where opportunity and preparation meet.

I'm only saying to you that if you begin by assuming you can't do whatever it is, or that you've got to have this or that special opportunity or career—if you're going to be a crybaby or a grouch or tell people how bad it is that you're blind, then you'll get a lot of sympathy but relatively few jobs and still fewer promotions. You will live as miserable a life as you believe you will live— and all needlessly, except that society has taught you to feel that way, and you haven't been able to break out of the stereotype. Many of us who are blind could get jobs that we don't get, and we don't simply because we have been told by society that we can't perform, and we have believed it. We have fallen into all of the traps of the stereotype: We have been told that we're geniuses for doing the simplest of routine tasks, and we have taken pride in the so-called "compliment." Too often we have sold our potential equality for a trifle: If, for instance, it is raining and luggage is to be loaded into a car, which is right in front of a door and easily accessible, almost nobody would think anything of it if a perfectly healthy blind person waited under shelter while a sighted person said, "Just stand here. I'll load the car." It isn't pleasant to get wet, especially if you have on freshly pressed clothes. I know. I've been there. And there is a temptation, if nobody expects you to do whatever it is, to take advantage of it.

There is also something else: You can become so obnoxiously independent that you are intolerable. If a sighted person is sitting at one end of a table and wants the salt which is at the other end, he or she doesn't insist on getting up and going to get it to prove the ability to walk. The normal sighted person will allow someone near the salt to pass it. But I know blind people who insist that "Nobody's going to touch *my* arm! Nobody's going to help me! I'm independent." They are so unpleasant and so offensive that people turn away in disgust—or, even worse, pity.

It is a matter of having sense enough to know how to behave to get on in the world. If your motive in standing in that doorway is that since only one person is needed to load the car and that there is no point in everybody getting wet, that's fine. But if your motive is to stand and wait because you're blind, don't complain the next time you don't get equal treatment when the goodies are being passed out. You have behaved as if you can't compete on terms of equality. Now, accept it.

I believe that we as blind people are capable of competing on terms of real equality with others in jobs. I believe that the reason we have not done so in the past is that society has custodialized us and held us down. But I believe also that this has not happened because society has wanted to be vicious or unkind or mean. It is because people have taken for granted that that's the way blind people are, that blind persons can't be expected to do this or that kind of thing.

Furthermore, I believe that since we are part of society, we have accepted the public views about us and have done a great deal to reinforce those views. I believe we must begin to change that. I believe we are beginning to change it, and that's what Job Opportunities for the Blind (JOB) is about.

More and more we have the opportunity for our future to be in our own hands if we will only take advantage of that opportunity and make it so. Not all sighted people have good will toward us, but most do—and most want to be of assistance, once they really know that we can compete on terms of equality and that we want to! But before we can convince anybody else, we must convince ourselves. We must really believe that we are capable of equality—that we can get along as well as others similarly situated in society. Unless we believe that, how can we expect other people to believe it? To a great extent, the sighted public will treat us like what we believe in our heart of hearts we are.

In the same year, 1992, he edited *As the Twig is Bent*. In this volume he spoke of the need to think of blind children, to plan for their future and to help them (and blind adults) gain maturity. The "Editor's Introduction" and his article, "To Park or Not to Park," contain the following information.

EDITOR'S INTRODUCTION

by Kenneth Jernigan

There is a well known saying that as the twig is bent, so grows the tree.

What is true of plants is also true of people. The poet Wordsworth said, "The child is father of the man."

He meant, of course, that our behavior and beliefs as adults are, to a large extent, determined by what happens to us when we are growing up.

This third Kernel Book is largely focused on that theme—what today's blind children are being taught about themselves and what happened to yesterday's blind children, those who are today's adults. As we of the National Federation of the Blind have so often said, the real problem of blindness is not the blindness itself but the mistaken notions and misunderstandings about blindness which are so widely prevalent in society. The first two Kernel Books (*What Color is the Sun* and *The Freedom Bell*) also dealt with this theme, but the present volume has a particular emphasis on blind children and what lies ahead for them. Every day all of us are, at least to some degree, bending the twig that will determine the final shape of their lives.

In this book I have tried to acquaint you with quite a number of blind children and adults, and I have tried to do it at something more than merely the surface level. These are people I know—friends, former students, and colleagues. I think they are people that you, too, will want to know. In the process I hope you will gain an increased understanding of what blind people are like. Mostly we're just like you. We cry if we have reason to—but not because of blindness. And we laugh if something's funny—but, again, not because of blindness. Our lives are as varied, as interesting, or as dull as yours. It all depends on how the twig is bent, how the tree grows, and what opportunities and environment we have.

I don't know how many more Kernel Books we will print, but if this one gets the warm reaction which the first two have received, there will probably be others. Meanwhile the present volume is now being widely distributed, hopefully to do its bit to help improve the climate of public opinion about blindness. Every day we bend the twig.

TO PARK OR NOT TO PARK

by Kenneth Jernigan

As those who have read previous Kernel books know, I have been blind since birth and grew up on a farm in Tennessee. After attending the state school for the blind and going to college for undergraduate and graduate degrees, I returned to the Tennessee School for the Blind for four years as a teacher, hoping not only to teach something useful to blind youngsters but also (if I could) to serve as a role model and a stimulus to accomplishment.

Then, from 1953 to 1958 I taught at California's training center for blind adults—again, trying to act as a role model and provide stimulation and encouragement. In fact, my primary task was to help those who came to the Center to examine blindness and their attitudes about it; to understand that they could still be competitive, productive members of society; and that they could not have the privileges of full citizenship without also assuming its responsibilities.

In 1958 I went to Iowa to become director of the State Commission for the Blind, which administered a training center and other programs. Once more, I found myself examining with my trainees and students what blindness was really like, not just what it was thought to be like. How many special privileges should we take— or, for that matter, even want? What did we owe to society, and what to ourselves? How important was it to avoid offending well-intentioned sighted people who offered help that we felt we didn't need and what long-term effect would our actions have upon us and other blind people, as well as upon the members of the sighted public? Such discussions led to difficult soul searching— especially as we related them to our daily behavior. Of course, I was not just dealing with what my students felt and did but also with my own attitudes and conduct. Self-deception is one of the easiest and most dangerous mistakes that a person can make.

As director of the Iowa State Commission for the Blind, I frequently had business at the State Capitol. Ordinarily there was no trouble finding a parking place quite close to the building. However, from January until some time in the late spring or early summer the legislature was in session, and the Capitol was always crowded. Correspondingly, the Capitol grounds and parking areas were filled with cars, and if one arrived after 7:30 in the morning, he or she was likely to have to walk several blocks. If one is not in a hurry and the weather is pleasant (as, for instance, in early May with the birds singing, the sun shining, and the appropriations settled), such walking may be good for both body and soul, evoking thoughts of a just providence and a well-ordered world; but if the time is January and the snow lies deep on the ground (with legislators to meet and appropriations to justify), the perspective changes.

Now, it so happens that in the Iowa of that day I was a public figure of considerable note, treated with respect and deference. Therefore, when I traveled by automobile to the Capitol to transact this or that piece of business, the security guards were pleased to see me and offer assistance. There was at the very door of the Capitol a parking place reserved for the handicapped, and I was a blind person. The security guards insisted that I take the parking place. More than that: They were hurt and offended if I indicated that I would park elsewhere and walk back in the snow like everybody else.

The problem was not the guards or my colleagues in government or the general public. All would have been glad to have me use the handicapped parking place. No, that is an understatement. They would have felt downright good about it.

The problem was not with them. It was with me. I knew that I could walk as well as anybody else and that (regardless of technicalities or public misconceptions) the intent which had led to the enactment of the handicapped parking permit law was to provide easy access to the building for those who had trouble in walking and truly needed it. Yet, I like comfort and approval as well as the next person. It was not pleasant to walk through the cold, wet Iowa snow in January, and it was not satisfying to hear the tone of disappointment and hurt in the voices of the security guards when I declined the use of the space, regardless of how courteously and appreciatively I did it. And it was not a matter which could be faced, settled once and for all, and then put behind me. It happened over and over—because, as I have already said, I had frequent business at the State Capitol in January, and the snow storms came with discouraging regularity. So my Federationism and my bodily comfort, my wish to be honest and consistent and my wish to be polite and thought of as a good fellow—in short, my spiritual aspirations and my bodily desires— were in continuous conflict.

What do you think I did? In the circumstances what would you have done? Whoever says that the world is not filled with temptations (for the blind as well as for the sighted) is either a naive nincompoop or a barefaced liar. Of such is humanity made—neither angel nor devil but somewhere between, and always becoming.

In 1993, Dr. Jernigan wrote about "making hay" in a Kernel Book of the same name. One of the major concerns of the blind (as is true for the rest of the population of America) is how to earn a little money. In doing this, Dr. Jernigan taught himself an important lesson—one that would stand him, and the blind students he taught, in good stead for decades thereafter. Here it is:

MAKING HAY

by Kenneth Jernigan

As a blind child growing up on a farm in the hills of Middle Tennessee in the late 1920's and early 1930's, I did a lot of thinking. This is not surprising since there wasn't much else to do. We lived in a four-room house on a gravel road, and I doubt that an automobile a week passed our door. We had no radio, no telephone, no newspaper, no magazines, and no books except the Bible and the textbooks my brother (four years older than I) brought home from school.

The world of the late '20's and early '30's in rural Tennessee was a totally different place from what we know today. Nobody thought about atom bombs, pollution, or jet planes. About the hottest topic I heard discussed by my elders was whether it was a sin for a woman to bob her hair and what the likelihood was that you would go to hell if you played cards. I had better explain that last remark. I am not referring to playing cards for money, just ordinary games around the family table. And while we are on the subject, there was no question at all about whether you would go to hell if you danced or played pool. You would.

The difference between the world of then and there and the one of here and now was not limited to the rural areas. Let me give you an example. When I went off to the Tennessee School for the Blind in Nashville at the age of six (that would have been January of 1933), one of the more charming customs of the place was a Saturday morning ritual involving the Scriptures. Shortly after breakfast the small boys (I don't know what happened to the girls since there was strict segregation) were plopped down on a bench and given the task of memorizing a chapter from the Bible. It didn't do any good to protest, object, or try to resist. You sat there until you memorized it, after which you were free to go play.

One's religion had nothing to do with it, nor did one's interest or aptitude. When you got the task done, you could (within limits) go where you pleased and do what you liked. Meanwhile you couldn't. And whatever time you spent trying to beat the system was just that much of the morning gone. I suppose I need not tell you that I quickly concluded to learn my chapter with minimum delay, which I religiously (no play on words intended) did. As a result, I have been a devout Bible quoter ever since—and much, I might add, to my benefit and long-range satisfaction. Ah, well, children are not always in the best position to know what will stand them in good stead.

I don't want to leave you with the impression that everything in that Tennessee world of the '20's and '30's concerned the Bible or religious matters. It didn't. We popped corn in a pan of bacon grease on the wood stove in the kitchen or in a long-handled popper at the fireplace in one or the other of the two bedrooms. (The house had a kitchen, a dining room, and two bedrooms.) We visited our neighbors and relatives, either walking or (if the distance was too far) riding in a wagon drawn by two mules; we gathered hickory nuts and walnuts; and now and again the family sang songs or listened to a neighbor play a banjo. At Christmas time there was a great deal of cooking, but no convenience foods, of course, and as little as possible bought from the store. For instance, we didn't make fruitcake. That would have cost too much. Instead, we made jam cake. The black walnuts, the homemade blackberry jam, and most of the other ingredients came from our farm and required no outlay of cash.

As to my personal situation, it was (if you want to be high-toned about it) what you might call anomalous. Nobody in the neighborhood had ever known a blind person, so there was no one to give advice. My parents loved me, but they didn't know what to do. This led to some strange inconsistencies. For instance, my mother and dad didn't want me to carry wood for the fireplace or stove or water from the spring, which was only a few feet from the house. They didn't want me to play in the yard or go any farther than the porch. They were afraid I might get hurt. Yet, they had no objection at all to my shooting firecrackers at Christmas time.

It was regarded as a natural thing for boys in that part of the country to shoot firecrackers, and I suppose my parents just never thought about it. One of my earliest memories is of me standing on the front porch with a match and a firecracker in my hand and of my father, saying as he went past me into the house, "You'd better be careful, or you'll blow your hand off with that thing." Young as I was, I knew that he was right and that nobody would stop me if I was careless—so I wasn't careless. I developed a technique of holding the match just below the head and pressing the firecracker fuse against it. Match and fuse were held between my thumb and index finger, so there was no possibility of the firecracker's exploding in my hand since my fingers were between it and the flame. Never once did I get hurt, and I think the experience helped me learn something about risk taking and proper caution.

As I have already said, I did a lot of thinking as I was growing up. I also did a lot of planning, for I didn't want to spend the rest of my life in close confinement in that four-room house on the farm. As I reasoned it, I needed to read all the books I could, and I needed to go to college. Therefore, as Braille and recorded books became available to me through the books for the blind program of the Library of Congress, I followed through on the matter and crammed my head as full of book learning as I could. Later I went to college and put the limited environment of the farm behind me.

Meanwhile, I wanted to do productive work and make some money. This wasn't easy since my family (though loving me) thought I was virtually helpless. My first effort (caning chairs at the School for the Blind) brought more labor than cash, but I had to start where

I could. Also, we had cows on the farm, and we sold their milk to a nearby cheese factory. During summer vacations I milked cows night and morning and got ten cents a week for it. At the time I was probably eleven or twelve.

During the first part of the Second World War (I would have been fourteen or fifteen), I made a little money collecting peach seeds. I sold them to a man who came by twice a week in a truck. I was told that the kernels were used for filters in gas masks, but I don't know whether that was true or not. What I do know is that I got a penny a pound for them and that there were a tremendous number of peaches eaten in the neighborhood.

Then, there was the NYA (the National Youth Administration), one of Franklin Roosevelt's New Deal programs. Beginning in 1943 I washed windows, scrubbed floors, shined the small boys' shoes, and did other chores at the School for the Blind for three dollars a month—fifteen hours at twenty cents an hour. I thought I was rich.

And there was even an extra dividend. I was not the only boy at the School for the Blind who got three dollars a month for working for the NYA. There were quite a number, which meant that we now had a cash economy, with more money in circulation than the boys at the School for the Blind had ever known. It stimulated business. I was one of those who profited. I established a relationship with a local wholesale house and walked there once or twice a week to carry large boxes of candy and chewing gum back to the School. I bought the candy for three cents a bar and sold it for a nickel. Going for the candy was not only good exercise but also good profit. My roommate and I did a thriving business. It helped me get some of the money to start to college.

There was also my broom-making project. A neighbor in the country raised broom corn, and I took it with me to the School for the Blind and made it into brooms. (All blind boys in those days were taught chair caning and broom making regardless of their aptitudes or wishes, and I think I could still do a creditable job at either task.) My neighbor supplied the broom corn, and I made and sold the brooms. We split the profits.

During the latter part of the Second World War (by this time I was sixteen or seventeen) I got a chance during the school year to make some money by sorting aircraft rivets. The Vultee Aircraft Company established a plant near Nashville to make dive bombers, and there were many thousands of rivets in each plane. The workers would drop rivets on the floor; and when the dirt, cigarette stubs, and other leavings were swept up, the assorted mixture was brought to the students at the School for the Blind for sorting. We separated the rivets from the trash, sorted them into sizes and types, discarded any with rough spots on them, and sent them back to the aircraft plant. It was a messy job, but it was a way to make some money. I think I got two and a half cents a pound for it.

But all of these various jobs were preliminary to my first truly big opportunity. It happened like this: In the summer of 1944 (I was seventeen) I wanted to expand my horizons. Farm laborers in our neighborhood made $1.25 per day, working from sunrise to sunset, and I wanted to join their ranks. The pivotal event occurred when they began making hay. We had no power machinery. There was a mule-drawn mower, and after the hay was cut, there was a mule-drawn rake. The men would follow the rake with pitchforks, putting the hay into shocks and then tossing it into the mule-drawn wagon. Then it would be taken to the barn and put into the loft.

I tried to get my dad and the other decision makers to let me try my hand at making hay. They were not only unwilling but didn't even want to talk about it. In fact when I insisted, they indicated to me that they were busy and had work to do and that I should stop bothering them.

Since I was unwilling to spend the summer doing nothing, I looked around for other opportunities. It occurred to me that I might try my hand at making furniture. Lumber was cheap in those days, and I also had the idea of using spools. At that time thread was wound on wooden spools, plastic not yet having come into use, and almost everybody sewed. Spools were throw-aways, and I got all my relatives, plus department stores in surrounding towns, to save them for me. I got them in every conceivable size and then sorted them and strung them on iron rods to make table legs.

The design was simple, but the product was both durable and graceful. I could make a table in a day and could sell it for $10. It cost me $1.75 in materials, so I had a profit of $8.25. My rejection became a triumph. While the men did back-breaking labor in the hay fields for $1.25 a day, I stayed in my workshop, listened to recorded books, and produced tables for a profit of $8.25. No matter how fast I made them, I could never keep up with demand. It was as regular as clock work—$8.25 net profit day after day, not the $1.25 I would have made in the hay field.

I also designed and made floor lamps from spools. The lamp had an old steering wheel for a base with a pipe running up the center, surrounded by four columns of spools, with a fixture and shade on top. I could make it in a day, and I sold it for $25, with a cost for materials of a little over $8. This was twice as much profit as I made from a table. The trouble was that the lamps were harder to sell, so I got relatively few orders.

By the end of the summer I had more money than I had ever seen, and I did it again the following year. I went to college in 1945 and never returned to the furniture business, but it taught me a valuable lesson, as did the other jobs I have described. There are many ways to make hay, and if you lose $1.25, you may make $8.25 if you put your mind to it. As I have already said, the world of fifty years ago was a different place from the world of today—but many of the lessons still hold. They probably always will, and one of them is that making hay is a lifelong process.

Also in that year, 1993, Dr. Jernigan edited *The Journey*. In it he talked about the need to think for tomorrow—the value of planning. His article, entitled "The Value of Planning" and the "Editor's Introduction" contain this information:

EDITOR'S INTRODUCTION

by Kenneth Jernigan

This is the second Kernel Book to be issued this year, and the fifth in the series. The first Kernel Book was published in 1991, just over two years ago.

When we started the series, we hoped it would reach a wide audience and bring a new understanding about blindness—that it would show blind people as they really are, ordinary human beings with the normal range of wants and wits, strengths and weaknesses. I think it is fair to say that we are well on the way to achieving that objective—or, at least, that we have made substantial progress toward it.

We have now published more than two million Kernel Books, and the demand for them shows no sign of diminishing. An increasing number of people (very often strangers I meet as I travel over the country) tell me they have read more than one of these books and now feel that a great deal of the mystery has gone out of blindness for them. These strangers (they usually don't stay strangers) feel comfortable in asking me questions about blindness—how a blind person travels from place to place, how clothes are selected, and how the ordinary tasks of daily living are performed. But they also feel comfortable talking about personal matters—how it feels to be blind, and everything from perception of color to courtship and marriage.

This, of course, is what we hoped would happen. The people whose stories appear in these pages are mostly just like you except that they can't see. This doesn't give them unusual talents, such as improved hearing or special musical ability; nor does it curse them with unbearable burdens. If those of us who are blind have appropriate training and equal opportunity, we can get along as well as anybody else—earning our own way, having a family, and leading a regular life. And, after all, isn't that really the way it is with you? If you didn't have a chance for an education and if everybody thought you were incompetent and inferior, isn't that pretty much the way it would be? That's how it is with the blind. In short, if we have a chance and good training, we'll do all right, neither needing nor wanting custody or care.

And one more thing: We want you to know about the National Federation of the Blind. Established in 1940, this organization has, in the opinion of most of us who know about such things, been the single most important factor in helping blind people stand on their own feet and do for themselves. We who are blind still have a long way to go, but we are getting there—and the Kernel Books are helping.

Some of you already know many of the people you will meet in this volume. Others will be new to you. Whether you are a first-time reader or have been with us from the beginning of the series, I hope you will find the present volume interesting and informative. If you have questions about blindness or know somebody who needs our help, let us know. Meanwhile, here is the fifth

Kernel Book. It tells of a journey—a journey which, in its own way, is as significant as the trek across the prairie in the last century by the pioneers, or the landing on the moon in the present century. It is the journey of the blind from second-class status to hope and opportunity.

Kenneth Jernigan
Baltimore, Maryland
1993

THE VALUE OF PLANNING

by Kenneth Jernigan

Blind children are as different from each other as sighted children, but this may not hold for every characteristic. If, for instance, blind children want to get along and do well, they have to learn to plan. At least I did.

As I have often said, living on a farm in rural Tennessee in the late twenties and early thirties was altogether different from what we know today. Not only did we not have a radio, a telephone, electricity, running water, indoor plumbing, or a newspaper. We didn't have automobiles either. It wasn't that we didn't know what a car was. It was just that one didn't pass our house on an average of more than once a week. When we wanted to go somewhere, we walked, rode a horse, or traveled in a wagon drawn by two mules.

Besides me, there were three others in that four-room house, my father and mother and a brother, who was four years older than I. Visitors were rare, and the other members of the family were usually busy. As to entertainment, it was scarce—and even reading wasn't available until after I went away to school in Nashville when I was six.

In the circumstances I had to make my shots count, both for the short run and the long run. Early on, I knew that an education was essential if I didn't want to spend the rest of my life in isolation on the farm, which I didn't. I also knew that there would be a fairly brief window of time to set things in motion.

After I started school, I spent nine months of every year in Nashville and three months at home on the farm. That meant that I pretty much lost contact with any local children who might have grown up as friends, and it also meant that I would have three months of isolation and boredom if I didn't find something productive to do. And I didn't just want entertainment. Well, that too—but something more, something that would help me get an education, something that would help me get off the farm.

By the time I was in the sixth grade I had started getting Braille and recorded books from the Library of Congress. I ordered from the main library in Washington, from a library in Cincinnati, and from another in Illinois. I don't know whether I was supposed to use only one, but I didn't think it was safe to ask, believing I had better let well enough alone. I spent my summers reading, sometimes (not always but sometimes) twenty hours a day—and I took notes on every book I read, planning to be able to make top grades when I got to college, with time left over for participation in extracurricular activities. I thought this would help me build a record of not just being a book worm. By the time I finished high school I had read hundreds of books and had stacks of bulging folders of Braille notes.

In my senior year of high school (that would have been 1945) I had my first contact with the federal-state rehabilitation program. A counselor came to the School for the Blind, and he and I sat down for a chat in what was called "the parlor." (The school was in an old southern mansion, and the amenities lingered, high-ceilinged parlor and all.) When we got past the niceties, the counselor asked me what I wanted to major in when I went to college. I told him I wanted to be a lawyer. He left the subject, talked for a while about the crops and the weather, and then circled back to it. He asked me to tell him three or four things I might like to do.

I was a late teenager (maybe a brash one), so I told him I didn't need to give him three or four. I wanted to be a lawyer. He was not an unkind man, but when you cut through the verbiage, what he said was clear. I could either be a lawyer and pay for it myself, or I could be something else and the rehabilitation agency would help. Academically I was prepared for college, and I had done what I could as a blind boy growing up on a farm to save money. Also, my dad and mother were willing to do what they could to help. But all of it together wasn't enough, in addition to which I didn't feel right about putting strains on the family finances. In short, I went to college and was something else.

As I have said, the rehabilitation counselor was not an unkind man, and he undoubtedly thought he was acting in my best interest; but I now know that he was wrong. There are, to my personal knowledge, hundreds of successfully practicing blind lawyers in this country today. If the National Federation of the Blind had been stronger at the time and if I had known of its existence, maybe things would have been different. Or, maybe they turned out all right after all.

In any case I started college in the fall of 1945, but the day before I was to enroll, I became seriously ill with a ruptured appendix. So I was six weeks late.

Tennessee Tech is located in the hills of upper middle Tennessee, and before the Second World War it had only four or five hundred students. Now, in the fall of 1945, it suddenly had a student body of 2,000, most of them combat hardened veterans. I was the only blind student on the campus, and even though my rigorous planning stood me in good stead, there were touchy moments.

When I went to my first English class, for instance, the teacher said to me publicly: "Young man, you there on the back row, I don't object to your being in my class, but I think it is only fair to tell you that you will fail. A blind person can't do college English." I said I hoped I would get a fair opportunity to try, and he assured me that I would.

Later, the biology teacher was blunter and more terse. I had decided to sit on the front row this time, and the teacher was neither gentle nor kindly disposed. He had obviously had a run-in with the college administration because of me, and he wasn't happy. His speech went to this effect:

"You can sit in this class if you want to, but I can tell you right now that you will fail. I didn't want you here, but the dean made me take you."

When I ventured to say that I hoped I would have an equal opportunity, he replied with what I can only call menace, "Don't worry! You will!"

The next day in laboratory I learned what he meant. There were four of us at each lab table, and I was handed a microscope along with the rest. When I asked what he wanted me to do with it, he said, "It's not my problem. You said you wanted an equal opportunity. Here's your microscope."

Let me not be misunderstood. Almost uniformly I was treated with understanding and respect, and even the English and biology teachers eventually came around. The first quarter each of them gave me a B, but after that I got A's. As a matter of fact, the biology teacher became as belligerently my defender as he had been my detractor.

As the college years went by, I made the grades I had hoped and planned to make, but an experience in my senior year is worth noting. I had become so accustomed to being able to make A's that perhaps I had become careless, or maybe just a little too big for my pants. I had all of the credits I needed to graduate, but just for fun I enrolled in a class for advanced athletes. I was reasonably good at standing on my hands and other gymnastics, but I was totally outclassed. When the coach told me he was going to have to give me a B, I was not disappointed but grateful. Inwardly I felt that I probably deserved an F for presumption. I had no business enrolling in the class in the first place. From that experience I learned a valuable lesson, one that has stood me in good stead for the rest of my life.

I not only made the good grades for which I had prepared during the summers of my boyhood on the farm, but I took part in intercollegiate debating, became a member of the editorial staff of the college newspaper, and got elected to a variety of club and class offices. In addition, I helped pay my college expenses by selling candy, tobacco products, and sundries.

When I finished my degree at Tennessee Tech, I went on to graduate school and later into teaching and other activities, but the basis of it all (the underpinning which made it possible) was the early preparation, the habit of planning I developed as a child.

Today's blind youngsters are, by and large, not discouraged from going to college, and Braille and recorded books are more plentiful than they have ever been. But there are still major obstacles to the blind person seeking a career and a full life. The National Federation of the Blind is now strong enough in every part of the land to play a major role, and public attitudes are better than they used to be. Even so, one thing is unchanged. Planning is still the essential foundation of success.

The 1994 book, *Standing on One Foot,* describes an episode in which Dr. Jernigan caught himself believing in the stereotypes that he had been trying to eradicate. The "Editor's Introduction" and his article, also called "Standing on One Foot," tell us these things:

EDITOR'S INTRODUCTION

by Kenneth Jernigan

When we started publishing the Kernel Books in 1991, we thought the series might run to three or four volumes and a modest circulation. Now, over three years later, we are issuing the sixth Kernel Book, and our circulation is approaching two and a half million. This represents a substantial amount of both work and resources, but we think the effort has been eminently worthwhile.

I have been asked why we chose the name Kernel Books, and there are a number of answers. In the first place, I suppose it has to do with whim. I thought the title was catchy, so I used it. But there is something more. We wanted to go to the very heart of blindness, trying to show our readers what it's really like—and, for that matter, what it isn't like.

If you are blind, what do you think and how do you look at things (not how do you look at them physically, but your point of view and perspective)? How about dating and marriage? What about children, recreation, work, and relations with others? In short, how do blind people live and feel on a daily basis? What we are trying to do is to cut through the sentimentality and misconceptions to the very "kernel" of the subject.

I do a lot of traveling throughout the country, and until recently, people in airports and on the streets who struck up conversations recognized me (assuming that they recognized me at all) because they had heard me on radio or seen me on television talking about the National Federation of the Blind.

Now, that has largely changed. More often than not, I meet people who have read one or another of the Kernel Books. They tell me that they feel personally acquainted with those whose stories have been told. They also feel comfortable talking about blindness—asking about the little things, such as how clothes are selected and matched, or how a blind person does grocery shopping.

This is exactly what we hoped would happen, and I think the present Kernel Book will be no exception. In its pages you will meet a blind father and a sighted mother who, with some difficulty, adopted a baby. You will experience with a blind college student his attempts to come to terms with himself and his blindness, and you will go to the courtroom with a blind woman as she is called to serve on a jury. Of course, you will also get further acquainted with people you have met in previous volumes.

As to the title of this book (*Standing on One Foot*), it comes from one of my own experiences. All of us are products of the culture in which we live, and that is true of me as well as anybody else. Therefore, although I have spent most of my life trying to help people understand the facts about blindness, I found myself sometime ago falling into the same trap that I have been urging others to avoid. It caused a good deal of soul-searching—but enough! You'll find the details in the following pages.

As I have already said, we want you to know about blindness, but we also want you to know about the National Federation of the Blind. Established in 1940, the Federation has, in the opinion of most of us who know about such things, been the single most important factor in helping blind people live normal lives and do for themselves. We who are blind still have a long way to go, but we are getting there—and the Kernel Books are helping. The reason they are helping is that they are one of the major factors in our campaign to increase public understanding and awareness. We are truly changing what it means to be blind, and you who read these books are helping. May you enjoy this book, and may you find it worthwhile.

Kenneth Jernigan
Baltimore, Maryland
1994

STANDING ON ONE FOOT

by Kenneth Jernigan

We who are blind are part of the larger society. We tend to see ourselves as others see us. We tend to accept the false views about our limitations and, thus, do much to make those limitations a reality.

I can offer a personal example. Quite sometime back, an article written by R. H. Gardner appeared in the *Baltimore Sun*. It was headlined: "'Ice Castles' A Little Hard to Swallow," and this is what it said:

Several years ago, I was at a party when a friend, for reasons I cannot recall, bet me I could not stand on one foot 15 seconds with my eyes closed. I had been quite an athlete in my youth (10 years old), during which period I could stand on practically any part of my anatomy—head, hands, ears, or toes—for an indefinite length of time.

I accepted the bet.

To my astonishment, at the count of five I began to waver. At seven, the waver turned into a stagger; and at ten I was lost. It was a great shock for a former athlete (even a 10-year-old one), and I have never forgotten it.

For something happens to your balance when you close your eyes. And how much worse it must be if you're blind!

Being blind, a scientist-friend once pointed out to me, cannot be compared to closing your eyes. When you close your eyes, you still see. You see the undersides of the lids with the light behind them.

But what you see when you're blind is what you see out of the back of your head. There's neither light nor sight of any kind.

I was reminded of all this while watching 'Ice Castles,' a film about a blind figure skater.... I'm told there is a blind figure skater upon whose career the film is loosely based. But it's hard to believe, in view of my experience trying to stand on one leg...

When I read that article, I pooh-poohed it and laughed it to scorn. So did one of my sighted associates. Then, just to show how silly it was, she closed her eyes and stood on one foot. But the laughter stopped, for she wobbled and fell. Then, she opened her eyes and tried it again. There was no problem. She kept her balance without difficulty.

"Nonsense!" I said. "Let me show you"—whereupon, I stood on one foot—and immediately lost my balance.

That incident occurred many years ago, but I still remember it as if it had happened yesterday. Was I shaken? You bet!

After getting over the shock, I did some serious soul-searching. We know that the tests which are made by blindfolding sighted people to determine what the blind can do are totally invalid. I have been among the most vocal in pointing that out. I knew (or, at least, I thought I knew) that balance is a matter of the inner ear, not the eye. Why, then, did my associate fall when her eyes were closed but keep her balance when they were open? Perhaps the fact that she was accustomed to seeing things around her as part of her daily life made the difference, or perhaps (even though she is well versed in our philosophy) the matter went deeper. Perhaps (reacting to social conditioning) she subconsciously expected to fall and was tense. I suggested that she practice a few times with her eyes closed. And what do you know? It worked. In four or five times she could stand on one foot as easily with her eyes closed as open.

But what about me? I have never had any problem with balance. In fact, I was formerly able to walk across an entire room on my hands. So I tried standing on one foot again—and I could do it with perfect ease. If anybody doubts it, I will be glad to demonstrate. Then why did I fall the first time? I reluctantly conclude that (despite all of my philosophy and knowledge to the contrary, despite all of my experience with this very sort of situation dressed out in other forms) I fell into the trap of social conditioning. I hope I won't do it again, but I can't be sure. There is probably not a blind person alive in the world today who has not, at one time or another, sold himself or herself short and accepted the public misconceptions about how limited blind people are, usually without ever knowing it. Prejudice is subtle, and tradition runs deep.

Which brings me back to Mr. Gardner and his newspaper article. He was not trying to hurt the blind, but just to make a living. Nevertheless, based on his single false experience as a simulated blind person, he made sweeping generalizations about our lacks and losses. Do you think he would believe we are capable of equality—that we can travel alone, compete with others for a regular job, and live full and normal lives? Of course not. And his opinions count. He is a member of the press, a molder of thought. And how do you think he would react if one of us brought all of this to his attention?

Probably with defensiveness and resentment. Perhaps he would even help stimulate unfavorable publicity about us, not realizing or admitting why he was doing it—or, for that matter, that he *was* doing it. Of course, he might not behave that way at all. He might learn from the experience and be a better person for it.

A few years ago I went to a cafeteria with a sighted friend. We took our trays and moved down the line. When we turned from the cash register and started for the table, an accident occurred. A glass of water fell from the tray and splashed on the floor. "There will be those," I said, "who will see this and think the reason I spilled that glass of water is because I am blind."

"You are right," my sighted friend replied; "for you didn't spill it. I did. It fell from my tray, not yours."

All of this was bad enough, but there was more, and worse. I didn't leave it there: "How did you do that?" I asked.

This time my friend (who is as well versed in our notions about blindness as I am) responded with more than a touch of acid: "I did it the same way anybody else would," she said. "I tipped my tray. Do you think it is normal for the blind to be clumsy and the sighted to be graceful? Do you think sighted people don't have accidents? Why did you automatically assume that you were the one who spilled the water?"

It was a fair question, and it caused a lot of reflection. I reluctantly concluded that (despite all of my philosophy and knowledge to the contrary, despite all of my experience with this very sort of situation dressed out in other forms) I fell into the trap of social conditioning. I hope I won't do it again, but I can't be sure. The force of cultural conditioning is powerful, and changes in public attitudes about blindness are hard to set in motion.

If I, who have spent most of my life dealing with the problems of blindness, make such mistakes, how can I blame sighted people when they misjudge or fail to understand? Even though there are still a lot of wrong notions about blindness and what blind people can't do, we are learning and truly making progress. Whether sighted or blind, we should take pride in our accomplishments, but we should mix that pride with a little humility. We should have faith in ourselves and keep both feet firmly on the ground, but we should also know that sometimes we will be found standing on one foot.

When the Blizzard Blows, also printed in 1994, contains an article by Dr. Jernigan describing an incident in which the practitioners in a doctor's office misjudged their patient, Dr. Jernigan, because of his blindness. Dr. Jernigan was not only a successful administrator of extensive and imaginative national programs, he dressed to look the part. Nevertheless, he was regarded as almost helpless because of his blindness. His article, "The Hook on the Doctor's Door," says this:

THE HOOK ON THE DOCTOR'S DOOR

by Kenneth Jernigan

Not long ago when I went to a doctor's office for an examination, I had two or three things happen to me during the course of a few minutes that showed me how far we still have to come in changing public attitudes about blindness. In the examining room I was taking off my shirt and getting ready to hang it on a hook on the back of the door. I had my hand on the hook, so there was no question that I knew where it was.

The nurse said: "If I close the door, will you be able to find it?"

I don't know whether she was talking about the door or the hook, but it really doesn't matter. I had my hand on both of them, and the door was only going to move for a short distance. There is no way that I could have lost it.

I later learned that the nurse had gone out to the waiting room and asked my secretary, who had come with me so that we could work while I was waiting, whether she wanted to come back and help me take my clothes off. That is not all. When I was leaving, the receptionist said to my secretary: "Does he need another appointment?"

What should I have done? How should I have reacted? What I *didn't* do was become upset or hostile. The nurse and the receptionist were well-intentioned and kindly disposed. They were doing the best they could to be of help to me. Moreover, if I am so touchy and insecure that I can be upset by people who are trying as best they can to give me assistance, then I had better look within. Confrontation was certainly not called for.

On the other hand, I shouldn't just leave the matter alone. I was pleasant and unperturbed, but I also took the occasion to talk about things I was doing and accomplishments blind persons were making. And I let the nurse see me tie my tie and find the door, trying to teach by example and not by sermon.

One thing that may have helped me keep my cool was an experience I had almost thirty years ago with a young blind fellow named Curtis Willoughby. He had just graduated from high school and was planning to go to college. He wanted to be an electrical engineer, and he didn't know whether a blind person could do it—and, particularly, whether he could do it. Of course, I didn't know whether he could do it either—but I hoped, put on a brave face, and did everything I could to encourage him.

Even though there were technical problems to overcome, he did extremely well in college. I continued to encourage him and talked now and again to his professors, assuring them that there would be no difficulty in a blind person's functioning as an electrical engineer. In reality they probably knew more about it than I did. Certainly they knew more about the technicalities of electrical engineering. But they seemed to need the reinforcement.

When Curtis graduated from college, I helped him make contacts and write job resumes. I talked to potential employers, assuring them that Curtis was competent and could do the work of an electrical engineer. I also continued to encourage Curtis and talked positively to everybody I met.

After about three months, Curtis was hired by Collins Radio of Cedar Rapids, Iowa. He apparently did his work in a satisfactory manner since he received commendations.

A little while later, I was talking with a friend of mine who was a newspaper reporter, and he said to me: "Do you think Curtis is really pulling his weight at Collins, or do you think they are just keeping him for public relations purposes?"

I said, "I believe he is doing the job. I certainly hope so, but how can I be sure?"

The next spring another blind person graduated as an electrical engineer from Iowa State University, the same school from which Curtis had received his degree, and this blind person didn't have to wait three months for a job. He was hired immediately, and by Collins Radio. I hunted up my newspaper friend and said to him:

"I can now give you a firm answer. I think Curtis is pulling his weight at Collins for if they need one blind person for public relations purposes, they don't need two."

A few years went by, and Collins fell on hard times. They cut their work force by more than half and were in serious financial trouble. Engineers were laid off according to seniority, and when Curtis's number came up, he didn't ask for special privileges—which is the way it should have been. He took his layoff like the rest. We of the National Federation of the Blind don't try to have our cake and eat it too. We want equal opportunity, but we are also willing to make equal sacrifices and accept equal responsibility.

Anyway, Curtis took his layoff, and then he applied for a job as an electrical engineer with the telephone company. As director of programs for the blind in the state of Iowa, I had the responsibility of trying to help Curtis get another job. I thought he was a good electrical engineer, but I didn't know whether he was as good a salesman as I was. So I scheduled a lunch with top engineering officials at Northwestern Bell in Des Moines and talked about Curtis. I said he was a whiz at electrical engineering, and I did it with enthusiasm. They apparently believed me, for before we left the lunch, it was agreed that Curtis would go to work for the phone company.

He did, and after a time he was invited to spend a year at Bell Labs in New Jersey. This is a prestigious appointment, one that is only given to the best.

When Curtis finished at Bell Labs, he came back to Des Moines and resumed his work as a systems design engineer. One day without comment I received from Curtis a copy of a letter. It was written by top engineering officials with AT&T, and it said something to this effect:

"Mr. Willoughby has been dealing with Problem X, and his work is some of the best we have seen. Please put this letter in his personnel file."

I called Curtis and said, "Tell me in two or three sentences what you did. If you make your explanation longer, I probably won't understand it."

As I remember it, he said that in large installations, such as manufacturing of farm equipment and the like, there were tremendous loads of electrical current and that these interfered with the phone system. There would be pixie effects—sometimes causing static and other interruptions and sometimes creating no problem at all. The filtering equipment necessary to remedy the problem was bulky and expensive. It would cost many tens of thousands of dollars if used widely throughout industry. Curtis had discovered a way to redesign the telephone system at these large installations so that the bulky filtering equipment would not be needed and another piece of equipment which had routinely been used could also be eliminated. The new design permitted more clarity in telephone conversations than would have occurred with the expensive filters or with the standard equipment.

After finishing this conversation with Curtis, I went into my office and literally locked the door. I sat at my desk and said to myself:

"You helped Curtis through college. You encouraged him in his search for employment. You did one of the best selling jobs in your life, convincing phone company officials that he could perform as well as anybody else as an electrical engineer. But deep down in your heart, have you ever really believed that he was fully, completely equal to a sighted electrical engineer?"

I wish I could say that my answer was an unequivocal yes. The truth is that I don't know. I had said it, and I had thought I believed it. But did I? After receiving the letter, I am certain that I did. But before that? I can't be sure.

This brings me back to the hook on the doctor's door. I have spent most of my life trying to convince blind people that they can compete on terms of equality with others, and trying to bring sighted people to the same belief. If under these circumstances I was still not certain that I believed in my heart that Curtis was pulling his weight, how can I possibly feel hostility, or blame others who fail to comprehend? What we need is compassion and understanding, not blame or bitterness. Although there are times when we must speak out and not equivocate, let me always remember the telephone company when I am annoyed by the hook on the doctor's door. I will fight if I must, but usually it won't be necessary—especially, if I remember Curtis and the phone company.

In 1995, the Kernel Book is called *Toothpaste and Railroad Tracks*, and the article by Dr. Jernigan "Of Toothpaste and Shaving Cream." Here are the "Editor's Introduction" and that article:

EDITOR'S INTRODUCTION

by Kenneth Jernigan

What do toothpaste and railroad tracks have in common? Just about the same that axes and law books do—nothing and everything. They are the building blocks of the routine of daily existence. In a very real sense they are the essence of humanity itself.

When I was younger (maybe 40 years ago), there was a popular song called "Little Things Mean a Lot." It dealt with what the title implies, but its message was much more than that. It was that each little incident (relatively unimportant in and of itself) combines with all of the other trivial events that are constantly happening to us to form the pattern of our lives. It is not the major events but the recurring details that make us what we are—that determine whether we will succeed or fail, be happy and productive or sad and miserable.

This is the eighth Kernel book, and it is the logical extension of those that went before it. Some of you have been with us from the beginning, but for those who haven't, let me give you in the order of their production the titles of the first seven Kernel books. We began with *What Color is the Sun* in 1991. Then we followed with *The Freedom Bell, As the Twig is Bent, Making Hay, The Journey, Standing on One Foot,* and *When the Blizzard Blows.* Now we come to *Toothpaste and Railroad Tracks.*

The Kernel books have a constant theme and a common purpose. It is to let you know something about the details of everyday life as blind persons live it. Mostly we are not world-famous celebrities but ordinary people just like you—people who laugh and cry, work and play, hope and dream—just like you.

The stories that appear in these pages are true. They are written by those who have lived them. These are people I know personally—former students, colleagues in the National Federation of the Blind, blind men and women of almost every age and social background. There is, of course, one exception. I did not know the blind beak of Bow Street. He lived before my time, but his story is so interesting that I wanted you to have it.

Since I am blind myself, I think I know something about blindness; and since I am a member of the National Federation of the Blind, I think I know what blind people as a group are trying to do and how they feel.

We feel about the same way and want about the same things that you do, and when we fail (which all of us do now and again), it usually isn't because of our blindness. Rather, it has to do with lack of opportunity and the fact that too many of the general public believe we are unable to make our way and do for ourselves. Since we are part of the broader society, we sometimes tend to accept the public view of our limitations, and thus do much to make those limitations a reality.

But overwhelmingly the future is bright for the blind. Because of our own efforts and because of help and understanding from an increasing number of sighted friends, we are changing what it means to be blind. And the Kernel books are helping make it happen—just as you who read them are helping make it happen.

The National Federation of the Blind is a nation-wide organization primarily composed of blind people. It is the blind speaking for themselves with their own voice, and the Kernel books are an important part of that voice.

I hope you will enjoy this book and that through its pages you will make new friends. I also hope that you will also gain new insights concerning both toothpaste and railroad tracks.

Kenneth Jernigan
Baltimore, Maryland
1995

OF TOOTHPASTE AND SHAVING CREAM

by Kenneth Jernigan

Almost everybody who thinks about blindness begins with the assumption that if you are blind, you are at a tremendous disadvantage in dealing with the everyday tasks of getting along and managing your life. To some extent, of course, that is true.

Regardless of other things, the world is structured for the sighted. Most books are in print, not Braille; an increasing number of electrical appliances have lights that flash and flicker instead of knobs that turn and click; and pictures are replacing words on everything from the cash register at McDonald's to the sign on the bathroom door.

Most of these items and appliances could be marked and produced in nonvisual ways, but the fact that they aren't (and that they won't be) is not an overwhelming problem. There are techniques for dealing with the reading, the flickering lights under transparent plates, and the pictures that tell you where to go and what to do.

Functioning as a blind person in a world designed for the sighted keeps you on your toes, but with a little thought and ingenuity you can manage. In fact, you can manage quite well.

But that isn't the way most people look at it. They figure that if you are blind, your days are miserably bleak and limited. I've been blind all of my life, and I think I am about as happy and successful as most of the sighted people I know. It is true that I haven't made a million dollars or been elected president of the United States—but I get along, pay my bills, and look forward to a good dinner and a Sunday afternoon. So do the majority of blind people I know. And I know a lot of them—some successful, some just managing to get by, and most somewhere between.

And let me hasten to add that I am not just talking about people who have been blind from birth but about all of the other variations—those who became blind as children, those who became blind as young adults, and those who became blind in middle age or later.

But if blindness is how I say it is—if you can have as much fun, make as much money, and be as successful as anybody else—why do people think blindness is so tragic and limiting? I have given a lot of thought to that question, and I believe the answer is less involved with the major activities of life than with the insignificant details.

It is true that over seventy percent of working-age blind people are unemployed—not because they can't do the job but because people think they can't do it and because they haven't had opportunity. But most people don't know that. More to the point, they don't think about it, and even if they did, they would simply take it for granted that the majority of blind people are not unemployed but unemployable, and then they would pass on to something else.

No, it is not the big things that cause the average member of the public to think of blindness as tragic and limiting. It is the routine activities, the details.

More specifically, it is the fact that when there is more than one way to do a thing and when one of those ways involves using sight, the sighted person will almost inevitably use the visual technique. It will be done without a second thought, with the automatic assumption that the visual technique is superior. Some visual techniques are superior, of course; some are approximately equal; and some are inferior.

Let me give you an example. A few mornings ago, my wife (who, incidentally, is sighted) expressed some annoyance that her toothpaste had fallen off of the brush. I was quite surprised, for I realized that something I had always taken for granted wasn't so.

"Do you squeeze your toothpaste on to your toothbrush, looking at it as you do it, and then put the toothbrush loaded with toothpaste into your mouth?" I asked.

"Why, yes," she said. "Doesn't everybody do it that way?"

"I don't," I said. "I put the tube up to my mouth, bite off what I want, and then put the brush on my teeth and go at it."

My wife was as surprised by my technique as I was by hers. "It makes sense," she said. "I'll try it."

She did, and she said how much more efficient my technique was than the visual method she had been using. About a week later I asked her if she was still using my toothpaste technique, and she rather sheepishly said that she wasn't. When I asked her why, she thought about it a minute and then said, "I guess I'm so used to looking at it that it's just too hard to change."

Here's a case where the nonvisual technique is clearly superior but where the visual method is automatically used even though it is not as good. My wife (along with most of the other sighted people I have asked) has always, without even thinking about it, taken it for granted that the sighted technique is superior.

If she had considered it at all before our conversation, she would probably have felt that my method of putting toothpaste on the brush would be the same as hers except that I would need to feel for the brush, which would be a little harder than just looking at it.

Certainly the world doesn't turn on whether you bite your toothpaste or squeeze it onto a brush, but life is a matter of daily routine, not dramatic events. So let me move from toothbrushes to razors.

I shave every day (or almost every day), and I do it with an ordinary razor with a blade. Many of the sighted men I know tell me that they shave in front of a mirror. Yet, I have known a great many sighted men who have worked at schools or training centers for the blind and who, after seeing blind boys and men shaving in the shower, have tried the technique and adopted it. I have never known one of them to return to the visual technique. In fact, even those who shave in front of a mirror almost always rub their hand across their face to feel if it is clean shaven. Even so, the average person tends to think that shaving without sight is difficult. It isn't. The nonvisual method is easier and offers more flexibility.

Like most men who shave with a blade, I use shaving cream, the kind that comes from a can under pressure and makes a big pile of foam. Since I have to wash my face anyway, I combine the operation with shaving. I get my face (including my forehead) wet, and I then spread shaving cream all over it. When I am finished, I rinse and am done.

A few years ago, when I was making television announcements for the National Federation of the Blind, I thought it might be interesting to demonstrate different techniques used by the blind. I had shots made of me walking down the street, carrying wood to a fireplace, tying my tie, and shaving.

As the TV editors looked at the pictures, everything was all right until they came to the shaving sequence. One of them said, "We can't show that. It would look like a vaudeville act, like somebody throwing a pie at your face."

I gathered from my questions to them that they were accustomed to seeing TV commercials about shaving and that in those commercials a small amount of shaving cream is put on a part of the face. Those commercials, it would seem, had formed their image of what was normal and acceptable. As with some of the other things I have been discussing, I had always assumed that other men used shaving cream the way I did. Apparently such is not the case.

I said to one of the TV editors: "Don't you wash your face in the morning?"

"Yes," he said, "but I don't do it with shaving cream. I wash my face and forehead with soap. I rinse my face; and then I put shaving cream on and shave." It seemed to me that this was a time-wasting, inefficient way to do it, but I thought I would keep my opinion to myself.

When I was director of Programs for the Blind in the state of Iowa, we bought an old YMCA building for a headquarters and training center. It had seven floors, and the only way to get from the basement to the top was either by climbing the stairs or by using the elevator.

It was, to say the least, not a modern elevator. In fact, it was one of the old-fashioned kind using direct current. It had a grille-work at the front of the cab and a lever that you pushed one way to go up and the other way to go down. There was no way to tell when you got to a given floor except by looking—or, at least, that's what we thought when we moved in.

But those of us who were blind had the strongest possible incentive to devise a nonvisual technique, for we couldn't afford to hire an elevator operator—and we didn't want to walk up and down the stairs between the seven floors all day.

My first thought was that if we couldn't see the floors, perhaps we could string a cable from the top to the bottom of the elevator shaft with some kind of tabs on it that would brush the elevator car and make a noise at each floor. That would have been expensive and complicated and we never got around to it. In the meantime we walked—at least, those of us who were blind did.

Then, one of the blind trainees found that he could stick a knife or comb through the grille-work and touch the bar on the elevator door at each floor, thus allowing a blind person to operate the elevator easily and efficiently. A little later we learned that we had been going about the whole thing wrong. If we paid attention, we could feel the air currents coming off of the floors as we passed them and could level the elevator without any mechanical devices at all.

Why did it take us so long to discover this technique? I believe it was because it never occurred to us to think in any other way except in visual terms. We thought that if we couldn't see the floors, we needed to devise a substitute to do the same thing, to touch them in one way or another. Only when we opened our minds and let our imaginations run free did we get the solution.

The elevator technique we developed was not superior to the visual technique used by the sighted occupants of the building, but it was just as good. The fact that it was different didn't make it inferior. It just meant that it was different.

There is more opportunity for blind people today than there has ever been in the history of the world, and we are only beginning to realize our possibilities. We are truly changing what it means to be blind, and one of the ways we are doing it is by coming to understand that visual techniques are not necessarily superior to nonvisual techniques. And it isn't just blind people who are learning this. It is also an increasing number of the sighted public. We who are blind must lead the way and do for ourselves, but we must do it in partnership with the sighted. And we must do it with imagination and new ways of thinking.

Also in 1995, Dr. Jernigan edited *Tapping the Charcoal*, and included an article by that name. So often blind people (and some sighted ones too), refrain from seeking experience because they believe it is too dangerous for them. Dr. Jernigan has shown thousands of blind people how to cook over an open fire. Here is his article:

TAPPING THE CHARCOAL

by Kenneth Jernigan

When you come right down to it, most people give more attention to food and things related to eating than to almost anything else. At least, that's the way it is with me. My wife Mary Ellen and I live in a big house, and the biggest room in it is the dining room. We like to entertain, and I like to cook on the charcoal grill.

My wife is sighted, and I am blind; but that hasn't changed the fact that our roles in the food department are what once would have been called "traditional." She generally takes responsibility for organizing the kitchen and doing most of the cooking, and I handle the barbecuing and related outside chores. I also have a number of specialty dishes that I like to prepare—a mean kettle of butter beans, a unique homemade salad dressing, and an occasional stew or soup.

As to setting the table, she probably does more of it than I do, but either of us will take care of it as needed. The point is that we do a lot of cooking and have a great many guests and that blindness (except for a few specialized techniques we have devised) makes relatively little difference in how we function.

But you might think otherwise if you heard some of the conversations that occur. Not long ago, for instance, a sighted friend of mine was at our home for dinner; and before we went to the table, I was putting batteries into a talking clock. I use the clock (which will tell me how many seconds have gone by) to time the burgers on the charcoal, and its batteries were dead. As will sometimes happen in such cases, the plate that covers the batteries was acting as if it didn't want to slide back into place. My friend said:

"Here, I'll do that." Saying this, he reached for the clock.

"That's okay," I said. "I'll take care of it."

Up to that point, my friend's behavior was, at the very worst, maybe a little pushy. But his next comment was more than that.

"All right," he said, "I'll let you do it. I know how independent you like to be."

What kind of response should I have made? Certainly I shouldn't have become upset or angry, and I didn't. In fact, I passed off what he said with a smile and a general flow of conversation. But I wonder how he would have felt if the circumstances had been reversed. Suppose I had gone to his home and behaved exactly as he did in mine.

He was a guest in my house, a house I had demonstrated the competence to buy and pay for. We were dealing with my clock and my batteries, a clock and batteries I had bought and paid for. The task was not difficult. The cover went on almost immediately, but even if that hadn't been the case, my friend's conduct was inappropriate.

Even though he knows me quite well and often almost embarrasses me with his praise of my ability when we are talking with mutual acquaintances, he still thought that my blindness meant that I couldn't put a simple cover-plate on a clock. Moreover, I am sure he felt that there was no impropriety in his statement about my "liking to be independent." But if I had been in his home and had reached for his clock as he did for mine, and had then said to him, "All right—you do it; I know how independent you like to be," he would have thought I was losing not only my manners but also my mind.

On another occasion that same friend (and he is a friend) was having dinner at my home, and when I started to pour the coffee, he reached for it, saying: "Here, let me pour that."

Suppose I had been in his home and he had started to pour the coffee, and further suppose that I had reached for it without so much as a by your leave. He would have felt that I was overstepping the bounds of the relationship between guest and host, and he would have thought it doubly inappropriate since I am blind.

His tone and words were those you might use in dealing with a small child, but he was in no sense trying to put me down. He is fond of me, and we're the best of friends. Incidentally, if you wonder how I pour coffee, how I know when the cup is full enough, I do it by listening and by long experience in knowing how heavy the cup feels as the liquid goes into it. It's a simple matter, just one more technique that has become automatic with time and use.

My friend's behavior (not just what he said but also the attitude behind it) illustrates to perfection the dilemma we as blind people face. Very often our friends and associates treat us as if we were children, and not very competent children at that. If we object, we appear to be proving the point of our immaturity. And if we do nothing, we permit the misconception to remain unchanged. But the situation is not static.

We are making steady progress. Day by day and step by step we are changing what it means to be blind.

The public misunderstandings with which we deal are often not grim. In fact, they can be downright funny. I think of the time when I went to a cafeteria, where you carried your tray through the line but a waitress then took it to your table. I was with a sighted associate, and both of us had put iced tea on our trays. When we got to the table and the waitress had put our trays down and was turning away, I reached out toward my plate and turned my tea glass over. It made a mess.

The waitress was very gracious about it and said she would bring me another. She did—but just as she turned around and was leaving, my sighted friend reached across my tray (probably to get salt or pepper) and hit my tea glass and turned it over. The waitress heard the splash and turned around.

In a very solicitous voice she said: "I'm sorry. I'll get you another glass."

Do you think I told her that I hadn't spilled that second glass of tea, that it was my sighted friend who had done it? Certainly not. She wouldn't have believed me and would probably have thought that I was just embarrassed.

"No," I told her, "I think I'll just drink this glass of water. I think I wasn't meant to have tea today." Still insisting that she would bring me more tea, the waitress left—but I am sure that she was puzzled by our prolonged laughter. Explanations wouldn't have helped. The incident brightened our day.

I remember an evening almost twenty years ago when a sighted professor of journalism and his six-year-old son were my dinner guests. We were cooking on the charcoal, and I was explaining to the professor that you can tell when your hamburgers are done by timing them and by how hot your fire is.

I was showing him how the burgers are put into a wire rack with a handle on it, which makes them easy to turn. When they are done on one side, you simply lift the rack and turn it over.

He wanted to know how I could keep the rack straight on the grill, and I explained that I do it by touch. You can even touch a hot stove without burning yourself if you do it quickly. I illustrated by touching the top of the hot grill, hitting it lightly and then quickly taking my fingers away. The professor seemed thoroughly convinced that the technique would work. After all, he was watching me do it. But when his six-year old son decided to try it, he wasn't so sure.

"That grill's hot!" he said. "Be careful! Don't do that! You'll burn yourself!"

The boy (such are the ways of children) was ecstatic. "Chicken!" he cried to his dad. "Chicken!" He danced to the other side of the grill and kept tapping the top of it with his fingers. I was laughing and doing the same thing, and by and by, the professor was trying it too. I then said to him, "Now, let's tap the glowing charcoal."

The boy was all for it and skipped out of his father's reach. I hoped he was mature enough not to burn himself, and he was. It wasn't long before he, his dad, and I were playing the game of quickly and lightly tapping the glowing coals.

There is no great virtue, of course, in tapping a hot grill with your fingers, but it does make the point that visual techniques are not the only ones that can be used in the activities of daily living. There are many others that work just as well. And, by the way, I doubt that my friends (the professor and his son) will ever forget the experience. Most alternative techniques are not as dramatic as tapping the charcoal, but they can be just as effective.

The real problem of blindness is not the blindness itself—not the acquisition of skills or techniques or competence. The real problem is the lack of understanding and the misconceptions which exist. It is no accident that the word *blind* carries with it connotations of inferiority and helplessness.

The concept undoubtedly goes back to primitive times when existence was at an extremely elemental level. Eyesight and the power to see were equated with light, and light (whether daylight or firelight) meant security and safety. Blindness was equated with darkness, and darkness meant danger and evil. The blind person could not hunt effectively or dodge a club. In our day, society and social values have changed.

In civilized countries there is now (except perhaps in certain American cities) no great premium on dodging a club, and hunting has dwindled to the status of an occasional pastime. The blind are able to compete on terms of equality in the full current of active life. The primitive conditions of jungle and cave are gone, but the primitive attitudes still linger.

Even so, we who are blind have come farther in the last thirty or forty years than ever before in all of recorded history. This is so largely because of the work of the National Federation of the Blind, which has done more than any other single thing to help make life better for blind people. And we are only at the threshold.

For the blind of this country tomorrow is bright with promise. We believe in the future; we believe in ourselves; and we believe in the goodwill of our sighted friends and associates. We will put the batteries in our clocks; we will pour coffee for ourselves and others; and we will tap the charcoal—but we will do it quickly and with a light touch.

In 1996, the book and Dr. Jernigan's article in it were entitled, *Beginnings and Blueprints*. Dr. Jernigan remodeled buildings throughout his long career. How does a blind person do this? It is easy when the techniques are known. This is what he said:

BEGINNINGS AND BLUEPRINTS

by Kenneth Jernigan

When does a beginning turn into a blueprint? I don't know, but of one thing I am certain. Blueprints have played an important part in my life. And not just in the work I have done managing and remodeling buildings but also in the disappointments and opportunities that have shaped my being and made me what I am.

As readers of the Kernel Books know, I have been blind since birth. I grew up on a farm in Tennessee in the late twenties and early thirties, and as might be imagined, jobs and money were much on the minds of my parents and their neighbors. Such things were on my mind too, but not from the perspective of my elders. I knew that there was a depression, of course, and that things were bad. But that wasn't what mainly concerned me.

From my earliest hazy memories, I recall wondering what would happen to me when I grew up. My blindness didn't bother me (I took it for granted—just as I did that I was a boy and not a girl), but I didn't ignore it. It was there. It was part of me. My mother and dad didn't believe I would have very many options. They didn't say so, but I could tell how they felt.

They had seen a blind person preaching once, so they thought I might do that. They also thought I might be able to play some kind of musical instrument. In fact, they went so far as to buy me a second-hand piano somewhere along the way; and early on, my Aunt Ethel (she was my dad's sister) gave me a violin that had belonged to her husband's brother Scott.

But all of this was to come to nothing. For although I was required to memorize a great many chapters from the Bible when I went to the Tennessee School for the Blind, and although some of the speeches of my adult years have been likened (sometimes happily and sometimes not) to sermons, preaching was not for me. Nor was music.

Soon after I entered the Tennessee School for the Blind in Nashville in January of 1933, I was enrolled in the violin class. After all, I had a violin of my own. Simultaneously (or soon thereafter) I joined the school band, vainly moving from horn to horn in a futile attempt to find my niche. But for me, trying to learn the notes was like memorizing a string of telephone numbers. I couldn't play the simplest melody, and I still can't today. I continued band and violin for five years, being thoroughly bored with both.

I ultimately quit band to take what was called manual arts, which in reality was a high-toned name for chair caning and broom making; and I quit violin to take piano, an even greater disaster since I spent the bulk of my practice time disassembling the piano and engaging in similar mischief. Occasionally I tried sleeping, but the bench was too short. In brief, neither music nor preaching fit the blueprint.

In previous Kernel Books I have talked about my activities in high school and college, my building and selling of furniture, and my work as an insurance salesman; so I will not deal with those things here. Suffice it to say that (although furniture and insurance were rewarding, both financially and otherwise) they did not suit the ultimate blueprint of my life. Nor did real estate, which I considered for a while—going so far as to get a broker's license once. No, it was not to be music or preaching or furniture or insurance or real estate even though I made beginnings in some of them.

After college, I did a stint of high school teaching for a few years, and then I had my first formal acquaintance with blueprints. It happened like this.

There was an opening for the superintendency of the Kentucky School for the Blind, and I applied. Happy Chandler (former baseball commissioner and erstwhile senator) was governor of Kentucky at the time, and I had his support; so it seemed likely that I would get the job.

But a snag developed. When I talked with the hiring officer (I think he was called Superintendent of Education or some such), all went well until we came to the question of working with architects. Some 300,000 dollars' worth of remodeling was to be done at the school, and the hiring officer wanted to know how I as a blind person would read blueprints.

I told him I had never thought about the matter but that I was sure it wouldn't be a problem. That wasn't good enough, and I didn't get the job—a fact that is laughable in light of my later experience.

When I became director of state programs for the blind in Iowa in the late 1950's, we bought an old YMCA building (it was seven stories tall) and made it into a training center and headquarters. As the years went by, we did many millions of dollars of remodeling, and I directed it all.

As to the matter of blueprints, it was amazingly simple. The architects and I sat down one morning for a couple of hours and worked it out. The architects did their normal measuring and drafting, and then produced their regular blueprints. All that was necessary for me to read them was for the architects to trace each line with a narrow piece of plastic tape.

Most people think of blueprints as mysterious and complex, but they aren't. A series of parallel lines close together indicates stairs, and a line drawn at an angle in a doorway shows which way the door is to swing. Narrow lines represent windows, and wider lines represent walls, with squares or rounds appropriately placed marking columns. All of this can be done with tape of proper width, and it can be done in a very short time. The resulting blueprint is completely accurate and easily useable by both the sighted and the blind.

Yet, in the attempted beginning in Kentucky a few years earlier my lack of experience cost me the job. Maybe that is the way it always is. If beginnings and blueprints don't go hand in hand, there isn't much chance of success.

When I came to Baltimore in 1978 to establish the headquarters of the National Federation of the Blind, we got a complex of old factory buildings and began the process of remodeling. By now, working with blueprints was routine, as easy for the blind as the sighted. I could in a few minutes teach any architect how to prepare blueprints for me, and as the Baltimore years have gone by, I have done it repeatedly. The National Center for the Blind is visible proof of how it works. The buildings are the envy of all who see them, attractive and well-proportioned.

So far, I have said almost nothing about the National Federation of the Blind, but in a very real sense it is key to everything—the beginnings, the blueprints, the career, the full life, and all of the rest. I first became acquainted with the Federation in the late 1940's, and it gave me a whole new perspective about blindness and what I could hope to be and do.

It was not just an organization for the blind. It was the blind, speaking, thinking, and doing for themselves—helping and encouraging each other, exchanging ideas, and working to bring new insights to the public.

With its more than 50,000 members throughout the country, the National Federation of the Blind has, in my opinion, been the biggest single factor in improving the quality of life for blind people in the United States in the twentieth century.

Most of the work of the Federation is done by volunteers, by those of us who are blind and by our sighted friends. On a daily basis we do our work with new beginnings and expanding blueprints, and the encouraging thing is that we who are blind are no longer doing it alone. An increasing number of sighted friends and associates are helping us change what it means to be blind. In the circumstances how can we do other than to look forward to the future with hope and confidence?

In the same year, 1996, Dr. Jernigan spoke to the Convention of the National Federation of the Blind on the topic of the revolution of the Kernel Books. Sometimes a very simple straightforward writing can make a dramatic change, and the Kernel Books have done just that.

In his address to the Convention, Dr. Jernigan included (along with other material) his "Editor's Introduction" and the title article from the Kernel Book *Old Dogs and New Tricks*. This is what he said:

THE REVOLUTION OF THE KERNEL BOOKS

An Address Delivered By Kenneth Jernigan
At the Convention
Of the National Federation of the Blind
Anaheim, California, July 2, 1996

Revolution, the dictionary tells us, is "sudden or momentous change." It is "activities directed toward bringing about basic changes in the socioeconomic structure, as of a minority or cultural segment of the population." By these standards, what we have achieved during the past five years in writing, publishing, and distributing the Kernel Books is a revolution. We have brought about a "sudden" and "momentous change" in attitudes about the blind, our own attitudes and those of society. We have initiated "activities directed toward" causing "basic changes in the socioeconomic structure of a minority, a cultural segment of the population." And we have done it in half a decade.

We produced the first Kernel Book (*What Color is the Sun*) in 1991. In 1992 we published *The Freedom Bell* and *As the Twig is Bent*. In 1993 it was *Making Hay* and *The Journey*. In 1994, *Standing on One Foot* and *When the Blizzard Blows*. Last year it was *Tooth-*

paste and Railroad Tracks, and *Tapping the Charcoal*; and today, we are releasing *Old Dogs and New Tricks*. The eleventh Kernel Book (*Beginnings and Blueprints*) is already written and ready for publication. It will be released sometime this fall. More than three million of the Kernel Books are now in circulation, and the demand for them grows every day.

These are the facts, the statistics, easily gathered and quickly told. But revolutions are made of more than facts. They consist of intangibles—burdens that tax the spirit, toil that has no drama, belief that buoys hope, and dreams that cross the night to span the day. Revolution? From these little books? Yes, revolution. Never mind that the tone is gentle and the message nonconfrontive. The effect is felt, and basic changes are being made in the socioeconomic structure. Here are samples of typical letters:

Fall, 1993

Dear Sir:

To read this valuable little book, *The Journey*, and to learn of the great accomplishments of the blind in spite of the odds, and to learn how we the members of the sighted public are sometimes unwittingly detrimental is a shock, but an eye opener. This should be read by everybody, and I am loaning my copy to various acquaintances. God bless the work you do.

November, 1994

Thanks so much for the books. As I sat reading *Making Hay*, nonstop with the use of my magnifier, I felt comforted as if by an old friend. I have lived with what I have called "eye problems" all of my life, but now I think I can begin adjusting to my blindness.

I'm not really familiar with NFB since it was only by chance that I got your address to begin with, so being new, I need all the help I can get. The NFB sounds like a wonderful family to belong to, an inspiration to all and a place where people can be understood. You speak of four books. May I now receive the others?

Thank you again for giving me hope.

February, 1992

I received a book called *What Color is the Sun* about six months ago, and since I have read it, my life has been changed. I wasn't going to read it at first. I just tossed it onto the nightstand.

However, one night I decided to read a few pages to see what it was about. I started reading, and I was so interested in the different stories that before I knew it, I was halfway through the book. I have read it three times. And every time, I feel that I'm in each story. I was wondering if there is any other material like this that I can get. I never have liked to read, but these stories touch my heart. I'm only twenty-two years old, but after reading your books, I feel that I have lived in the thirties and forties.

May, 1995

Recently I discovered your little book *The Freedom Bell*. I picked it up from a table in a retirement home. I can't tell you how much it means to me to discover somebody who cares enough to answer our questions. My sight has been deteriorating rapidly, and it is very scary. I am desperately serious. I need your help. I neglected to tell you my age. I am eighty-three, but that doesn't mean I'm not sharp.

July, 1995

The course that I taught this past spring at the university was a real success. I had thirty-four students—most of them studying special education. The course was entitled: The Education of Sensory-Impaired Children.

I began each class period with a discussion of an assigned essay from *What Color is the Sun*. The discussions were lively and valuable. I felt that my students learned a great deal about blindness—mostly what blindness does not mean. I am sure that the articles had quite an impact upon their view of blindness. We read every article in the book.

Will I use one of your books next year? I certainly will—either the same one or another Kernel Book.

September, 1991

Thank you, thank you for the book *What Color is the Sun*. I am sighted but can't find the words to describe what that book has done for me. It really opened my eyes!

Never again will I gaze upon blindness with a sort of indifference, which I am afraid I have done most of my eighty years. Sighted people NEED the exposure this book gives, and thank God it came my way.

September, 1991

My name is April, and I am twelve years old. I'm not blind, but I have read your book *What Color is the Sun*. I now think I should thank you for publishing it. Out of the one hundred twenty pages I learned a lot about blindness. I used to feel sorry for blind people. Now I realize that I made a big mistake.

I just felt I should thank you from the bottom of my heart. THANK YOU!

These are just a few of the many letters that we are increasingly receiving. They tell, as nothing else could, of a new way of thought about blindness that is sweeping the land, and they speak of the effectiveness of the Kernel Books. Since we are releasing the tenth Kernel Book today (*Old Dogs and New Tricks*), let me use its introduction and first article to show you how the revolution is being accomplished. Here is the introduction:

With this volume we publish the tenth Kernel Book. The first nine have been well received. No, they have been more than that. The comments have been nationwide and enthusiastic. I think it is not too much to say that these little books are playing a significant part in changing what it means to be blind in America in the last decade of the twentieth century.

And what are the Kernel Books about? They deal with blindness, but not in a medical or professional way. They are a departure from what is usually written, an attempt to take the mystery out of blindness by giving firsthand accounts of how blind people live on a daily basis. Other firsthand stories about blindness have been written, of course, but not in such large numbers and not in this format.

Year after year and book after book we are building a picture that shows what blind people are really like and how they feel. The details differ, but the pattern is the same. In effect, the people who are writing in these pages are saying:

Blindness is not as strange as you may think it is, and it doesn't have to be as terrifying. I am blind, and this is how I lead my daily life—not just in broad terms but in my activities. Here is how I know whether a light is on when I enter a room—how I cook my food, raise my children, and participate in church activities. Mostly my life is just about like yours. It has more detail than drama about it, being a mixture of joy and sorrow, laughter and tears.

I don't spend most of my time thinking about blindness. It is simply one of the facts of my life. I remember it when I need to, but that's about all. I think about who is running for president, last night's dinner, and today's discussion with a friend.

This is what the people who appear in this book are saying. I know them. They are friends of mine, colleagues in the National Federation of the Blind. Some have been my students. I have met others in a variety of ways. But by and large, our common bond is the National Federation of the Blind.

In fact, the National Federation of the Blind has been the vehicle for improving the quality of life for blind people throughout the country. It has certainly changed my life, teaching me to think about my blindness in new ways and helping me understand what I can do and be.

The Federation is a nationwide organization primarily composed of blind people. It is a self-help and self-support organization, believing that blind people should take responsibility for their own lives and that what they need is training and opportunity, not dependence and lifelong care. The Federation believes that blind people can and should do for themselves, that they should work with each other and cooperate with their sighted neighbors to make the world a better place than it was when they entered it.

As to the specifics of the present Kernel Book, the title pretty much says it. It is never too late to learn new techniques and new ways of thought. This is true for the blind as well as the sighted, the old as well as the young. We hope you will enjoy these stories and that whether your goal is to climb a mountain or knit a sweater, you will succeed—and that along the way you will learn new tricks.

Kenneth Jernigan
Baltimore, Maryland
1996

That is the introduction. Now, let me share with you the first article. It is written by me (editors take such prerogatives), and it is the title story of the collection. Here is what it says:

Old dogs, we are told, can't learn new tricks. Maybe—but dogs aren't human. What about humans? Can they learn new tricks? Specifically, can a person who becomes blind in adult life learn to function independently? And what about children? A blind child grows up in a world designed for the sighted. If the child is to learn to get along, he or she must find different techniques from those used by sighted associates and friends.

Can it be done? Of course it can. It happens every day. The question is not whether but how. Make it personal. What about you? If you became blind tomorrow, could you manage? How would you handle the hundreds of details of your daily life?

When I was a child, I had a little sight—not much, but a little. If it wasn't too bright or too dark, I could see step-ups. I couldn't see step-downs, but I could see the lines and shadows of the step-ups. I could see the contrast between a sidewalk and grass, and I could see the difference between the country road that ran by the farm where I lived and the vegetation on either side of it. At night I could see the moon if it was full, but not the stars.

It wasn't much, but it helped. I could go into a room at night, for instance, and immediately tell whether the light was on; and in the daytime I could tell whether there was a window, and where it was. Under the right lighting conditions, I might be able to see an open door, and I might be able to tell where a person or a tree was. Sometimes yes—sometimes no. It was deceptive, and it caused me bumps and bruises—but I managed.

When I was in my early thirties, I lost all sense of dark and light. It happened so gradually that I wasn't aware of it until I thought back a few weeks and realized what I wasn't seeing. For all intents and purposes I was totally blind from childhood, but shortly after I became thirty, there was no doubt about it. I was—and almost forty years later, I still am.

With that background, let me talk about techniques. How do blind people function? How do they manage the nuts and bolts of daily life? More particularly, how do I do it? I can't give you a complete catalogue, of course, but I can give you a sample.

Let's begin with whether a light is on in a room. When I was a boy on the farm in Tennessee, it was a kerosene (or, as we called it, a coal oil) lamp. Today in my home in Baltimore it is an electric light. But the problem is the same. How do I know whether the light is on?

In most situations there is a switch on the wall, and if it is up, the light is on. If it is down, the light is off. But there are three- and four-way switches, allowing a person to turn a light on in one part of the house and turn it off in another.

I have just such an arrangement in the house where I now live. You can turn the hall light on at the front door, at the back door, or on the stair landing. The ceiling is too high for me to reach the light bulb to know whether it is giving out heat, so unless I come up with some kind of non-visual technique, I won't be able to tell. Yet, there are times when sighted people visit me and then leave without telling me whether they have turned off the light. If my wife has gone to bed (which sometimes happens), I either have to have some way to know whether the light is on, or else take a chance on letting it burn all night.

The technique I use is really quite simple, and it is quick and efficient. Several years ago a friend gave me a set of musical teacups for Christmas. If you pick one of them up, it plays *You Light Up My Life*. When you set it down, it stops. I was curious about this and, after experimenting, found that when light hits the bottom of the cup, it starts the music.

I think the cups cost six or seven dollars apiece, and I have a half-dozen of them. I also now have a perfect light detector. I have stored five of the cups in the attic and have left one of them sitting on the kitchen counter.

Now, if I want to know whether a light is on anywhere in the house, all I have to do is pick up my teacup and walk through the rooms. It's quick, and it works. There are fancy light detectors that have been invented for the blind (detectors that cost a good deal more than six dollars), but I don't need them. My teacup works just fine.

Before leaving the kitchen, let me deal with carrying liquid. If the glass or cup isn't full, there isn't any trouble. It doesn't matter if the container isn't exactly level. But if you want a full glass of water as a measure for cooking rice or something else, it does matter.

In such cases I used to have difficulty in carrying the container level and keeping the water from spilling. But not anymore. The technique I use is amazingly easy, and I think it will work for anybody. I wish I had thought of it sooner. I pick up the glass in one hand with my thumb on one side of it and my index finger across from it on the other side of the glass. I am holding the glass at the top, outside of the rim. My hand is above the glass, and I hold it loose enough for it to find its own level. It works well, and I rarely spill a drop. Try it.

There isn't any magic about these techniques. It is simply a matter of thinking them up and doing a little experimenting. I know a blind woman, for instance, who doesn't pour vanilla or other similar liquids into a quarter teaspoon—or, for that matter, a teaspoon or a tablespoon. She puts the liquid into a small jar, bends the spoon handle until the bowl of the spoon is parallel with the floor, and then dips the liquid. It gives a perfect measure, and it's no trouble at all. Of course, if your measuring spoons are plastic, it won't work. Get spoons that are metal.

Then there is the matter of cooking eggs. If you want them scrambled, there isn't any problem, but what if you want them fried? The same woman who taught me about the measuring spoons also taught me about egg frying.

Take a tuna can, or some other can about that size, and cut both ends out of it. Get your frying pan to the temperature you want; place the open-ended can or cans in the pan; and break the egg into the can.

You can touch the top of the can to tell where it is, and when you get ready to turn the egg, slide a spatula under the bottom of the can, and pick the egg up. It will be perfectly formed, and you can turn it without difficulty.

I understand that blind persons are not the only ones who sometimes have trouble turning the eggs they are frying. Some sighted persons have the same difficulty. Egg templates are sold commercially, I am told, using essentially the technique I have described—but why bother? The tuna can works just fine, and there isn't any point in wasting money or going to extra trouble.

Some commercial gadgets are really an advantage in cooking. Earlier, I mentioned rice. Commercial rice-cookers solve a lot of problems—at least, the one at my house does.

My wife is sighted, and I am blind, but we both use and like the rice-cooker. You put twice as much water as rice into it, and you turn it on. You don't do anything else. When the rice is done, the cooker knows and it turns itself off—no sticking, no stirring, no wondering about how long to cook or when to take it up.

That rice-cooker also knows other things, and it has a mind of its own. Once I was cooking oatmeal, and the cooker turned itself off before I thought the oatmeal was ready. I turned it back on, but it dug in its heels. It turned itself right off again. The cooker was right. The oatmeal was done.

As I think about it, I suppose the cooker has a thermostat, which begins to show a rise in temperature when a given quantity of the liquid has boiled away. At that stage it probably turns itself off, but I really don't know. After all, I am not interested in the mechanics of rice-cookers. I just want to get a good bowl of rice or oatmeal or whatever else it is I want for breakfast or dinner.

Sometimes the techniques I devise almost get me into trouble. Last summer is a good example. As you know I plan conventions and make hotel arrangements for the National Federation of the Blind. The meeting I have in mind was to be held in Chicago last summer.

A lot of hotels have stopped using regular metal keys and have gone to a plastic card with a magnetic strip on it. I can see their point. The cards cost almost nothing while metal keys are expensive, and if somebody carries a hotel key away or loses it, the hotel has to go to the expense of changing the lock and replacing the key.

The combination on the magnetic lock, however, can be changed from the hotel's front desk by a computer that is connected to all of the rooms. It is inexpensive and efficient. But the card must be inserted into the door lock in exactly the right way, the proper end and the proper side being placed just so.

The card is shiny plastic, so how does a blind person know which side of it to place up and which end to insert? One way to do it, of course, is by trial and error. After all, there are only four ways it can go—but sometimes even if you have the card right, it doesn't work on the first try. So the whole thing can be a nuisance if you can't tell which side of the card is which.

But in most cases you can. Ordinarily the magnetic strip is slightly slicker than the rest of the card, and quite easy to feel. Usually it goes on the bottom and toward the right. Even if you couldn't tell by this method, any enterprising blind person would make a little nick in the card or do something else just as simple.

When I was planning for last summer's convention, I met with the hotel staff to talk to them about the do's and don'ts. Mostly I wanted to put them at ease and help them realize that they didn't need to go to extra expense or trouble just because they were dealing with blind people.

In this context I told them about the hotel keys and showed them that the magnetic strip was easy to identify by touch. I said that they didn't need to spend any time or money making extra marks on the cards for those attending the convention. They said they understood, and we passed on to other things.

When the date of the convention arrived and I checked into the hotel, the man behind the desk handed me a magnetic key and told me with great satisfaction that he had specially marked it with tape so that I could tell which side of it was which. What was I to do? If I told him that I didn't need the marking and showed him how easy it was to feel the magnetic strip, he would likely be embarrassed and maybe even angry. If I didn't tell him, the hotel would spend time and money on marking the keys and doing similar things, and then probably feel that our meeting was less valuable than others because of the extra trouble and expense.

I handled it as gently and as well as I could, talking again to all of the hotel staff the next day and mentioning the matter in general terms. In one form or another this is a problem that blind people face again and again. It has no easy solution.

Most people have great good will toward us. They think that if they were blind, they wouldn't be able to do anything at all, so they try to figure out ways to help us. The situation is complicated by the fact that sometimes the help is needed, but very often it isn't. I don't know of any way to deal sensibly with the matter except to try to get people to approach us straight on and without a lot of emotion. If somebody wonders whether we need help, ask us. If we say no, accept it. If we say yes, accept that too.

As a further complication, what happens if a blind person is rude or touchy when help is offered? Most of us aren't, but unfortunately (just as with the sighted) a few of us are. Whether sighted or blind, not everybody is an angel—or, for that matter even a responsible, everyday citizen.

My answer is that we who are blind should be treated the way you would treat anybody else. How would you deal with a sighted person who behaved rudely toward you? Deal with the blind person the same way. Hopefully, most of us (blind or sighted) will treat each other with consideration and respect.

The techniques to permit a blind person to function on a daily basis are worth knowing. No, they are more than that. They are key to real independence and comfortable daily living. But they are not the most important thing that a blind person must learn. This brings me to the reason I have devoted so much of my life to the work of the National Federation of the Blind. In my opinion the National Federation of the Blind has done more than any other single thing to make life better for blind people in this country in the twentieth century.

I first became acquainted with the National Federation of the Blind in the late 1940's when both it and I were a great deal younger than we now are. It and its brilliant president, Dr. Jacobus tenBroek, helped me learn a whole new way of thought about what I was and what I could be. Dr. tenBroek taught by example. His blindness did not keep him from earning graduate degrees and being a respected college professor and Constitutional scholar. The same was true of others I met.

The National Federation of the Blind meant then (as it means today) that it is respectable to be blind, that blindness will not keep you from doing what you want to do or prevent you from being what you want to be if you have reasonable training and opportunity and if you do not think of yourself as a victim.

A core principle of the organization is that we as blind people do not want or need custody or paternalistic care, that we can and should do for ourselves, that we should not ask others for assistance until we have done all we can to solve our own problems, and that we (not the government) should have prime responsibility for our welfare and support.

Does this mean that we do not want or need help from others? No—quite the contrary. If we are to go the rest of the way to full participation and first-class status in society, it is true that we must do for ourselves, but it is equally true that we must have help and understanding from our sighted friends and the larger public. Without it we will fail.

Meanwhile, we will do what we can to help ourselves. And despite the old proverb, we think that (whether we are old or young) we can continue to learn.

That is the first article in the tenth Kernel Book. The others are: "The Sliding Board," "Tending to My Knitting," "Roller Coasters," "Serving Communion," and "Loving Elizabeth." Six articles plus the introduction, ninety-one pages. A little book—a revolutionary message.

When we think of the revolution of the Kernel Books and look back through the years to understand the present and reckon the future, we need to consider the accuracy of our past predictions. The exercise may give us both insight and humility. In 1973 (at that time I was still President of the Federation), I spoke at our convention banquet in New York City. The subject was blindness and history, and those who were there will remember that I ventured a prediction. I was talking about future historians and what they would say about our movement.

In the context of that '73 Convention my prediction seemed unlikely and far from the mark. Dr. tenBroek had died five years earlier, and the second generation of the movement was just coming to maturity. NAC (the National Accreditation Council for Agencies Serving the Blind and Visually Handicapped) had been established in the mid-sixties, and with more than a hundred accredited organizations, it was threatening to sweep all before it. The agencies dominated the field—and we (unlike today) had scant resources, few friends, and many opponents. In such an atmosphere the prediction I made at the 1973 banquet seemed nothing less than visionary. This is what I said:

While no man can predict the future, I feel absolute confidence as to what the historians will say. They will tell of a system of governmental and private agencies established to serve the blind, which became so custodial and so repressive that reaction was inevitable. They will tell that the blind ("their time come 'round at last") began to acquire a new self-image, along with rising expectations, and that they determined to organize and speak for themselves. And they will tell of Jacobus tenBroek—of how he, as a young college professor, (blind and brilliant) stood forth to lead the movement.

They will tell how the agencies first tried to ignore us, then resented us, then feared us, and finally came to hate us—with the emotion and false logic and cruel desperation which dying systems always feel toward the new about to replace them.

They will tell of the growth of our movement through the forties and fifties and of our civil war. They will tell how we emerged from that civil war into the sixties, stronger and more vital than we had ever been; and how more and more of the agencies began to make common cause with us for the betterment of the blind. They will tell of our court cases, our legislative efforts, and our organizational struggles—and they will record the sorrow and mourning of the blind at the death of their great leader Jacobus tenBroek.

They will also record the events of the 1970's when the reactionaries among the agencies became even more so, and the blind of the second generation of the NFB stood forth to meet them. They will talk of how these agencies established the National Accreditation Council for Agencies Serving the Blind and Visually Handicapped (NAC), and with it tried to control all work with the blind, and our lives. They will tell how NAC and the other reactionary agencies gradually lost ground and gave way before us. They will tell of new and better agencies rising to work in partnership with the blind, and of harmony and progress as the century draws to an end. They will relate how the blind passed from second-class citizenship through a period of hostility to equality and first-class status in society. But future historians will only record these events if we make them come true. They can help us be remembered, but they cannot help us dream. That we must do for ourselves. They can give us acclaim, but not guts and courage. They can give us recognition and appreciation, but not determination or compassion or good judgment. We must either find those things for ourselves, or not have them at all.

That was 1973 (twenty-three years ago), and in broad terms the prediction has come true. The century draws to a close, and there is unprecedented harmony among agencies and organizations of and for the blind. But what about the future? What will our situation be like when we meet twenty-three years from now, in 2019?

By then the members of the first generation of the movement will almost certainly be gone, and so will many of those of the second, my generation. Even the numbers of the third generation will be thinning, and the fourth generation will be coming to dominance. And the fifth generation will be knocking at the door. The Federation will be seventy-nine years old, approaching the end of its first century. If I am still here, I will be ninety-two, undoubtedly more symbol than substance. Marc Maurer will be sixty-eight, either no longer President or coming close to the end of his time in office.

So what will the movement be like when we meet in 2019? The past five years have taught me that there will be undreamed-of surprises, for no one could possibly have foreseen the two most important events of this decade—the establishment of the Newsline Network® and the coming of the Kernel Books. But if I am not sure of specifics, I am absolutely certain of the general direction our organization will take. Our mutual faith and trust in each other will be unchanged, and all else will follow. I never come into the convention hall without a lift of spirit and a surge of joy, for I know to the depths of my being that our shared bond of love and trust will never change and that because of it we will be unswervable in our determination and unstoppable in our progress.

As I said in 1973, we have come a long way together in this movement. Some of us are veterans, going back to the forties; others are new recruits, fresh to the ranks. Some are young; some are old. Some are educated, others not. It makes no difference. In everything that matters we are one; we are the movement; we are the blind.

And through the Kernel Books we are telling our story, in our own voice and our own way. My brothers and my sisters, let us continue to make it come true!

In 1997, the Convention address was entitled "The Day After Civil Rights." It combined a philosophical understanding with the experiences of everyday life, and it reached an astonishing conclusion. Contained in this address are the articles written for two Kernel Books along with the introductions. Both of these books, *Like Cats and Dogs* and *Wall-to-Wall Thanksgiving,* were published in 1997. Here is what Dr. Jernigan said:

THE DAY AFTER CIVIL RIGHTS

An Address Delivered by
Kenneth Jernigan
At the Banquet of the Annual Convention
of the National Federation of the Blind
New Orleans, Louisiana, July 4, 1997

It has been said that all knowledge consists of definition and classification, and even definition may be just another way of classifying. History, for example, can be classified (or divided) into ancient, medieval, and modern; secular and ecclesiastical; American, English, European, African, Asian, and Latin American; political, economic, and social. And there are hundreds of other ways of doing it.

As to our history, the history of the organized blind movement, I classify or divide it into four stages. Of course, I could add a fifth—the centuries and eons before our founding in 1940. But I prefer to think of that time as the dark ages, the pre-history before hope and enlightenment.

When the National Federation of the Blind came into being almost six decades ago, our problem was simple. It was to find enough food to keep body and soul together—not for all of us, of course, but for many. If you are hungry, it is hard to think about anything else. And the blind were hungry.

And then we moved to a second stage, the attempt to find jobs. Call it rehabilitation. It wasn't that poverty had been eliminated, but it had been so reduced that we could now begin to think about something else, about jobs, about how to earn and not just be given. Naturally, the desire for jobs was there from the beginning, but it now moved to the center of the stage. This was in the late '50's, the '60's, and the '70's. We wanted jobs—and we found them. Not always according to our capacity and not always with equal pay—but jobs.

And then we moved to a third stage. Call it civil rights. After a person has satisfied hunger and found a job, there is still something else—the search for self-esteem and equal treatment—the yearning to belong and participate—to be part of the family and the broader community. And for us, as for other minorities, there was only one way to get there—confrontation. The status quo always fights change.

Many people think that civil rights and integration are the same thing. They aren't. The concept of civil rights precedes integration and is a necessary precursor to it. As used in the late twentieth century, the term civil rights (although some will deny it) always means force—an in-your-face attitude by the minority, laws that make somebody do this or that, picketing, marches in the street, court cases, and much else. And we have done those things, all of them. We had to.

But there comes a day after civil rights. There must. Otherwise, the first three stages (satisfying hunger, finding jobs, and getting civil rights) have been in vain. The laws, the court cases, the confrontations, the jobs, and even the satisfying of hunger can never be our prime focus. They are preliminary. It is not that they disappear. Rather, it is that they become a foundation on which to build.

Legislation cannot create understanding. Confrontation cannot create good will, mutual acceptance, and respect. For that matter, legislation and confrontation cannot create self-esteem. The search for self-esteem begins in the period of civil rights, but the realization of self-esteem must wait for the day after civil rights.

It will be easy for me to be misunderstood, so I want to make something very clear. We have not forgotten how to fight, and we will do it when we have to. We must not become slack or cease to be vigilant, and we won't. But we have now made enough progress to move to the next stage on the road to freedom. I call it the day after civil rights.

If a minority lives too long in an armed camp atmosphere, that minority becomes poisoned and corroded. We must move beyond minority mentality and victim thinking. This will be difficult—especially in today's society, where hate and suspicion are a rising tide and where members of minorities are encouraged and expected to feel bitterness and alienation and members of the majority are encouraged and expected to feel guilt and preoccupation with the past. Yes, it will be hard to do what I am suggesting, but we must do it. We must be willing to give to others as much as we want others to give to us, and we must do it with good will and civility. We must make the hard choices and take the long view.

Let me be specific. If a blind person tries to exploit blindness to get an advantage, or tries to use blindness as an excuse for failure or bad behavior, we must not defend that blind person but must stand with the sighted person that the blind person is trying to victimize. This will not be easy; it will not always be politically correct; and it will frequently bring criticism, not only from those blind persons who claim to want equality but are not willing to earn it, but also from some of the sighted as well. But we must do it anyway. If we want equal treatment and true integration, we must act like equals and not hide behind minority status. Yes, blind people are our brothers and sisters, but so are the sighted. Unless we are willing to have it that way, we neither deserve nor truly want what we have always claimed as a birthright.

That birthright, equal responsibility as well as equal rights, is the very essence of the NFB's philosophy. It is what we set out to get in 1940; it is what we have fought for every step of the way; it is what we are now close to achieving; and it is what we are absolutely determined to have. Equal rights—equal responsibility.

We are capable of working with the sighted, playing with the sighted, and living with the sighted; and we are capable of doing it on terms of complete equality. Likewise, the sighted are capable of doing the same with us—and for the most part, I think they want to. What we need is not confrontation but understanding, an understanding that runs both ways. This means an ongoing process of communication and public education.

It is for that reason that in 1991 we introduced the Kernel Books. As I said at last year's convention, what we have done in writing, publishing, and distributing these books is nothing short of revolutionary. More than three million of them are now in circulation, and the difference they have made in public attitudes about blindness would be hard to exaggerate.

This year, following our usual pattern, we are issuing two more Kernel Books. Book twelve, *Like Cats and Dogs*, is available now; and book thirteen, *Wall-to-Wall Thanksgiving*, will come this fall. There are, of course, many other elements in our educational program, but the Kernel Books are the centerpiece of it. As you hear the introductions to the two 1997 books and excerpts from the articles I wrote for them, keep in mind the context and the reason for publishing them. They must carry a message without being so preachy that nobody will read them, and they must be entertaining without blurring the purpose:

LIKE CATS AND DOGS
EDITOR'S INTRODUCTION

In the early and mid 1930's, when I was a boy in grade school, I dearly loved to read poetry—or, more properly speaking, have poetry read to me. And my teachers often obliged. One of my favorites was a poem by Eugene Field called the "Gingham Dog and the Calico

Cat." Although it will never be a classic, I liked it. It begins like this:

"The gingham dog and the calico cat
Side by side on the table sat;
'Twas half-past twelve, and (what do you think!)
Nor one nor t'other had slept a wink!"

The poem goes on to tell how the cat and dog had an awful fight and concludes by giving the outcome:

"But the truth about the cat and pup
Is this: they ate each other up!"

Thus, we come to the title of this book, *Like Cats and Dogs*. Maybe I chose it because I once had a dog that I dearly loved, or because I currently have some adorable kittens—or maybe because of the well-known saying about people fighting like cats and dogs. Regardless of the reason, the title is chosen, and we come to a question: Exactly how do cats and dogs behave toward each other?

If they don't understand each other, they fight "like cats and dogs." But if they have the opportunity to get acquainted, they can live in harmony and become good friends.

As it is with cats and dogs, so it is with the blind and their sighted neighbors. There can either be harmony and friendship or misunderstanding and frustration. This little volume (the twelfth in the Kernel Book series) is meant to promote understanding, the ultimate framework of all true friendship and mutual respect.

As with past Kernel Books, the stories here are real-life experiences, told by the blind persons who lived them. The one exception is the article by Theresa House, who is the sighted wife of a blind man. Her parents feared that a blind person could never be an adequate

husband for their daughter, and certainly not a suitable father for her children. You will see how it is turning out as they live their lives and raise their family.

As a matter of fact, marriage and children are major themes of this book. Bruce Gardner, blind and preparing to be a lawyer, dates and falls in love with a
young sighted woman. She has questions, and so do
her father and mother.

And there is the matter of blind parents and sighted
children. As the boy and girl grow up, how do they feel?
Do they think their parents can take care of them—and
how do the parents feel? What ambitions do the parents have for their children?

There is another theme relative to children (blind
children). Many are not given the chance to learn
Braille. What does that do to them, and how do they
feel about it as they come to adulthood?

There is more—the article I wrote about the difference between the sounds and smells of today and sixty
years ago; and there is the story about a blind kitten
(told by the owner, of course, not the kitten); an account
of a blind woman's experience with pouring coffee; and
much else. But I think I have told you enough to give
you an inkling of what to expect.

At the core, all of the people represented here are
talking about the same thing. What they are saying is
this: In everything that counts we who are blind are
just like you. As you read, you will recognize yourself
in the story of our experiences. We laugh and cry, work
and play, hope and dream, just like you. And although
we don't forget that we are blind, we don't constantly
think about it either. We are concerned with the routine business of daily living—what we plan to have for
dinner, the latest gossip, and the current shenanigans
in Washington.

Around fifty thousand people become blind in this country each year. That means that it may happen to you, a member of your family, a neighbor, or a friend. So we want you to know what blindness is like—and, more to the point, what it isn't like. That is why we are producing the Kernel Books. We hope you will find this volume both informative and interesting. If you do, we will have accomplished our purpose. We want to live in harmony with our neighbors—not the way most people think cats and dogs live.

Kenneth Jernigan
Baltimore, Maryland
1997

That is the introduction. Now here are excerpts from my article called *The Sounds and Smells of Sixty Years*:

Everybody knows that change is probably the only constant in life, but I think we don't fully understand what that means until after we are fifty. At least, that is how it has been with me.

As readers of the Kernel Books know, I grew up on a farm in Tennessee in the 1920's and '30's, and it seems to me that almost nothing today is the way it was then. Since I have been blind all of my life, I am not talking about how things look but how they smell, taste, sound, and feel.

Start with smell. The world smells different today from what it did then. Nowadays I spend much of my time indoors, breathing conditioned air, whether heated or cooled. But that wasn't how it was when I was a boy.

Since we didn't have electricity, we couldn't have had air conditioning even if we could have afforded it.

So in the summer the windows were open, and usually so were the doors. The air was rich with odors—the smells of growing things, of the barnyard, of the dust and gasoline from an occasional passing car, and of creeks. These were the smells of summer, but there were also the smells of winter—wood, burning in a fireplace, the smell of the unheated portions of the house, and the smell of the country in winter.

And it was not just the smells of that time but also the sounds—the mixture of stillness, bird songs, distant cattle, and the aliveness of the land. Today, whether indoors or out, one thing is always present—the sound of motors. There are automobiles, office machines, fluorescent lights, power tools, lawn mowers, vacuum cleaners, kitchen appliances, air conditioners, and heating units. When I was a boy, I might go a whole week without hearing a motor—but not today. In the world of the '90's, there is never a minute without a motor. Sometimes it is an avalanche of noise, and sometimes only a vibration in the background—but it is always there—always a motor.

And I mustn't omit taste and touch. At first thought, it might seem that there would be no difference between then and now, but there is. It isn't necessarily that I can't touch most of the things today that I touched in the 1930's. It is just that I don't. And as to taste, it may simply be my imagination or my aging taste buds, but it certainly doesn't seem that way. Food is prepared differently, and the ingredients take a different path from origin to table.

But what does all of that have to do with blindness? After all, that is what this book is about. Certainly blindness and blind people are not treated today the way they were sixty years ago. The blind of that generation had almost no chance to get a job, and very little chance to get an education.

In my case (many of you know this story as well as I do, so you can judge for yourselves whether it fits our purpose in the Kernel Books), I was allowed to go to college, but I wasn't permitted to take the course of study I wanted. I attended elementary and high school at the Tennessee School for the Blind in Nashville, graduating in 1945. One day in the spring of my senior year, a state rehabilitation counselor came to talk to me about what I wanted to do and be.

I remember it well. We sat in what was called the parlor—a room, incidentally, which deserved the name. The School was housed in an old southern mansion, and the parlor, which was used as a general reception area, was the very essence of elegance.

The counselor and I sat on the elaborately carved sofa, and he asked me to tell him two or three areas of study that I might like to pursue when I went to college. I told him that I didn't need to pick two or three, that I wanted to be a lawyer.

He said that he wouldn't say that a blind person couldn't be a lawyer but that he thought it wasn't realistic. I would not be able to see the faces of the jury, he said, and would not be able to do the paperwork and the travelling. I argued, but I was only a teen-ager— and I didn't have any money.

Ultimately he told me (with big words and gently, but with absolute finality) that I could either go to college and study law and pay for it myself, or I could go and prepare to be something else and be assisted by the rehabilitation agency. Since I was a teen-ager and didn't have any money, I went and was something else.

Of course, I now know that he was wrong. I am personally acquainted with hundreds of successfully practicing blind lawyers, and most of them are not noticeably more competent than I am. But I would not want to create the wrong impression. This man was not trying to do me harm. Quite the contrary. He truly believed that what he was doing was in my best interest. He was trying to help me. He was acting in the spirit of the times and doing the best he knew.

Today it wouldn't happen that way. Many things have made the difference, but principal among them is the National Federation of the Blind. Established in 1940 by a handful of blind men and women from seven states, the Federation has conducted a never-ending campaign to educate the public and stimulate the blind. I joined the organization in 1949, and it changed my life.

Today the Federation is the strongest and most constructive force in the affairs of the blind of this country, but its work is by no means finished. The job that still has to be done is not so much a matter of legislation or government assistance as of handling the interactions of daily life. We have come a long way in public acceptance, but sometimes the attitudes of sixty years ago are still with us.

Let me illustrate by what at first may seem to be trivial examples. (Again, some of you are familiar with the details surrounding the story I am about to tell, so you can judge whether it meets our test of suitability for the Kernel Books.) Over fifty years ago, when I was a boy on the farm in Tennessee, I often found time heavy on my hands during the summer months when I was not in school. To relieve the tedium, I would sometimes ride with a truck driver, who collected milk from the local farmers to take to a nearby cheese factory.

The days were hot, and when we could afford it, we sometimes bought a bottle of Coca-Cola. (Incidentally, it cost five cents.) I didn't have much money, but now and again I had a little, and I wanted to pay my share. One day I said to the driver (a young fellow about twenty), "I'll buy a coke for each of us."

"Okay," he said, "stay here. I'll go in and get it."

"No," I said. "I'll go with you."

He was obviously uncomfortable and didn't want me to do it. Finally he said, "I can't do that. How would it look if people saw a blind person buying me a coke?"

I was a teen-ager, not yet accustomed to the ways of diplomacy. So I told him in blunt terms that I would either buy the coke publicly or I wouldn't buy it at all. After greed and pride had fought their battle, he decided not to have it, and we drove on—after which I was not welcome in the truck.

But that was more than fifty years ago. It couldn't happen today. Or could it? Well, let me tell you about an incident that occurred less than six months ago. My wife and I were entering a restaurant—an upscale, classy place with plenty of glitter and lots of manners.

It so fell out that another couple and we reached the door almost simultaneously. I happened to be positioned so that it was natural for me to open the door and hold it while the other couple entered, but the man was obviously ill at ease. He insisted that he hold the door and that my wife and I go first. Since I already had my hand on the door and was holding it open and since I was not in the mood to be treated like a child or an inferior, I dug in my mental heels and stayed put. It was all done on both sides with great politeness and courtly manners, but it was done. As I continued to hold the door, the other couple preceded us into the restaurant. But the man was obviously uncomfortable, showing by his comments and demeanor that he felt it was inappropriate for a blind person to hold a door for him and behave like an equal.

Trivial? Not related to the daily lives and economic problems of the blind? Not a factor in determining whether blind people can hold jobs or make money? Don't you believe it! These incidents (the one fifty years ago and the one this year) typify and symbolize everything that we are working to achieve.

But again I must emphasize that we are not talking about people who are trying to cause us harm. We are talking about people who, almost without exception, wish us well and want to be of help. Our job is not one of force but of giving people facts.

And key to it all is the National Federation of the Blind—blind persons coming together in local, state, and national meetings to encourage each other and inform the public. Sometimes we are tempted to believe that our progress is slow, but in reality it has been amazingly rapid. We have made more advances during the past sixty years than in all previously recorded history. And there are better days ahead.

It is true that the smells, sounds, touch, and taste of today are not what they were sixty years ago—but it is equally true that, despite occasional nostalgia, we wouldn't want them to be. We wouldn't because today is better—and not just in physical things but also in the patterns of opportunity and possibility. I say this despite all of the problems that face our country and our society. We who are blind look to the future with hope, and those who are sighted are helping us make that hope a reality.

That is my article for the first of this year's Kernel Books. Here are the introduction and the article for the second:

WALL-TO-WALL THANKSGIVING
EDITOR'S INTRODUCTION

Most American holidays have a double significance—what they are, and what they imply. New Year's Day, for instance, means just that, the beginning of another year. But it also means reviewing the past, planning for the future, and hoping to do better.

The Fourth of July commemorates the establishment of the nation. But over the years it has picked up a whole host of other meanings—everything from summer picnics and fireworks to how we should live, and the current state of American values.

And then there is Thanksgiving—and also the present Kernel Book, the thirteenth in the series. When we started publishing the Kernel Books almost seven years ago, we didn't know how successful they would be, but our goal was to reach as many people as possible with true-life first-person stories told by blind persons themselves—how we raise children, hunt jobs, engage in courtship, get an education, go to church, cook a meal, meet friends, and do all of the other things that make up daily living.

And we wanted to do it in such a way that the average member of the sighted public would read and be interested. The results have been better than we could possibly have hoped. More than three million of the Kernel Books are now in circulation, and I rarely travel anywhere in the country without being approached by somebody who has read them and wants to talk about them or ask questions.

As to the present volume, *Wall-to-Wall Thanksgiving*, it is much like what has gone before. It tells about blind people as they live and work.

What does a blind boy do to earn summer spending money, and what do his sighted parents expect of him? What of the Viet Nam veteran who loses his sight in the war and comes home to build a new life? And what about the self-conscious youngster and young man with a little sight, who is ashamed of blindness and yet has to live with it?

What of the small details that come together to make the days that form the years—learning to ride a bicycle, cook a steak, read a book, get a job? This is what *Wall-to-Wall Thanksgiving* is about. I know the people who appear in its pages. They are friends of mine. Some have been my students. All of them are fellow participants in the work of the National Federation of the Blind.

If you wonder why so many of us give our time and effort to the Federation, it is because the Federation has played such an important part in making life better for us. In fact, the National Federation of the Blind has done more than any other single thing to improve the quality of life for blind persons in the twentieth century. It is blind persons coming together to help each other and do for themselves. That doesn't mean that we don't want or need help from our sighted friends and associates, for we do. But it does mean that we think we should try to help ourselves before we ask others for assistance. And we should also give as well as take. All of this is what the National Federation of the Blind stands for and means.

I have edited the Kernel Books from the beginning, and I have contributed a story to each of them. My present offering deals with help I have received from sighted people. Sometimes my reactions have been appropriate and mature; sometimes not. As you read, you will see that my views have changed as I have grown older. Perhaps my article, "Don't Throw the Nickel," sums it up.

As to the title of this thirteenth volume in the Kernel Book series, *Wall-to-Wall Thanksgiving*, it is taken from the story of the same name by Barbara Pierce. But like the various holidays, it has more than a single meaning. With all of the difficulties we have had and with all of the problems we still face, we who are blind have more reason for Thanksgiving now than ever before in history.

Unlike many in today's society, we do not think of ourselves as victims. We feel that our future is bright with promise. That is so because we intend to work to make it that way, and because more and more sighted people are joining our cause and helping us.

I hope you will enjoy this book and that it will give you worthwhile information.

Kenneth Jernigan
Baltimore, Maryland
1997

That is the introduction. Now for the article. As I have already said, it is called "Don't Throw the Nickel."

When is it appropriate for a blind person to accept help from a sighted person, and when is it not? If the offer is rejected, how can it be done without causing embarrassment or hurt feelings? Since most sighted people are well-disposed toward the blind, these are very real questions—questions that I as a blind person have faced all of my life. As you might imagine, my answers have changed as I have grown older and gained experience.

When I was a teen-ager, filled with the typical self-consciousness of adolescence, I frequently rode city buses. This was in Nashville. The school for the blind, where I was a student, was located on the edge of the city, and I liked to go downtown. Incidentally, in those days a bus ride cost a nickel, as did a lot of other things— a hamburger, a Coca Cola, an order of French fries, a full-size candy bar, a double-dip of ice cream, and much else.

One day I was standing on the corner waiting for a bus when an elderly woman approached me and said, "Here, son, I'll help you." She then put a nickel into my hand.

I could tell that she was elderly because of her voice. There was quite a crowd at the bus stop, and I felt acute embarrassment. I tried to give the nickel back, but she moved out of my way and kept saying, "No, that's all right."

Everybody stopped talking, and my frustration mounted. Each time I stepped toward her to try to give back the nickel, she moved out of the way. It must have been quite a spectacle, me with my hand extended holding the nickel, and the woman weaving and dodging to avoid me. Finally, in absolute exasperation, I threw the nickel as far as I could down the street.

That was over fifty years ago, but the memory is still clear. Once the woman had placed the nickel in my hand, there was really no way I could have given it back. If I had simply and quietly accepted it and thanked her, very little notice would have been taken. As it was, I created quite a show. The elderly woman, who was only trying to help me, was undoubtedly embarrassed, and I did little to improve the image of blindness. Instead, I did the exact opposite.

Ten years later, when I was in my twenties, I was teaching at the California training center for the blind in the San Francisco Bay area. One of my principal duties was to help newly blind persons learn how to deal maturely with loss of sight and the attitudes of the public about blindness.

Late one afternoon, after a particularly hard day, I was leaving the Center to go home. When I came to the corner to cross the street, an elderly man (he sounded as if he might be in his eighties) approached me and said, "I'll help you across the street."

"No, thanks," I said. "I can make it just fine." I was polite but firm.

"I'll help you," he repeated, and took my arm. As I have already said, it had been a hard day. I made no discourteous response, but I speeded up my pace as we crossed the street.

Clearly the man could not keep up, and if I am to be honest, I knew that he couldn't. He released my arm and said with a hurt tone, "I was only trying to help."

When I got to the other side of the street, I came to a complete stop and said to myself, "Are you really so insecure about your blindness that, even if it has been a hard day, you can't afford to be kind to somebody who was only trying to help you?"

As with the nickel-throwing incident, there was a lesson to be learned. I should have accepted the man's offer of help, and should have done it graciously. We would both have profited, each feeling that he had done the other a kindness. As it was, both of us experienced pain, even if only a little and even if only temporarily.

By the time another ten years had passed, I was in my thirties and directing programs for the blind in the state of Iowa. My job required me to do a great deal of traveling, and one day when I was checking into a hotel, a bellman carried my bag to my room. As he was leaving, I gave him a tip.

"Oh, no," he said, "I couldn't take a tip from you. I'm a Christian."

Unlike what I did in the other situations I have described, I did not refuse or resist. I simply thanked him and let it go at that. Of course, I might have tried to get him to change his mind, but I didn't think it would be productive. And besides, I didn't feel so insecure or unsure of myself that I needed to prove either to him or me that I was equal.

So far, I have talked about help that has been courteously offered and probably should have been accepted. But what about the other kind? Blind people don't have a monopoly on rudeness or bad manners. Sighted people are human, too.

I think of a time when I was standing on a street corner in Des Moines, minding my own business and waiting for a friend. A big husky fellow with the momentum of a freight train came along and scooped me up without ever even pausing. "Come on, buddy," he said, as he grabbed my arm, "I'll help you across the street."

As it so happened, I didn't want to cross that street. I was going in another direction. But he didn't ask. And he wouldn't listen when I tried to tell him. He just kept walking and dragging me with him.

In the circumstances, I planted my feet and resisted—and I should have. All of us, whether blind or sighted, owe courtesy and consideration to each other, but in this case I was being treated like a none too intelligent child. No, worse than that—for children are rarely manhandled in public.

Not long ago I entered an elevator, and a man standing next to me reached out and placed his hand on my arm, between me and the elevator door, in a protective manner. He probably felt that I might lean into the door as it was closing or that I might have difficulty when the door opened. It was a sheltering gesture, totally inappropriate but meant to be helpful. He would have been shocked at the thought of behaving that way toward a sighted adult passenger, but in my case he saw no impropriety.

When the door opened, he restrained me with his hand and said, "Wait. You can't go yet." Since I was standing immediately next to the door and since there was no traffic outside, it is hard to know why he felt I should wait. Maybe he thought I should take a moment to get my bearings, or maybe it was simply more of the protectiveness. Who knows?

He treated me very much as he would have treated a small child. How should I have reacted? It all depends on how insistent and how obtrusive he was. There is something to be said for restraint and not hurting other people's feelings, but there is also something to be said for recognizing when enough is enough.

In what I am about to say next, I am not just talking about persons who are totally blind but also about those who now see so poorly that they cannot function the way a sighted person normally does—persons who may be losing sight and who may be having trouble accepting it. I am also speaking to relatives.

As I have indicated, most blind people appreciate help when it is offered. When a blind person is walking through a crowd or down the street with somebody else and trying to carry on a conversation, it is easier to take the other person's arm. This is true even if the blind person is quite capable of traveling alone.

All of us like to do things for ourselves, but there are times when refusing to take an arm that is offered constitutes the very opposite of independence for a blind person. If, for instance, a blind person is walking with a sighted person through a crowded restaurant, the sensible thing to do is to take the sighted person's arm and go to the table without fuss or bother.

As you can tell, my views about independence and help from others have changed over the years. Probably the single most important factor in helping me come to my present notions has been the National Federation of the Blind. Having chapters in every state and almost every community of any size, the Federation is the nation's oldest and largest organization of blind persons.

As it is with me, so it is with thousands of other blind people throughout the country. We work together to help each other and ourselves. We give assistance to parents of blind children, to blind college students, to the newly blind, to the senior blind, and to blind persons who are trying to find employment. Above all, the Federation teaches a new way of thought about blindness. We want to take the mystery out of blindness. Mostly, we who are blind are very much like you.

This is the message of the National Federation of the Blind, and it has made a great difference in my life. If I had to sum up my personal philosophy in a single sentence, it would probably be this: Do all you can to help yourself before you call on somebody else; try to make life better for those around you; and don't throw nickels.

There you have excerpts from the two Kernel Books for 1997. I believe our efforts at self-improvement and public education will be advanced by these books and that we will go the rest of the way to full participation and first-class status in society.

While I am talking about the future, let me say something else. I never come into one of our convention sessions without feeling a lift of spirit and a surge of joy, for I know to the depths of my being that our shared bond of love and trust will never change, and that because of it we will be unswervable in our determination and unstoppable in our progress.

Through our public service announcements on radio and television, through newspaper articles and personal contacts, through gatherings like this, through our mail programs, through our publications, through public speaking engagements, through meetings with government officials and corporate leaders, and especially through our Kernel Books, we are telling our story—and we are doing it in our own way and with our own voice. The day after civil rights is fast approaching, and we will meet it as we have met every other challenge we have ever faced—joyously, actively, and triumphantly. My brothers and my sisters, we are truly changing what it means to be blind—and the Kernel Books are helping us do it.

The last of Dr. Jernigan's convention addresses regarding the Kernel Books was presented to the 1998 Convention of the National Federation of the Blind in Dallas, Texas. It contains the material prepared for *Gray Pancakes and Gold Horses* and *To Touch the Untouchable Dream*, both books released in 1998. This is Dr. Jernigan's address, entitled "The Continuing Saga of the Kernel Books":

THE CONTINUING SAGA OF THE KERNEL BOOKS

by Kenneth Jernigan

During the 1990's the Kernel Books have been at the very heart of our program of public education, and 1998 is no exception. This year, as in the past, we are publishing two new volumes. The first will be available at this convention, and the second will be released this fall.

Today, as on previous occasions, I want to give you the introductions to the two books, as well as the first article in each. As you know, I edit these books, and I also usually write the first article. So here is my Editor's Introduction to the book that will be available to you at this convention:

EDITOR'S INTRODUCTION

This is the fourteenth volume in the Kernel Book series. Its title, *Gray Pancakes and Gold Horses*, is taken from the first two stories and symbolizes the theme of the book.

How do blind children learn the details of the hundreds of small daily acts that sighted children pick up without ever even knowing they have done it? A blind boy sits in a farm house on a summer night and wonders which way to shake his head to mean yes and no. He guesses and loses, and his mother's feelings are hurt. I know, for I was that boy.

A blind father cooks for his two sighted children, and the pancakes are gray, causing the children to reject them. Small incidents, things of no great moment. Yet, the stuff of daily living, the patterns and realities of life.

This Kernel Book is much like those that have gone before it. It contains first-person real-life stories, told by those who have lived them. It talks about going to school, communicating with others, and living from day to day. I know the people who appear in its pages. They are friends of mine. Some have been my students.

The one thing all of us who appear in this book have in common is our shared participation in the work of the National Federation of the Blind, the organization which has been the strongest single factor in making life better for the blind of this country during the twentieth century. With more than 50,000 members, the National Federation of the Blind is primarily composed of blind people, who are trying to make life better for themselves and other blind people, while at the same time making the world a better place in which to live for everybody.

We who are blind have a major job on our hands in trying to get members of the general public to see us for what we are—not especially blessed or especially cursed but just ordinary people, exactly like you. The only difference is that we don't have eyesight, which is not as big a factor in our daily lives as most people think it is.

So how do we get the job done? How do we get people to see us for what we are and not just what they have always thought we are? One of the most important ways is through the Kernel Books. This is why we write and publish them. They must be entertaining enough that people will read them, but they must do more than that. They must carry the message of what blindness truly is, and what it isn't.

We hope you will enjoy this book and that it will give you new insights about blindness. Since more than 50,000 people become blind in this country each year, the information you get from these pages may be useful to you in a personal way at some future time—and if not for you, then for a family member or friend.

As you read, remember that we who are blind have more hope today than ever before in history. We believe that when we can, we should do for ourselves before calling on others for assistance, but we also recognize the value of the help which a growing number of sighted friends and associates give us. We want to live the full lives of free, participating citizens, and we know that we can.

All of this you will see reflected in the pages of this book. We hope you will find it of interest and that it will cause you to rethink some of your notions about blindness.

Kenneth Jernigan
Baltimore, Maryland
1998

There you have the introduction to Kernel Book fourteen. Now, here is my opening article. It is entitled "The Barrier of the Visible Difference."

THE BARRIER OF THE VISIBLE DIFFERENCE

Catchy titles and clever phrases are the stuff of big business. As every advertising agency knows, fortunes are made or lost by the way the public reacts to a jingle or a slogan.

Once I heard a liquor distributor say that his company had a thoroughly mediocre wine that was going nowhere, and then somebody got the bright idea of giving it a sparkly name (I think it was Wild Irish Rose). After that, he said they couldn't make enough to meet the demand, operating three shifts a day.

Whether that story is true or false, the underlying message is right on target. It is not just what a thing is but how it sounds and feels that sets the tone and gives the value.

When most of us come across the term "visible difference," we think of the trademark of the beauty expert and cosmetics manufacturer Elizabeth Arden. "Visible Difference" is the brand name of moisturizers, lotions, and other products. But for the blind the term means something else. It represents a barrier and a hurdle to be surmounted. Let me illustrate.

When I was a boy of about four, my mother and I were sitting in the front bedroom of our home. Even though more than sixty-five years have passed, I still remember every detail. It was a summer evening just after dark. My father and brother were sitting on the porch, and the night sounds (the frogs and crickets) were coming into full chorus. It was oppressively hot with a lot of dust in the air.

In those days we didn't have electricity, so my mother had just lit the oil lamp. The smell of the burning kerosene began to blend with the regular odors of food and plant life that permeated the four-room house. Of course, all of the doors and windows were open.

When my mother finished lighting the lamp and adjusting the wick, she sat down and put her arm around me. Then she kissed me on the left side of my face. Since she was sitting on my left, this was a natural (almost an automatic) gesture. Then she said:

"Do you like for mother to kiss you?" Now, this put me into a real dilemma—for I very much liked for mother to kiss me, but I felt shy and embarrassed to say it.

Hunting a way out, I thought perhaps I could say yes by shaking my head. From conversations I had heard, I knew that other people shook their heads to mean yes or no, but I didn't know which way the head should move to indicate which meaning. It had never before occurred to me to wonder about the matter since I had never needed to know. My mother or anybody else around the house would undoubtedly have been perfectly willing to tell me if I had asked, but that didn't help in the situation I was then facing.

Using the best logic I could muster, I thought that since my mother was sitting on my left, maybe if I moved my head that way, it would indicate yes. Unfortunately it didn't, and my mother (not understanding my embarrassment and lack of knowledge) thought I was saying no. She was hurt and cried, and I didn't know how to explain.

So what is the moral of that little story, that minor tragedy of childhood? It is not that blind people are less competent than others of their age and circumstance. It is not that blind persons are slow learners or inept. It is that sometimes something that can be seen at a glance must be learned a different way by a blind person. The learning can be just as quick and just as effective, but it won't happen unless somebody thinks to explain, to help the blind child cross the barrier of the visible difference. There is no great problem in knowing how to shake one's head or in doing a hundred other things that sighted children learn without ever knowing that they have done it. It is only that the blind child must either be unusually persistent and inquisitive or have somebody constantly at hand who thinks to give information. Otherwise, insignificant details will multiply to major deficits.

And this is not just a matter of childhood. After seventy years I keep learning new things about the barrier of the visible difference. Recently when I told a blind friend of mine who is a lawyer about my head-shaking episode, he asked if I knew how you are supposed to hold your hand in a court when you are told to raise your right hand. I said that I had never thought about it but had always assumed that you simply raise your hand above your head, which is what would seem logical in the circumstances.

"No," he told me, "that isn't the way it is done. You raise your hand to shoulder level with the palm out." He went on to tell me that when he was being sworn in to be admitted to the Bar, he had raised his hand above his head and that later, one of his classmates had told him how the customary ritual is performed.

It is important to understand the significance of this incident. There is nothing better about raising the hand to the shoulder than over the head. It doesn't make one a better lawyer or a better witness in court. My friend is an excellent attorney, and I have testified in court on more than one occasion. We are simply dealing with a custom of society, a visible difference.

More than anything else (at least, unless one is aware of it and thinks about it) meaningless visible differences can lead to confusion and misunderstanding, and sometimes even to misplaced feelings of superiority or inadequacy. A thing that looks beautiful to the eye, for instance, can feel ugly and dirty to the touch. Again, let me illustrate. Once when I was four or five, my mother and father took me to the county fair. This was a big event.

We lived about fourteen miles from the county seat, and we didn't have a car. Very few people did in those days, so friends and neighbors pooled their transportation and helped each other with rides.

On this particular occasion my mother and I were standing at one of the booths at the fair. In retrospect it must have been one of those places that give prizes for throwing darts, tossing rings, or something of the sort. Regardless of that, the woman in charge gave me a small statue of a horse. As I think back on it, she may have done it because I was blind, or simply because she thought I was a cute kid. For purposes of my story, it doesn't matter.

The horse must have been quite pretty, for both the woman and my mother kept exclaiming about it. It was apparently covered with some sort of sparkly gold paint.

To the eye I assume that it was extremely attractive, but to me it just felt dirty and grungy.

Now, I had never before had a small gold horse or, for that matter, any other kind of horse, or very many nice toys of any kind—so I was pleased and ecstatic with my treasure. But I thought I ought to clean it up and try to make it look nice.

Therefore, while my mother and the woman were talking, I busily scratched all of the rough-feeling gold paint off of it. It was quite a job. By the time I had finished, my horse felt clean and attractive. I was proud of it. Imagine, then, my disappointment and chagrin when my mother and the woman noticed what I had done and were absolutely dismayed. I couldn't understand why they were unhappy, and they couldn't understand why I felt that the horse was better for my effort. Again, I had bumped head-on into the barrier of the visible difference.

Unlike the head-shaking incident, this was not exactly a matter of learning correct information. If a thing looks better to the eye and feels worse to the touch, that doesn't make it better or worse. It simply means a different point of view, a visible difference.

I thoroughly understand that we live in a world that is structured for the sighted, so if a blind person intends to get along and compete in society, he or she must learn how the sighted feel and what they think is beautiful and attractive. But this has nothing to do with innate loveliness or quality. It is simply a visible difference.

As a matter of fact, although I wouldn't scratch the paint off of it if I met it today, that horse of my childhood would feel just as dirty to me now as it did then. A few years ago when I went to Athens, I was invited (no, urged) to handle a variety of sculptures. They may have looked beautiful, and I have no doubt that they did; but they didn't feel beautiful—at least, not to me. They felt dirty, and I wanted a good hand-washing after feeling them. Hopefully this does not mean that I am either a barbarian or a boor, only that my way of appreciating beauty may have something to do with the fact that I touch instead of look.

Do not make the mistake of thinking that it is only the blind who get stuck on the barrier of the visible difference. The sighted do it, too—repeatedly, every day. Recently when I was in the hospital, I was being taken to the x-ray department for tests. On the way I had to stop to go to the bathroom. As I came out, a hospital official (I think she was a nurse) saw me and exclaimed, in what I can only describe as panic:

"Catch him! He's going to fall. His eyes are closed."

My wife explained to her that I am blind and that my eyes are usually closed. It made no difference.

"It doesn't matter," she said. "Hold him. His eyes are closed. He will fall." This woman is not abnormal or unusually jumpy, nor (at least, as far as I can tell) is she stupid. She is simply so accustomed to the fact that sighted people look about them to keep their bearings that she cannot imagine that sight and balance have nothing to do with each other. If I had thought it wouldn't have upset her, I would have asked her if she believed she would be unable to stand up in a totally dark room.

During that same hospital stay, when I stepped into another bathroom, the nurse turned the light on for me even though I told her in a light and pleasant tone that I didn't need it. She said she would turn it on anyway. It was clear that she felt uncomfortable to have me in the bathroom in the dark. Obviously this is not a major matter. It simply shows that we feel uneasy when something violates (even benignly) our routine patterns.

And these are not isolated instances. Every day letters and articles come to my attention to prove it.

A journalist from Ohio writes to say that the blind need special fishing facilities—and he will lobby the government to help make it happen. He doesn't say why we can't fish in the regular way like everybody else, which many of us do all of the time.

A locksmith from Wisconsin believes the blind would benefit from specially shaped door knobs (oval and textured, he thinks), and he is willing to design them. A pilot from Pennsylvania thinks we should solve any problems we have with the airlines by setting up an airline of our own, and he will help fly the planes.

A man from Minnesota believes that blind alcoholics cannot benefit from regular programs used by the sighted and suggests separate services. Some years ago the *Manchester Union Leader*, one of New Hampshire's most prominent newspapers, said that the governor of the state was so bad that only the deaf, the dumb, and the blind could believe he was competent.

These few illustrations are not a complete list, of course, but only a sampling. Moreover, I am not talking about all of the sighted. An increasing number are coming to understand and work with us. They give us some of our strongest support.

Nor am I saying that the sighted are hostile toward us. Quite the contrary. Overwhelmingly the members of the sighted public wish us well and have good will toward us. It is simply that they are used to doing things with visual techniques, and when they look at a blind person, they see something to which they are not accustomed—what I call the barrier of the visible difference.

Most sighted people take it for granted that doing something with eyesight is better than doing it some other way. Visual techniques are sometimes superior to non-visual techniques, and sometimes not. Sometimes the non-visual way of doing a thing is better. Usually, however, it isn't a matter of better or worse but just difference.

This brings me to my experience with the National Federation of the Blind. I first became acquainted with the Federation almost fifty years ago, and it has done more than anything else in my life to help me gain balance and perspective—to understand that the barrier of the visible difference need not be a major obstacle, either for me or my sighted associates.

With more than fifty thousand active members throughout the nation, the National Federation of the Blind is leading the way in making it possible for blind people to have normal, every day lives. We of the Federation seek out parents and help them understand that their blind children can grow up to be productive citizens. We work with blind college students, giving scholarships and providing successful role models. Blind seniors make up an important part of the organization, helping and encouraging each other and exchanging ideas and information. We develop new technology for the blind and assist blind persons in finding jobs.

All of this is what we of the National Federation of the Blind do to help ourselves and each other, but the chief value of the organization is the way it helps us look at our blindness and the way it helps sighted people understand and accept. We who are blind know that with reasonable opportunity and training we can earn our own way in the world, compete on terms of equality with others, and lead ordinary, worthwhile lives. We do not feel that we are victims, or that society owes us a living or is responsible for our problems. We believe that we ought to do for ourselves and that we also should help others. These attitudes are the heart and soul of the National Federation of the Blind. They constitute its core beliefs and reason for being.

We go to meet the future with joy and hope, but we recognize that we need help from our sighted friends. If we do our part, we are confident that the needed help will be forthcoming. We also know that both we and the sighted can surmount the barrier of the visible difference and reduce it to the level of a mere inconvenience.

There you have the Editor's Introduction and the first article in volume fourteen of the Kernel Book series. Here is the Editor's Introduction to book fifteen, which will be released this fall:

EDITOR'S INTRODUCTION

This is the fifteenth volume in the Kernel Book series. Its title, *To Touch the Untouchable Dream*, comes from the article by Ed and Toni Eames, who recently went to South Africa. They tell of their visit to a game preserve and the techniques they used to experience the wonder of it.

The first of the Kernel Books was issued almost eight years ago, and since that time, more than three million have been put into circulation. If generalizations were effective, we could have saved a lot of paper, space, and time by writing a single paragraph or two to convey our message. It would probably go something like this:

Being blind is not what almost everybody thinks it is. Contrary to popular belief, the real problem of blindness is not the lack of eyesight but the misconceptions and misunderstandings which exist—misconceptions and misunderstandings by the public at large and also, unfortunately, sometimes by many of the blind themselves. However, we are learning new ways of thought about blindness, and every day our situation is improving. This is true because we have established our own nationwide self-help organization, the National Federation of the Blind, and because more and more sighted friends are doing what they can to help us.

We know that with proper training and opportunity the average blind person can do the average job in the average place of business and do it as well as a sighted person similarly situated. We know that blind children can successfully live and compete with sighted children, that blind seniors can function as well as sighted seniors, and that there is almost no job that some blind person is not competently doing. In short, through the work of the National Federation of the Blind and of our sighted friends and associates we are changing what it means to be blind.

If generalizations were effective, we could, as I have said, have saved a great deal of effort by simply writing and distributing these two paragraphs. But generalizations are not effective. They don't convey a sense of reality, so we give details and write the Kernel Books. The present volume is part of the process.

What happens when a blind man who has been an outdoorsman goes camping and climbs a tall tree while a passing tourist stops to watch? You will learn in this book, and I think you will find the interchange interesting. At least, I did since I was on hand to observe it.

And what happens when a blind father, waiting for his wife, is holding his baby in his arms and is approached by a sighted bystander, who believes that the blind are not competent to do such things? Then there is the blind person who teaches another blind person to operate a chain saw, and the blind woman who talks about baking bread. These and other true-life first person stories appear in this volume.

This is not the stuff of high drama. Rather, it is an account of the ordinary routine of daily life, the detailing of how average human beings live and work and play—perhaps as compelling in the long run as the most graphic international news story. I know the people who appear in these pages. They are friends and colleagues of mine.

Besides blindness, we have at least one other thing in common. We give our time and effort to the work of the National Federation of the Blind. We do this because the organization is the focal point for improving the quality of life for the blind of this country. Life has been good to us, and we feel the need to give something back—to help the newly blind, blind children, blind job seekers, blind seniors, and each other. We feel strongly that we must contribute as well as take, but we also realize that if we are to go the rest of the way to real equality, we will need help from sighted friends. These are our core beliefs, and we feel great hope and confidence in the future.

I hope you will find this book, the fifteenth in the series, both interesting and entertaining. If you do, we will have achieved our purpose and come one step closer to touching the untouchable dream.

Kenneth Jernigan
Baltimore, Maryland
1998

My opening article in book fifteen is called "Even I." Here it is:

EVEN I

Words play a more important part in our daily lives than we sometimes think. They allow us to communicate with each other with wonderful precision, and they are one of the principal features that distinguish humans from animals. It is not that words make us human but that they enhance our humanity.

For the blind, certain words have a special meaning. As an example, when I was a boy growing up on the farm in Tennessee, I learned early on of the significance of the words "Even I" used by my family and sighted neighbors.

As a case in point, consider the game of checkers. In those days (when none of us in that part of the country had either telephones or radios and when books and magazines were not part of the daily routine), the men and boys often entertained themselves by playing checkers. I wanted to play, too, but one or another of my family would invariably explain to me that I had to understand my limitations as a blind person. Eventually they would get around to saying something like this, "Even I find it difficult to play checkers."

The implication was that because they could see and I couldn't, I was obviously at a disadvantage, not only in checkers but in everything else. This, of course, was just plain foolishness. All I needed was some way to feel the squares on the checkerboard, a problem I solved by stretching a string across the squares and tacking it down at both ends. The job took only a few minutes, and my checker playing was not impaired by my blindness. However, in the face of all of the negatives, it took me a while to put the system into place. The "Even I" was a definite drawback.

And this attitude of believing that sight is always the deciding factor is not just a matter of fifty years ago or some isolated corner of rural America. In the 1950's when I was a teacher at the California Training Center for the Blind, we had a student who had always been an outdoorsman. He was now in his forties, had just become blind, and had come to us for training.

One day a number of us went to a wooded area for an overnight camping trip, and while we were there, the new student (feeling energetic in the fresh air) decided to climb a tree. He went up the tree with ease. A passing tourist stopped and marveled.

"That is amazing," he said. "Even I would have trouble climbing that tree, and I can see."

As best I could determine, the tourist was probably in his late sixties, and he was extremely overweight. I doubt that he could have climbed the tree if his life had depended on it, but he thought only in terms of sight and blindness. Of course, in the circumstances, blindness had nothing to do with the matter. The "Even I" was totally irrelevant.

Later, when I was director of programs for the blind in the state of Iowa, I was traveling to one of our district offices and stopped at a service station to get a Coca-Cola. While I was drinking it, a man who had just come in said:

"I can understand some of your problems, for I am handicapped, too. My handicap is not as bad as yours, but even I have trouble getting along."

After I left the service station and was continuing my trip, I thought about what he had said. So far as I could tell, he had at least three handicaps that would limit him in the competition of daily life. He had a speech impediment, which I think was what he was talking about when he said he had a handicap; he had a very limited education; and his intelligence did not appear to be very high.

I think his speech impediment was the least of his handicaps, but I am sure that he didn't see it that way. I suspect that I was much more employable than he and much better able to participate in the rough and tumble of the competitive world. But to him, because he could see and I could not, the edge was all in his favor. As he said, "Even I have trouble getting along."

In the early 1980's I appeared one night on the "Larry King" program. In those days it was entirely radio, and the studio was about nineteen floors up from street level in a downtown Washington, D.C., building. It was a lively program, and when we finished at midnight, my driver and I went out into the hall to take the elevator to ground level.

The problem was that the elevator wouldn't come. This seemed mightily upsetting both to Larry King and his assistant. I pointed out to them that there was a fire stair immediately next to the elevator and that there would be no problem in simply walking down to the street. It is no exaggeration to say that Larry King's assistant was shocked. Apparently it had never occurred to him that a blind person might take the stairs.

"Even I would not like to walk down those nineteen flights," he said, "and I am sighted."

What sight had to do with it was more than I could understand, but after a few minutes of trying to soothe him down and of waiting for an elevator that persistently refused to come, we took the stairs over his protest and walked without incident to the street.

This sort of thing happens every day, but it is not limited to the sighted. Let me go back to my teaching experience at the training center in California. In those days (1953 to 1958) I had not learned to sign my name. My students told me that I was creating a bad image of blindness because of this shortcoming and that I should get with it and learn to make a readable signature.

I argued that I rarely needed to sign my name, that I didn't need to learn how in order to improve my self-esteem, and that I could and would take an hour or two and learn to sign my name if the time came when I thought it would be useful to do so.

In fact, when I became director of Iowa's programs for the blind in 1958, I did just that. One evening as we were driving across the country from California to Iowa, my sighted wife worked with me for an hour, and I learned to sign my name. It is not the most elegant signature in the world, but it is legible and serves my purposes. Incidentally, as director of the Iowa programs for the blind, I did not sign my name as often as I thought I would, delegating routine paperwork and signatures to a deputy. However, the fact remains that I learned to sign my name in an evening and that I now do it without thought whenever I need to.

Yet, that does not end the matter. As I have thought about it through the years, my students were right, and I was wrong. I, who was teaching them that blindness need not mean inferiority, was not proving up. As later events would show, it would have been a simple matter to learn to sign my name.

So why didn't I do it? Reluctantly I conclude that it probably had to do with "Even I." From childhood I had been told in hundreds of ways every day that sight meant superiority. In the circumstances it would have been surprising if I had not absorbed and been affected by some of the mistaken notions.

Therefore, when I am tempted to be impatient or annoyed with sighted people who say "Even I," let me remember my own experience in learning to sign my name. What we need is not bad temper or blame but understanding and education.

This brings me to the National Federation of the Blind, the organization which has done more than any other single thing to make life better for blind people during the past century. The National Federation of the Blind has local chapters in every state and almost every community of any size. These state and local chapters come together to make up the national body.

Although we have sighted members, most of us in the Federation are blind. We give our time and devotion because we have seen what the National Federation of the Blind does in helping blind people lead normal, regular lives. Through its work with parents of blind children, with seniors, with blind college students, and with blind persons seeking employment, the National Federation of the Blind touches every aspect of the daily lives of the blind of the nation.

We in the Federation believe that we should stand on our own feet and do for ourselves before asking others for assistance, but we also know that our road to independence cannot successfully be traveled without help from our sighted friends and associates. And we have faith that this help will be forthcoming if it is reasonably requested and wisely used.

In fact, the future looks bright for those of us who are blind. We go into the new century with hope and confidence, and an ever-growing number of the sighted are moving with us as part of our cause. "Even I" is still one of our greatest problems—but that, too, is diminishing and fading into the past.

There you have the introductions and opening articles of this year's Kernel Books. When the National Federation of the Blind came into being in 1940, the problems we faced were overwhelming, but the most urgent and pressing of them was to find a way to relieve the immediate distress of poverty faced by most of the blind. After that (and it took years) we turned our attention to rehabilitation and jobs. Then, it was a question of dignity and civil rights—and although all three of those problems are still to some extent with us, we have now moved to a fourth stage of emphasis, that of public education.

For ultimately confrontation and legislation will not solve our problems. To some extent both confrontation and legislation will always be necessary, and we must certainly not forget how to do either. But in the final analysis, we cannot force people to accept us as equals, and I think we don't need to if we give them the facts. As somebody once said: It is not necessary to be loved, but it is extremely desirable not to be hated—and an overdose of confrontation and legislation can create backlash and hatred.

On the other hand, education properly done brings only good will and support. This is why we continue to invest the time and resources to produce and distribute the Kernel Books, and the results have richly justified our faith. We know that we are capable of living on terms of equality with the sighted and that the sighted are capable of accepting us as such—and for the most part they want to. All we need to do is present the facts in understandable terms.

Of course, the Kernel Books are no magic bullet. They will not solve all of our problems, and nobody thinks that they will. Certainly I don't. As I have already said, we must retain the option of confrontation and legislation, but these should be used sparingly and only when absolutely necessary. The better and more productive road is education.

As we move toward the next century, we as a movement are stronger and more confident than we have ever been. We choose peace and harmony if we can have it, but we will do what we have to do to go the rest of the way to equality. I have said it to you on previous occasions, and I will say it again now. The future is ours. We know who we are, and we will never go back.

Part IV:
We Know Who We Are:
From Confrontation to
Emerging Harmony

U nder the leadership of Dr. Jernigan, the National Federation of the Blind changed from a comparatively small organization of the blind into a powerful and mature social and political force. The techniques to achieve this transformation varied with circumstance.

During the 1970's, there was accelerating growth within the organized blind movement, and the Federation doubled in size. To manage the expanded scope of the Federation, a system of leadership training was adopted for individuals at the local, state, and national levels within the organization.

By 1978, a building had been identified in Baltimore, Maryland, to house the National Center for the Blind, and this facility soon became the focal point of programming for the blind throughout the United States. Visitors came from dozens of other countries each year to study the operation of Federation programs at the National Center for the Blind. Staff members were found and trained to promote the innovative programs of the Federation.

The Federation, during the 1980's, established training programs for the blind in several states, and many other programs for the blind studied the techniques and the structure of service delivery established by Dr. Jernigan. As Dr. Jernigan's leadership reached an increasing number of people and programs, there came to be increasing harmony and cooperation between programs for the blind and the consumers they serve. Even officials in agencies to serve the blind that had not actively accepted the value of partnership with blind consumers were affected by the style and the language of the Federation's great leader.

Although it is highly desirable to achieve harmony, this cannot be done simply by giving into everybody else's contrary view. Harmony can only occur when those who seek to harmonize have respect for each other. Furthermore, respect for a person or an organization cannot be reached unless the language of respect is employed. When certain self appointed arbiters of language told us that we must drop the honest, respectable, and forthright term "blind," Dr. Jernigan took up his pen. We are blind people, we know it is respectable to be blind, and we do not intend to accept somebody else's erroneous notion that we should try to hide from the fact. These are the sentiments in the article by Dr. Jernigan which appeared in the August 1993 *Braille Monitor* entitled "The Pitfalls of Political Correctness: Euphemisms Excoriated", this is what he said:

THE PITFALLS OF POLITICAL CORRECTNESS: EUPHEMISMS EXCORIATED

by Kenneth Jernigan

As civilizations decline, they become increasingly concerned with form over substance, particularly with respect to language. At the time of the First World War we called it *shell shock*—a simple term, two one-syllable words, clear and descriptive. A generation later, after the Second World War had come and gone, we called it *combat fatigue*. It meant the same thing, and there were still just two words—but the two syllables had grown to four. Today the two words have doubled, and the original pair of syllables have mushroomed to eight. It even has an acronym, PTSD—*post traumatic stress disorder*. It still means the same thing, and it still hurts as much or as little, but it is more in tune with current effete sensibilities.

It is also a perfect example of the pretentious euphemisms that characterize almost everything we do and say. Euphemisms and the politically correct language which they exemplify are sometimes only prissy, sometimes ridiculous, and sometimes tiresome. Often, however, they are more than that. At their worst they obscure clear thinking and damage the very people and causes they claim to benefit.

The blind have had trouble with euphemisms for as long as anybody can remember, and late twentieth-century America is no exception. The form has changed (in fact, everything is very "politically correct"), but the old notions of inferiority and second-class status still remain. The euphemisms and the political correctness don't help. If anything, they make matters worse since they claim modern thought and new enlightenment. Here is a recent example from the federal government:

United States Department of Education
Washington, D.C.
May 4, 1993

Memorandum

TO: Office for Civil Rights Senior Staff

FROM: Jeanette J. Lim, Acting Assistant Secretary for Civil Rights

SUBJECT: Language Reference to Persons with a Disability

As you know, the October 29, 1992, Rehabilitation Act Amendments of 1992 replaced the term "handicap" with the term "disability." This term should be used in all communications.

OCR recognizes the preference of individuals with disabilities to use phraseology that stresses the individuality of all children, youth, and adults, and *then* the incidence of a disability. In all our written and oral communications, care should be given to avoid expressions that many persons find offensive. Examples of phraseology to avoid and alternative suggestions are noted below.

"Persons with a disability" or "individuals with disabilities" *instead of* "disabled person."

"Persons who are deaf" or "young people with hearing impairments" *instead of* "deaf people."

"People who are blind" or "persons with a visual impairment" *instead of* "blind people."

"A student with dyslexia" *instead of* "a dyslexic student."

In addition, please avoid using phrases such as "the deaf," "the mentally retarded," or "the blind." The only exception to this policy involves instances where the outdated phraseology is contained in a quote or a title, or in legislation or regulations; it is then necessary to use the citation verbatim.

I hope this information has been helpful to you. If you have any questions about any of these favored and disfavored expressions, feel free to contact Jean Peelen, Director, Elementary and Secondary Education Policy Division, at (202) 205-8637.

That is what the memorandum says, and if it were an isolated instance, we could shrug it off and forget it. But it isn't. It is more and more the standard thinking, and anybody who objects is subject to sanction.

Well, we of the National Federation of the Blind do object, and we are doing something about it. At our recent national convention in Dallas we passed a resolution on the subject, and we plan to distribute it throughout the country and press for action on it. Here it is:

RESOLUTION 93-01

WHEREAS, the word *blind* accurately and clearly describes the condition of being unable to see, as well as the condition of having such limited eyesight that alternative techniques are required to do efficiently the ordinary tasks of daily living that are performed visually by those having good eyesight; and

WHEREAS, there is increasing pressure in certain circles to use a variety of euphemisms in referring to blindness or blind persons—euphemisms such as *hard of seeing, visually challenged, sightless, visually im-*

paired, people with blindness, people who are blind, and the like; and

WHEREAS, a differentiation must be made among these euphemisms: some (such as *hard of seeing, visually challenged*, and *people with blindness*) being totally unacceptable and deserving only ridicule because of their strained and ludicrous attempt to avoid such straightforward, respectable words as *blindness, blind, the blind, blind person*, or *blind persons*; others (such as *visually impaired*, and *visually limited*) being undesirable when used to avoid the word *blind*, and acceptable only to the extent that they are reasonably employed to distinguish between those having a certain amount of eyesight and those having none; still others (such as *sightless*) being awkward and serving no useful purpose; and still others (such as *people who are blind* or *persons who are blind*) being harmless and not objectionable when used in occasional and ordinary speech but being totally unacceptable and pernicious when used as a form of political correctness to imply that the word *person* must invariably precede the word *blind* to emphasize the fact that a blind person is first and foremost a *person*; and

WHEREAS, this euphemism concerning *people* or *persons* who are blind—when used in its recent trendy, politically correct form—does the exact opposite of what it purports to do since it is overly defensive, implies shame instead of true equality, and portrays the blind as touchy and belligerent; and

WHEREAS, just as an intelligent person is willing to be so designated and does not insist upon being called a person who is intelligent and a group of bankers are happy to be *called* bankers and have no concern that they be referred to as persons who are in the banking business, so it is with the blind—the only difference being that some people (blind and sighted alike) continue to cling to the outmoded notion that blindness (along with everything associated with it) connotes inferiority and lack of status; now, therefore,

BE IT RESOLVED by the National Federation of the Blind in convention assembled in the city of Dallas, Texas, this 9th day of July, 1993, that the following statement of policy be adopted:

We believe that it is respectable to be blind, and although we have no particular pride in the fact of our blindness, neither do we have any shame in it. To the extent that euphemisms are used to convey any other concept or image, we deplore such use. We can make our own way in the world on equal terms with others, and we intend to do it.

In 1994, Dr. Jernigan spoke to a gathering of leaders in the field of work with the blind. His message was that programs for the blind and blind consumers must recognize the power and value that each of them possesses. When we work together, there is the possibility for much greater progress than would be reachable if we insist on attacking problems alone. This is how Dr. Jernigan put it:

THE FUTURE OF SPECIALIZED SERVICES FOR THE BLIND

An Address Delivered by Kenneth Jernigan
At the Josephine L. Taylor
Leadership Institute
Washington, D.C., March 3, 1994

When Mr. Augusto asked me to appear on this panel, he told me that almost all of the people in the audience would be professionals, rehabilitators and educators; so my remarks are principally aimed at those of you who are professionals. Today we are talking about how to save specialized services for the blind and what kind of partnership can or should exist between the blind and service providers. The fact that we are considering this topic and that the discussion is being led by the consumer organizations and the agencies in the field implies that we think specialized services are in danger, that they are worth saving, and that the organizations of the blind and the professionals can work in partnership, and that the partnership can make a difference. There is no question that programs for the blind are in danger, but whether the professionals and the consumers can effectively cooperate to save the situation is still being determined.

Partners must be equals. You who are professionals need, in the modern lingo, to internalize that. You need to internalize something else, too. If an organization of the blind is not strong enough and independent enough to cause you trouble and do you damage (that is, jeopardize your budget, create political problems for you, and hurt your public image), it is probably not strong enough and independent enough to do you any good either. Likewise, if you as a professional don't have enough authority to damage the lives of the blind you are hired to help, you almost certainly don't have enough authority to give them much assistance.

Fifteen or twenty years ago you heard very little talk in our field about consumerism. Today that has all changed. The organized blind movement has now developed enough strength and presence that it must be taken into account in every decision of any consequence. How you as professionals react to that new reality may very well determine whether specialized services for the blind will survive.

Some time ago I was asked to speak to a group of agency professionals on the topic "Blind Consumers: Chattels or Choosers." It is not only a catchy title but a real issue, for we can't meaningfully consider the relationship between the blind and the agencies established to give them service without taking into account current public attitudes about blindness, and even more to the point, the truth or falsity of those attitudes. With all of our efforts to educate the public, the average citizen's notions about blindness are still predominantly negative; and since all of us (whether blind individual or agency professional) are part of the general public, we cannot help being influenced by public opinions.

Even so, we in this room (or at least most of us) profess to know that the blind (given equal training and opportunity) can compete on terms of equality with others; that the average blind child can hold his or her own with the average sighted child; that the average blind adult can do the average job in the average place of business, and do it as well as a sighted person similarly situated; that the average blind grandmother of eighty-four can do what the average sighted grandmother of that age can do. Of course, the above average can compete with the above average, and the below average will compete at that level. Blindness does not mean lack of ability, nor does it mean lack of capacity to perceive beauty or communicate with the world.

The techniques may be different, but the overall performance and the ability to experience pleasure are comparable. There are blind mathematicians, blind factory workers, blind dishwashers, and tens of thousands of just ordinary blind citizens to prove it. This is what I as a blind person, representing the largest organization of blind persons in the world, know and it is what you, knowledgeable professionals in the field, also know. Or, at least, this is probably what we would say we know if asked. But do we know it? Down at the gut level, where we live and feel, do we really believe it? As the poet Tennyson said, "I am part of all that I have met," and he was right.

Whether we are blind person or agency professional, it is very hard for us to contradict what our culture has taught us and what it reinforces every day. As
the German scientist Max Planck said, "A new truth
usually does not triumph by convincing its opponents
and making them see the light but rather because its
opponents eventually die and a new generation grows
up that is familiar with it."

On this critical issue we cannot afford to engage in
sophistry or deceive ourselves. If blindness is as limiting as most people think it is and as many professionals have traditionally said it is, then we should not deny
it but face it. On the other hand, if the real problem of
blindness is not the loss of eyesight but the misunderstandings and misconceptions which exist, we should
face that, too, and deal with it accordingly. In either
case the need for the professional in the field will be
equally great, but the services and the objectives will
be different.

Let me give you an example from my own personal
experience. When I was getting ready to graduate from
high school, I was interviewed by a rehabilitation counselor. He asked me what I wanted to do, and I told him
I wanted to be a lawyer. After changing the subject and
talking about other things, he returned to the question
and asked me to tell him three or four careers I might
like to consider. With the brashness of youth I told him
I didn't need to do that, that I knew what I wanted to
be—I wanted to be a lawyer.

He trotted out rehab jargon and told me that, while
he wouldn't say it was impossible for a blind person to
be a lawyer, he would say it wasn't feasible. A blind
man, he said, couldn't see the faces of the jury, couldn't
handle the paperwork, couldn't do the traveling. I argued—but I was a teen-ager; and he was the counselor,
who controlled the funds. He finally said (gently and
with big words, but very clearly) that I could either go
to college and be a lawyer, and pay for it myself—or I

could go and be something else, and the agency would help with the bills. I didn't have any money, and I was only a teen-ager—so I went and was something else.

I know now that he was wrong. I am personally acquainted with at least a hundred successfully practicing blind lawyers, and many of them are no better suited for the profession than I was. But I would not want you to misunderstand my point. That rehabilitation counselor was not being vicious or deliberately arbitrary. He was acting in what he believed to be my best interest. He was well disposed toward me and generously inclined. He simply believed (as his culture had taught him to believe) that a blind person couldn't be a lawyer.

What, then, should be the relationship between the blind and the agencies, the consumers and the professionals? As I see it, the answer must be given at two levels—the individual, and the institutional. The issue is easier to deal with at the individual level; for the choices are more personal, the alternatives more clear-cut, and the short-term consequences more obvious. If, for instance, a blind youngster should come to one of you today and say that he or she wanted to be a lawyer, I seriously doubt that you would resist or discourage. Law is now generally accepted as a suitable profession for the blind.

This does not mean that each of you in this room who is an educator or an agency employee will always make the right decision concerning careers and other life situations involving the blind persons with whom you deal. But make no mistake: You will and must make decisions. Money is not unlimited, and by funding one project you necessarily choose not to fund another. You have the responsibility for making decisions and for being knowledgeable enough to give correct information and advice to the blind persons who need your help. I have no doubt that, in most instances, your motives will be good, but your decisions will be wise only to the extent that you have a correct understanding of what blind people can reasonably hope to do and be, and what blindness is really like—what the limitations of blindness are and, perhaps even more important, what they are not.

Obviously this kind of decision making concerning individuals is not easy, but as I have said, it is far less difficult than the other sort, the institutional. Moreover, despite the fact that the decision making concerning individuals leads to successful lives or blighted dreams, it is not as important (even to those personally involved) as your institutional decisions. In the long run every blind person in this country will be far more affected (more helped or hurt) by your institutional than your individual decisions. For purposes of today's discussion I want to talk about your institutional decision making concerning the kinds of consumer organizations you will encourage or inhibit. And I urge you to resist the temptations of sophistry, for you cannot avoid making decisions in this area. You will make them whether you want to or not—and, for that matter, whether you know it or not. If in no other way, you will make such decisions by your daily attitudes and your subconscious behavior. Therefore, it is better to make them consciously and deliberately.

Of course, you cannot create an independent organization of blind consumers, for if the organization depends upon your permission and financing, it is by definition not independent. Freedom cannot be given by one group to another. It must either be affirmatively taken by the individual or group alleging to want it, or it cannot be had. It must be self-achieved, and the process must be ongoing and constant. But if you cannot create an independent organization of the blind, you can and will establish the climate that will encourage or inhibit it. And the stake you have is not solely altruistic or professional. It is also a matter of self-interest, and possibly survival.

In today's climate of changing values and hard-fought issues, the best possible insurance policy for an agency for the blind is a strong, independent organization of blind consumers. Regardless of how much blind individuals may like the agency and support its policies, they cannot achieve and sustain the momentum to nurture and defend it in time of crisis. That is the negative way of saying this: If there is a powerful, independent organization of the blind and if the members of that organization feel that the agency is responsive to their needs and sympathetic to their wants, they will go to the government and the public for funding and support. They will be vigilant in the advancement of the agency's interests. Its friends will be their friends. Its enemies will be their enemies. If it is threatened, they will feel that they have something to lose, and they will fight with ingenuity and determination to protect it.

Chattels, on the other hand, have very little to lose. They are at best indifferent and at worst resentful, always waiting for a chance to rebel in periods of crisis. In good times they rarely criticize, but they also do not imaginatively and effectively give support. In bad times they not only fail to defend—they *cannot* defend. They have neither the strength nor the know-how. Moreover, they lack the incentive. Having been taught that agency policy is none of their business, they cannot in time of danger suddenly become tough and resourceful. As many an agency has learned (the same is true of nations), chattels do not make good soldiers.

The agencies cannot have it both ways. Those that encourage independence, and help the blind achieve it, will prosper—and those that defensively cling to yesterday's power base will perish. If a sufficient number of agencies fail to recognize the new realities, then the whole blindness system may well be destroyed.

And what are these new realities, these vital issues of which I speak? There are at least three, interrelated and inseparable: funding, generic as opposed to specialized programs, and empowerment of clients.

There was a time (and not long ago at that) when agencies for the blind pretty much got all of the money they reasonably wanted, and sometimes more than they reasonably needed. Today, budgets are tightening; the environment is deteriorating; population is rising; and resources are dwindling. In addition, other disability groups (once disorganized and invisible) are finding their voice and reaching for power. Some say they took their lessons from the blind. Be that as it may, they are now a growing force to be reckoned with, and there is no turning back. The argument they make is deceptively alluring. Give us, they say, a unified program for people with disabilities—no special treatment for any segment of the group. We are one population. Despite superficial differences, our needs are essentially the same. Save money. Eliminate duplication.

You and I know that the logic is shallow and the promise false, but it will take more than rhetoric to save our programs. In the general melting pot of the generic disability agency the blind will have no useful training, no meaningful opportunity, no real chance. If the special training and rehabilitation needs of the blind are to continue to be met and if our programs are to survive, there is only one way it can be done. The agencies for the blind and strong, independent grassroots organizations of the blind must work together to make it happen. And the partnership cannot be a sham. It must be real. It must be a true partnership of equals—each giving, each supporting, and each respecting the other.

This brings me to the empowerment of clients. By this I do not mean that the clients should administer the agencies. This would not work, and it is not desirable. Rather, I mean that clients should be respected, that they should be given meaningful choices, that they should have access to information, and that they should be encouraged (not pressured but encouraged) to join independent organizations of the blind—organizations which are not company unions but which have both the power and the inclination to serve as a check and balance to the agency, to act in concert with it, to pursue reasonable complaints against it, to refuse to pursue unreasonable complaints against it, and to work in every way as a supporter and partner. Let these things be done, and both the blind and the agencies will prosper. Let them not be done, and I think the blindness system will perish.

There is something else: Workers in the blindness system must resist the growing tendency to hide behind the term "professionalism" and must stop treating "professionalism" as if it were a sacred mystery. There is a teachable body of knowledge which can be learned about giving service to the blind; but much of that knowledge is a matter of common sense, good judgment, and experience. Most thinking blind persons (certainly those who have been blind for any length of time and have had any degree of success) know at least as much about what they and other blind people want and need from the system as the professionals do, and it must also be kept in mind that not every act of a "professional" is necessarily a "professional" act or based on "professionalism." Just as in other fields in America today, the professionals in the blindness system must be judged on their behavior and not merely their credentials.

Whether you believe that the type of partnership and cooperative effort I have outlined will work depends on whether you believe in the basic tenets of democracy. It also depends on whether you believe the blind are capable of real equality. I *do* believe these things, and I hope you do, too. Otherwise, programs for the blind are probably doomed.

In 1996 the World Blind Union, the world organization focusing on the needs of the adult blind, held its Fourth General Assembly in Toronto, Canada. The keynote speaker was Dr. Kenneth Jernigan. In 1997 the International Council for the Education of the Visually Impaired, the world organization focusing on the needs of blind children and youth throughout the world, held its 10th World Conference in São Paulo, Brazil. Its keynote speaker was Dr. Kenneth Jernigan. In 1998 the National Council of State Agencies for the Blind gave its first-ever lifetime achievement award. The recipient was Dr. Kenneth Jernigan. In 1998, the American Foundation for the Blind International Leadership Award was established. It was presented to Dr. Kenneth Jernigan.

In the span of a quarter of a century a remarkable transformation had been achieved. A field once torn by bitter strife and confrontation had come to understand its unqualified need to combine forces in a common effort.

This is the text of the National Council of State Agencies for the Blind award and the comments of Dr. Fredric K. Schroeder, the federal Commissioner of the Rehabilitation Services Administration, regarding the striking new landscape that characterized the new reality:

The National Council of
State Agencies for the Blind, Inc.
with honor
presents this
lifetime achievement award
to

Dr. Kenneth Jernigan

in recognition of more than four decades
of exceptional leadership, advocacy and unwaver-
ing
dedication to promoting the capabilities and
fortifying
respect for the rights of individuals who are blind
worldwide.

This award is given in celebration of the life of
one who embodies the attributes of courage,
spirit and devotion.

Know the man—know the legend.

Jamie C. Hilton, President

April 22, 1998

Comments of Fredric K. Schroeder:

Dr. Jernigan's selection as the first-ever recipient
of the National Council of State Agencies for the Blind's
Lifetime Achievement Award represents an historic
moment in the affairs of blind people in America.

Not so very long ago blind people and agencies for
the blind found themselves on opposite sides of many,
perhaps most, major issues.

But that was twenty years ago, and that time is past. A transformation has occurred in work with the blind, and that transformation is due in no small part to Dr. Jernigan's leadership in bringing cohesive, focused action to formerly disparate elements in the blindness field.

Much of what is central to rehabilitation philosophy today is ideas (often unpopular at the time) which he pioneered decades ago. Indeed it is very nearly impossible to overstate the key role Dr. Jernigan has played in our field. His influence has been and continues to be immeasurable.

I know that it must have touched Dr. Jernigan very deeply to know that his many years of service, of pressing the system to do more, of faithful determination to fight for the rights of blind people (even when his views were unpopular) have resulted today in unprecedented harmony and cooperation in the blindness field.

By honoring Dr. Jernigan, you have honored the individual, and you have recognized the emergence of a new day, full of promise, in the lives of blind people everywhere.

So, what had changed? Quite simply, nothing and everything. Certainly not the National Federation of the Blind, whose constitutional purpose clause (authored in its current version by Dr. Jernigan in 1986) says in part:

The purpose of the National Federation of the Blind is to serve as a vehicle for collective action by the blind of the nation; to function as a mechanism through which the blind and interested sighted persons can come together in local, state, and national meetings to plan and carry out programs to improve the quality of life for the blind...

No, it is not the Federation, our vehicle for collective action, that has changed; but we ourselves. We the blind are a different people. No longer on the outside looking in. No longer in abject poverty. No longer without hope or belief. No longer without a literature which defines the nuance of our understanding and belies the nonsense of the naysayers. No longer without a corps of leaders hardened on the picket lines and tempered in the trenches. No longer without the possibility of training at superior centers. No longer without the right to have our blind children be taught Braille. No longer without the material resources of superb physical plant and cutting-edge technology. No longer the passive recipients of yesterday's charity but the active architects of tomorrow's promise. No longer without the legacy of Dr. Kenneth Jernigan and the tools he left us to finish the journey to full freedom and integration.

During the last year of his life, Dr. Jernigan fought a courageous campaign against cancer. It lasted many months—more than the medical people thought was possible. However, in October of 1998, Dr. Jernigan died. Even while he was battling the cancer, Dr. Jernigan continued to do what he had done during the rest of his life—he wrote, he inspired, he taught. During one painful night, when he was unable to sleep, Dr. Jernigan composed a touching, thoughtful, poignant article, which appeared in the June 1998 edition of the Braille Monitor. Entitled, "On the Nature of Mental Discipline and Sonnets," this is what Dr. Jernigan said:

ON THE NATURE OF MENTAL DISCIPLINE AND SONNETS

by Kenneth Jernigan

Recently in North Carolina, when I was undergoing cancer treatment and having a restless night, I put together a piece for the *Monitor* that I have been intending to do for more than thirty years. I doubt that I will ever write such an article again, but at least for once here goes.

From time to time I am asked what technique I use in writing speeches and articles, and I always give a general or cursory response. It is not a question of keeping secrets but of wondering whether the person (even though making the inquiry) would really want a full explanation if one were offered. Of course, I could (and usually do) say that writing requires a lot of time and hard work, but that is a platitude.

Let's get right to the meat of it. If I am to talk about how I write speeches and articles, I must discuss the sonnet, which is the most demanding verse form in the English language. It requires great mental effort while appearing to be amazingly simple. As a starter, a sonnet must have fourteen lines—not thirteen, not fifteen, fourteen. And each line must have exactly ten syllables—not nine, not eleven, ten. But wait! We are not through. Each syllable must be precisely placed.

To explain, I must leave the world of common sense and go to the rarified esoterica of graduate school literary classes. And more precisely I must talk about poetic feet. A poetic foot is a stressed and all associated unstressed syllables, much like a measure of music.

But there is more, much more! There are several kinds of poetic feet, but for our purposes we will deal only with the iambic. An iambic foot is an unstressed syllable followed by a stressed syllable. If a line consists of two feet, we call it dimeter. If it has three feet, we call it trimeter. If it has four feet, we call it tetrameter. If it has five feet, we call it pentameter. There is more, but for these purposes that is sufficient.

And now we can deal with the sonnet. As I have already said, it must have fourteen lines of iambic pentameter—not more, not less.

And if you think I have finished, be patient. I have only begun. The sonnet must have a particular rhyme scheme. The last part of the first line is called "a"—and so is everything that rhymes with it. Thus, if the first line ends with the word "cat," then "that," "hat," "mat," and anything of similar ilk will be called "a."

The last part of the first line that is not "a" will be called "b." Thus, if the line ends with the word "dog," then "log," "hog," "frog," etc. will be called "b." The next line that is not "a" or "b" will be called "c"; the next "d"; etc. And there you have the rhyme scheme for poetry.

In the English language there are two main kinds of sonnets—the Petrarchan, which came first and was named for the Italian who popularized it, and the Shakespearean, which is of obvious origin. Each has its own particular and demanding rhyme scheme, but both require fourteen lines of iambic pentameter.

The Petrarchan sonnet has a little (but only a little) flexibility. Its rhyme scheme is "abbaabba, cdecde." The "cde" lines may vary somewhat in placement, but the first eight lines may not. Thus, you may have "cc," "dd," "ee." Or you may have "cd," "cd," "ee." Or you may have any other arrangement you like for the "cde" lines—so long as you leave the first eight alone.

As to the Shakespearean sonnet, forget about flexibility. It isn't there. The rhyme scheme is "abab," "cdcd," "efef," "gg." Nothing more, nothing less. Take it or leave it.

Do you think I have finished? Not on your life. There is more. The first eight lines (I won't bother you with the technicality of their name) must pose a question or problem. And the last six (and again I won't bother you with their name) must give the answer or solution.

I first tried to write a Shakespearean sonnet in late 1944 or early 1945 when I was a senior in high school. You will observe that the language is romantic and the sentiment commensurate. Here it is:

From out the distant realm of higher grace
Your passing glance illumines all my thought,
And I do dream of how 'twould be, your face
With all its wondrous gleams of beauty wrought,

If could I but ascend the filmy clouds
That do obscure you from my closer view,
And pierce each vestige of the mist that shrouds
Each soft and perfect tint, each paling hue;

But could I breach the veil of clinging haze
That doth impair my vision's clearer sweep,
Perhaps 'twould serve but to reveal a maze
Of hidden flaws unseen across the deep.

Tis better thus to worship from afar,
Where naught but beauty gleams from out the star.

It was not until I was a sophomore in college that I undertook to write a Petrarchan sonnet. You will observe that by that time my language had become more down to earth. In fact, my journalism professor accused me of being a cynic. (I might insert here that—even though Freud would doubtless disagree—my sonnets have not primarily been written for philosophical but disciplinary purposes.) In any case, here is my first Petrarchan attempt:

> Often when I hear a great hero praised
> For some marvelous deed which he has done,
> And I see him basking in the warm sun
> Of fame, his name by all so fondly phrased,
> Or when I see some honest fellow, dazed
> By jeering insult, slandered, loved by none,
> Because of failure, or some goal not won,
> I muse upon the sad prospect amazed.
>
> Cannot mankind this truth of truths perceive,
> This one mighty immortal lesson learn,
> That what we have is ours by circumstance,
> That fate says who shall fail and who achieve,
> And even Solomon's glory did turn
> Upon a trick of near inheritance?

In recent times I have written only Petrarchan sonnets. A few years back, Mrs. Jernigan and I were driving home from one or another of the state conventions, and I suddenly heard her say to me: "Are you singing?"

"No," I said "I guess I was thinking out loud and trying to compose a sonnet." Here is what I wrote:

There is no slightest way to comprehend
The farther reaches of the stream of time,
Which is not stream but myth that birthed the slime
Which coalesced to form the thought I send
To probe the afterwhere of logic's blend
To seek to find some underlying rhyme
Or reason as a universal prime
To answer Einstein's search for means and end.

But if I cannot find the why and how
Of distant first and just as distant past—
Or, equal chance, of neither then nor now,
But circling stream that makes the future past,
Still must I seek and probe and try to know,
Because there is no other way to go.

My last effort at writing a sonnet was at least a
year or two ago. Here it is. You will observe that I even
went so far as to give it a name:

To Heisenberg

Perhaps my final breath will gently go
In restful sleep or age or other way,
As uneventful as the close of day
When only soft and quiet breezes blow
To mark the undramatic ebb and flow
Of all that lives and turns again to clay.
But just as like, my life may end in fray.
We dream and speculate but cannot know.

Yet, if the veil that hides what is to be
Could lift to show us at a single glance
The full procession of our future time,
The knowledge got would rob us of romance,
Would trade our will for one compelling prime.
We would be slaves, unable to be free.

There are two sonnets by American authors that I regard as outstanding. They are "Nature" by Longfellow and "Tears" by Reese. And even the Longfellow poem is flawed since two syllables have to be run together to make it scan. However, the sonnet that I have taken as my model of excellence was written by a Britisher. I committed it to memory when I was in high school and have referred to it ever since. It is "Remember" by Christina Rossetti:

Remember me when I am gone away,
Gone far away into the silent land;
When you can no more hold me by the hand,
Nor I half turn to go yet turning stay.
Remember me when no more day by day
You tell me of our future that you planned:
Only remember me; you understand
It will be late to counsel then or pray.

Yet, if you should forget me for a while
And afterwards remember, do not grieve:
For if the darkness and corruption leave
A vestige of the thoughts that once I had,
Better by far you should forget and smile
Than that you should remember and be sad.

So there you have my favorite sonnet and also some of my techniques for writing. Of course, there is much more to be said to round out the picture. I could, for instance, talk about dactylic, trochaic, and anapestic rhythms; about tercets and sestets; or about hexameters and other such. But I think I have said enough to make the point.

So what does all of this have to do with mental discipline and writing speeches and articles? If I have to tell you, it probably won't do any good. To those who say that I have gone over the edge and lost touch with reality, I reply that I have not forgotten how to engage in combat or street fighting and that I still know how to relate to the members at the National Convention. It can be put to the test. To those who say that madness is indicated, I respond that everybody has (or probably should have) at least a touch of insanity. If (assuming you choose to do so) you want to remember me in the future, think of the sonnet, for of such is the stuff of life—at least, of my life.

Yes, when we think of you, we will think of the sonnet. And we will also think of these words you spoke to us:

Our climb up the stairs to freedom has been slow and difficult, but we are nearing the top. We carry with us a trust—for Dr. tenBroek and for all of the others who went before us. We also carry a trust for those who will follow—for the blind of the decades ahead. Yesterday and tomorrow meet in this present time, and we are the ones who have the responsibility. Our final climb up the stairs will not be easy, but we must make it. The stakes are too high and the alternatives too terrible to allow it to be otherwise. If we fail to meet the challenge or dishonor our trust, we will fall far down the stairs, and the journey back up will be long and painful.

But, of course, we will not fail. We will continue to climb. Our heritage demands it; our faith confirms it; our humanity requires it. Whatever the sacrifice, we will make it. Whatever the price, we will pay it. Seen from this perspective, the challenges and confrontations are hardly worth noticing. They are only an irritant.

My brothers and my sisters, the future is ours. Come! Join me on the stairs, and we will finish the journey.

We will stay on the stairs. We will not fall. And the trust we carry, we now carry also for you. We will finish the journey, and when we do, in the words of the poem you loved so well,

The night shall be filled with music
and the cares that infest the day
shall fold their tents like the Arabs
and as silently steal away.